Humanizing the Narcissistic Style

By the Same Author

Characterological Transformation: The Hard Work Miracle
First Person Singular: Living the Good Life Alone

A NORTON PROFESSIONAL BOOK

Humanizing the Narcissistic Style

STEPHEN M. JOHNSON, Ph.D.

W · W · NORTON & COMPANY · *NEW YORK · LONDON*

Published simultaneously in Canada by
Penguin Books Canada Ltd, 2801 John Street,
Markham, Ontario L3R 1B4

Printed in the United States of America

Library of Congress Cataloging-in-Publication Data

Johnson, Stephen M.
Humanizing the narcissistic style.

Includes index.
1. Narcissism—Treatment. 2. Psychotherapy.
I. Title.
RC553.N36J64 1987 616.85′82 86-33329

ISBN 0-393-70037-2

W. W. Norton & Company, Inc., 500 Fifth Avenue, New York, NY 10110
W. W. Norton & Company Ltd., 37 Great Russell Street, London WC1B 3NU

4 5 6 7 8 9 0

For the teachers who light the way and pass the torch, and especially for my teacher and friend, Edward Muller.

Has anyone ever given anything to you
In all your darkest hours
Did you ever give it back
Well, I have
I have given that to you
If it's all I ever do
This is your song.

—Stevie Nicks
Has Anyone Ever
Written Anything for You

ACKNOWLEDGMENTS

I DEDICATED THIS BOOK specifically to Ed Muller for the reasons stated metaphorically in the dedication. I have learned a great deal from Ed, but, perhaps more importantly, he has rejoiced in my incorporation of what he has taught in my own self-expression. All true teaching is generative. It aims to add to the student's repertoire rather than restrict it. A great teacher encourages the student's separation and individuation and welcomes the blurring of roles in who teaches whom.

All the people mentioned on this page have echoed this pattern: They have been willing to teach me and willing to learn from me. Even when those transitions have not been entirely smooth they have hung in there—that commitment has meant the most of all.

Three of my closest friends, all psychologists, have participated in this kind of dialogue at close quarters for a long time. Their commitment and support have been invaluable to me and my commitment to them is for life. Thanks to Peter Alevizos, Larry King, and Janet Niven.

Three other professionals have served as direct guides in the processes of therapy and in stimulating my professional growth. They are Gypsy Frankl-Podolsky, Susan Rutherford, and G. Timothy Scott. And each of them has been a part of a larger group, the long-term members of which have provided much learning and support. Thanks to Debra Jackson, Pollyann Jamison, Richard Klotz, Judith Lindsay, Georgine Ollerenshaw, Mary Dwan, and John Stacey.

I have worked with two people who really made this book possible. Jane Gantor typed the manuscript and contributed editorial advice. Susan Barrows edited the work and shepherded it through production. Both understood the essence of the work, recognized its value and contributed more than they know to its completion.

Finally, there are two groups whom I must mention without names. For 18 years, my students at the University of Oregon have instructed and supported me in this work. Their questions, especially, provided the impetus to refine my thinking and writing. My clients, some of whom have written the best parts of this book, have shown the courage I wish to emulate and the faith I hope to justify. This is their song.

CONTENTS

Acknowledgments ix
Introduction 3

I. OBJECT RELATIONS AND THE FORMATION OF SELF 12
Developmental Psychoanalytic Psychology 12
Autism and Psychopathy 15
Mommy and I Are One 17
Optimal Frustration 20
Paradise Lost 22
Let the Good Times Roll 25
The Rapprochement With Reality 27
"No" and Identity Formation 32
Mama's Little Man, Daddy's Little Princess 34
Character and Temperament 37
The Conflict Model and the Deficit Model 37

II. THE USED CHILD: THE NARCISSISTIC EXPERIENCE 39
Etiology 39
Behavior, Attitude, and Feeling 46
Object Representations and Relations 49
Identity Formation 53
The Nature of the Real Self Formation 60
Defensive Functions 62
Energetic Expression 64
Therapeutic Objectives 67
Cognitive Objectives 67
Affective Objectives 71
Behavioral-Social Objectives 74

III. TREATMENT OF THE SYMPTOMATIC SELF 77
The Therapeutic Set and Countertransference 77
Countertransference and the Real Self 82
Worthiness, Grandiosity, and the Narcissistic Injury 84
Psychosomatic Illness and Hypochondriasis 85
Character Style and Character Disorder 87
Daniel: Character Style and Depression 92
John: Character Disorder and Depression 96

IV. TREATMENT OF THE FALSE SELF 114
Undoing 116
Energetic Interventions 120
False Self-Real Self Dialogue 128
Case Example: Phil 129
Necessary Versus Unnecessary Pain 134
What Is Working-Through? 135
Mobilization in the Borderline Narcissist 138
The Existential Shift 142

V. THE REAL SELF 145
Case Example: Larry 149
The Annihilation-Abandonment Crisis 153
The Real Self and Affect 156
The Real Self—Upside 159
Promoting Transformative Internalizations 170
Case Example: Chuck, The Trip Home 173

VI. THE INTEGRATION OF GROUP AND INDIVIDUAL THERAPY: THE NARCISSISTIC CHARACTER DISORDER 190
The Individual in Group: Part I 191
Individual Therapy: Part I 204
The Individual in Group: Part II 208
Individual Therapy: Part II 213
Commentary 217

VII. THE INTEGRATION OF GROUP AND INDIVIDUAL THERAPY: THE NARCISSISTIC STYLE 219
Individual Therapy: Part I 221

The Individual in Group: Part I 228
Individual Therapy: Part II 240
Complementarity of Individual and Group Treatment 247

VIII. TRANSFORMATION: POSSIBILITY OR FALSE PROMISE? 253

Appendix 261
References 272
Index 277

Humanizing the Narcissistic Style

INTRODUCTION

Some of my best friends are narcissists. Much of my most successful and moving therapeutic work has been done with individuals who can most accurately be understood by using the concepts of narcissism. But most of these friends and clients are not most readily recognized by their self-involvement, grandiosity, pride, entitlement, manipulativeness, etc., though these usually well-hidden features of their personalities certainly do exist. They are not those very disagreeable, self-centered, often noncontributing rip-off artists who come to mind when one thinks of the narcissistic character disorder. In the main, these people contribute a good deal to their fellow human beings, but they pay dearly in pain and aliveness for their driven achievements. They are too busy proving their worth—or more properly, disproving their worthlessness—to *feel* the love, appreciation, and joy of human connectedness which their good works could potentially stimulate in themselves and others. These people are not character disordered. They are people tortured by narcissistic injury and crippled by developmental arrests in functioning which rob them of the richness of life they deserve. They are good people, contributing people who are hurting—and often very badly. They are living and suffering the *narcissistic style*.

This form of narcissism is part and parcel of our life-denying culture, which places accomplishment over pleasure, status over love, appearance over reality. It is the endemic result of our culture's material perfectionism. It bridles a very significant proportion of our people and cripples some of our most gifted and giving individuals. Yet while the culture reinforces it, its breeding ground is the family. Though Madison Avenue plays on its existence and fosters its development, its roots are much deeper.

Individuals suffering from the narcissistic style can be profoundly helped by those who truly understand the underlying psychic structure of narcissism and who possess the human and technical skills to transform it. With psychological treatment which is able to meet them where they truly are and give them what they truly need, they can be brought to the experience of a real, emotionally connected life in which their contributions to the rest of us are, if anything, strengthened. That is not pedagogical psychoanalysis or short-term behavioral or cognitive modification or superficial scream therapy. Rather, it is a therapy informed by the deepest insights of psychoanalytic theory and practice and incorporating active as well as receptive techniques. These serve to help the individual both move beyond arrested development and work through emotional injury.

In a good deal of the literature, the narcissistic character disorder, as well as the narcissistic style, has been given a bum rap. Largely, the focus has been on those very disagreeable characteristics of the narcissistically disordered person rather than on the nature of his injury, the phenomenology of his pain, and the fragility of his self. A focus on these more phenomenological aspects of the narcissistic experience will promote far more empathy and understanding, an attitude which must be the touchstone of our therapeutic approach to all narcissistic persons. In this book, I will contrast the narcissistic character disorder with the narcissistic style, focusing on the similarities and differences along this *continuum* of ego functioning and describing the essential elements of the appropriate treatment for each.

I offer here an integrated psychoanalytic developmental theory which provides the underpinning for a synthesis of therapeutic techniques to be used with the character disorders and character styles. In the first book of this series, *Characterological Transformation: The Hard Work Miracle*, I presented this formulation for the psychological problems deriving primarily from difficulties in human bonding and attachment. The present volume deals primarily with disorders in individuation and the formation of self—the failure of normal narcissism which leads to a painful life of pathological narcissism.

In this integrated model, the presenting psychopathology is understood by appreciating the nature of the injury on the one hand and the nature of the arrest in the development of ego and self on the other. The nature of the injury is best elucidated by more traditional analytic understandings, particularly those offered by character and defense analysis. The understanding of the developmental arrest comes best from psychoanalytic developmental psychology, which I use here as an umbrella label for object relations, self, and ego psychology. This unified psychoanalytic theory then provides the groundwork for an integrated treatment approach which seeks to heal the emotional injury and work through to the maturation of the arrested ego.

Healing the original injury, particularly in its central pathological affects, often requires the use of treatment procedures which emphasize accessing and expressing these archaic and often catastrophic feelings. Such techniques range from calm genetic psychoanalytic interpretations to the more active and often engaging interventions of Gestalt and bioenergetic therapy. By contrast, therapeutic procedures aimed at remedying the arrested development of ego or self more often rely on explanation, reconstruction, and other supportive, cognitive, and behavioral interventions, which, while they may certainly access feelings and produce frustration, do not rely on unusual or active methods to deliberately do so.

It is my position that developmental psychoanalytic psychology and character analytic approaches need to be *informed* by one another. Each approach risks an overemphasis on one side of the etiological-treatment picture. The perspectives of the developmental model can lead to an overemphasis on explanatory, interpretive, and supportive interventions, neglecting the crucial role of the awareness and expression of primitive affects. But the more affective therapies can err in the direction of overemphasizing the importance of primitive emotional experience without a full understanding of ego and self development, thereby missing what is not so much psychological defense as *self*-preserving strategies necessary to functioning. Finally, both of these psychoanalytic approaches can be greatly enhanced when informed by the nondepth psychology strategies which come from the cognitive therapies, behavior modification, family and systems therapy, strategic therapy, neurolinguistic programming, transactional analysis, Gestalt therapy, and others. What I am advocating here is not a hodge-podge eclecticism. Rather, this is an integrated developmental theory and a synthesis of treatment approaches aimed at psychological deficit and conflict resolution.

The integration provided in this book is really at three levels. First, it represents an integration of developmental psychoanalytic psychology. This is the synthesis of ego psychology, object relations, and self psychology. This first integration is the easiest because these three schools share many similarities differing mainly in their point of emphasis. At this first level, however, I hope to make a contribution by disseminating what I view as incredibly important material which is very often inaccessible to anyone but the most analytically sophisticated reader. In both this work and *Characterological Transformation*, I have endeavored to translate as well as integrate the insights of developmental psychoanalytic psychology for those who might not otherwise be exposed to this rich body of knowledge.

The second level of integration maintains a psychoanalytic base but incorporates the insights of character and defense analysis within the more elaborate developmental structure provided by psychoanalytic developmental psychology. Here I hope to particularly serve those who have taught me so much in the area of character analysis and bioenergetic therapy by integrating this important body of knowledge within the larger theoretical context in which it really belongs. Reichian and bioenergetic therapies really do not need to be fringe movements seen by traditional therapists of nearly all other persuasions as just one more "flaky" fad of a libertine culture. Rather, character analysis is a branch of psychoanalysis incorporating energetic armoring as a part of classic defense analysis—a central element of traditional psychoanalytic theory. Indeed, without this arm of analysis, the contemporary emphasis on developmental theory pulls inexorably for a greater concentration on theoretical and cognitive understanding of psychopathology at the expense of the critical role of primitive affect in determining psychopathology and in effecting its cure. Many of us in the highly educated mental health professions tend to gravitate, almost automatically, to theoretical understandings and cognitive (i.e., insight and explanation) interventions, for they are safer than exploring the dark cauldrons of primitive emotion. Even when we acknowledge the critical roles of sex, aggression, grief, terror, etc., it is easier to talk *about* these feelings than to jump in among them.

I hope that the affective therapies (e.g., Reichian, bioenergetic, Gestalt, rebirthing, etc.) will persist through conservative times because they are essential for keeping us in the true human drama that psychotherapy is largely about. These therapies are often necessary for the very reasons they are resisted. The restrictive, emotion-denying, life-fearing aspects of our dominant Judeo-Christian culture create the very pathologies that these affective therapies are designed to remedy. They have been popular in the expansive, experimental, and questioning periods of the past. Now they have lost some of that popularity as the more reasonable and conservative forces in our society have become more dominant. Our culture is trendy. But the science that is psychotherapy must transcend trends and continue to provide a model for human growth which is both reasonable and yet truly human. In this work, then, I hope to integrate, legitimize, and contribute to the repopularization of these affective or expressive therapies. This process is easiest with Reichian and bioenergetic therapy because the underlying theory of character structure is so substantive and compatible with the new psychoanalysis.

The third level of integration involves the synthesis of various therapeutic techniques under this developmental-characterological umbrella, so that an eclectic treatment approach may be pursued with the guidance of a unified theory. I have endeavored here to exemplify the utility of this approach—first with a detailed practical description of the conflict and deficit problems of narcissism, and second with a theoretically consistent set of therapeutic procedures which may be applied to heal it. In this third level of integration—psychotherapy technique—I am also attempting to apply rich psychoanalytic concepts to the more common once-a-week therapeutic hour. When the patient is seen only weekly, the transference within therapy may be less pervasive, but the transference outside therapy may be differentially more important. Additionally, where therapy is less frequent and problems of character style are involved, active therapeutic techniques are often more appropriate, as the problem in these cases is more in accessing and expressing primitive emotions than in containing them.

In the developmental model presented here, characterological adaptations represent achetypal manifestations of core human issues. For narcissism, these archetypal issues are formed in that crucible created when the infant begins to become an individual, more autonomous and self-willed than the more passive and dependent suckling. As this individuation process unfolds, the child requires more freedom, more support for the development of autonomous functions, greater permission to experience and react to the frustrations of life, but with appropriate limits attuned to his developmental level. In some ways, this is the most difficult time for one to be a good enough parent in that there are inevitable conflicts, both within the child and with the surrounding environment. Perhaps the most difficult polarities of human existence are first encountered at this time and, as a consequence, some of the most universal of human dilemmas are often left chronically unresolved.

The *rapprochement with reality* is a most basic task of human life first encountered in that subphase of individuation which Mahler (1972) has called *rapprochement*. Though initially this label was used primarily to highlight the child's reemerging need to reconnect with the mother after his striking independence in the prior *practicing* subphase of development, the label has taken on a far more profound and enduring meaning for me. The rapprochement first called for by a mere 18-month-old child is really with some central realities of existence, including unity versus separation, dependence versus independence, grandiosity versus vulnerability, the desire to control versus the need to be controlled, limitlessness versus realistic limitations, etc. Many adults are still having temper tantrums, delusions, depressions, debilitating anxieties, perfectionistic obsessions and compulsions, and other painful adaptations to the failure to realize this rapprochement with reality. Due to developmental arrest during this subphase of individuation, many of us are still dealing with these dilemmas with quite limited and primitive ego functioning.

Most individuals who suffer such difficulties typically have little if any understanding of what they are really dealing with as they begin psychotherapy. And they often possess little if any awareness of the ways in which parental or other environmental figures made this rapprochement difficult or impossible. The emotions of the unresolved rapprochement were usually too painful to sustain, but they provided the powerful underlying motivation for a characterological adaptation *frozen* at a time of limited affective, behavioral, and cognitive resources. Through denying the realities of the self, the family, and the very instinctual needs of the organism itself, this characterological adaptation has typically been supported, at least in great measure, by the child's family or its substitute. Driven by the unremitting force of painful emotion and supported by the surrounding environment, the characterological adaptation became securely fixed. The emerging real self literally did not have a chance.

The synthesis of characterological, object relations, ego, and self psychology provides the best available map for current understanding of this common human tragedy. The task of contemporary psychotherapy is to develop from this understanding an environment in which the real self may be reclaimed and the rapprochement with reality achieved.

One central position set forth in these volumes is that achieving these goals requires an integration of therapeutic techniques so as to accomplish the building of ego resources, the phenomenology of a solid self, and the resolution of intrapsychic core emotional conflicts as required by classical psychoanalysis. This integrative, broad-spectrum approach to psychotherapy requires maximum flexibility in therapeutic technique. It demands that the therapist be comfortable with the most active of interventions characteristic of bioenergetic analysis, behavior modification, or neurolinguistic programming, on the one hand, and equally adept at the most receptive silence of psychoanalysis, which respects the necessarily creative process of self-discovery, on the other.

This approach integrates what, in *Characterological Transformation*, I refer to as the *conflict model* of human pathology suggested by traditional psychoanalytic theory with the *deficit model* contributed by the understandings of ego psychology, object relations, and self psychology. This integration allows one to consistently employ ego building techniques from cognitive and behavioral approaches on the one hand and conflict resolution techniques from psychoanalysis, Gestalt therapy, and bioenergetics on the other. This volume delineates the possible applications of this mixed model to the narcissistic character structure, which develops out of failures both in individuation and in the necessary rapprochement with reality.

In Chapter I, I have briefly sketched the entire developmental-characterological model, providing a unified theory to inform therapeutic intervention with the character disorders and character styles. Though this book is devoted to narcissism, at least some basic understanding of the whole model is necessary for effective therapeutic operation in any specific case. This is so, in part, because *pure* narcissism, unaffected by other characterological issues, is extremely rare, if it exists at all. So, it is essential in any given case to be aware of the other interactive characterological issues which surround the narcissistic expression. In a sense, all characterological adaptations are narcissistic, in that they are defensive compensations to early injury. Understanding each of the basic types of injury and the characterological adaptations which they typically create is necessary for differential diagnosis and treatment. In addition, this overall developmental view assists the therapist in determining the individual's resources, as well as his deficits. To do psychotherapy from the point of view of psychoanalytic developmental psychopathology, it is necessary to operate from an understanding of the entire developmental-characterological model.

In this first chapter, as in all that follows, I have relied more heavily than in my prior work on the insights of Heinz Kohut. Kohut's perspective is particularly useful when approaching the phenomenological understanding of the development of self—so critical in understanding narcissism. In addition, this more internal, phenomenological approach assists us in understanding the experience of the narcissistic client and helps us humanize our approach to him.

In Chapter II, I describe the narcissistic character structure. As in *Characterological Transformation*, the narcissistic conditions are discussed employing the following outline:

- Etiology
- Affect, behavior, cognition
- Energetic expression
- Therapeutic objectives
- Therapeutic techniques

Thus, in Chapter II, the archetypal etiological picture derived from character analysis, object relations, ego, and self psychology is presented in detail. This is followed by a description of the archetypal presentation of character as demonstrated in the individual's apparent and latent affect, characteristic behaviors, and characteristic attitudes, beliefs, and defenses. Following this, the insights of the bioenergetic therapists are used in a discussion of the energetic armoring characteristic of narcissism. Following this description, an outline of therapeutic objectives is offered. Finally, the greater substance of the book is devoted to the psychotherapy appropriate to narcissism.

Relative to *Characterological Transformation*, however, this book is less a basic text; it assumes more practical knowledge of psychotherapy and is less explicitly technique oriented. Here I present models of human pathology and formulas for therapeutic technique. However, I want you to know that I know that these models and formulas are only that—maps of the territory to be understood, not the territory itself. While they may guide the largely improvisational interaction of psychotherapy, they fail to fully capture the essentially artistic form that is the therapeutic process. It is my intent to free up, rather than to constrain, our understanding and practice of psychotherapy, so that more and more we are limited only by the reality of what our clients can use and less and less by the inherent constraints of our models.

The material on treatment technique is organized around the triadic presentation of self shown by the narcissistic person. Chapter III discusses therapeutic responses to the *symptomatic self*, which includes depressive, somatic, and cognitively disordered symptomatology. Chapter IV is devoted to treating the mobilization of the narcissistic defenses—the false self. Chapter V elucidates the treatment of the emotions and demands of the archaic *real* self functioning in the maturing patient.

Chapters VI and VII illustrate, through transcripts of recorded sessions, the group and individual therapy of narcissistic patients. These extended case reports present an integration of group and individual treatment modalities in two cases—one exemplifying the narcissistic style and the other the narcissistic character disorder. For me, this is the richest part of the book because it gives a moment-to-moment account of a dramatic process that otherwise can only be conceptualized. Further, the chapters are largely written by those people I mentioned at the outset—my *narcissistic* clients who have given to one another and to me so freely, who have shared their pain so openly, and who in that process have found their long-lost selves.

Chapter VIII addresses the issue of transformation. I now know that the transformation of narcissism is possible through a usually long and often painful process of psychotherapy employing the mixed model of conflict resolution and deficit repair. Is this possible with less pain and in less time? Or is the promise of that simply the narcissistically motivated, self-serving delusion of a few con artists? These are good questions better considered at the close of the work you will be doing by engaging, not just reading, this book.

CHAPTER I

OBJECT RELATIONS AND THE FORMATION OF SELF

DEVELOPMENTAL PSYCHOANALYTIC PSYCHOLOGY

DEVELOPMENTAL PSYCHOANALYTIC psychology is based on the direct observation of the evolution of children's behavior and consciousness informed by the most broadly based psychoanalytic theory. It is further supplemented by the results of long-term psychoanalytic psychotherapy in which the analysis of transference relationships have been used to reconstruct early childhood experience and relate it to adult psychopathology. All of this is further confirmed, refined, and corrected by other nonanalytic sources of developmental research.

The developmental observations begin with the infant in utero or at birth and follow its cognitive, behavioral, and affective development from the undifferentiated matrix of early infancy to the highly differentiated consciousness of the well-functioning young adult. Though this entire period of development is covered, the role of the first few years of life is emphasized by psychoanalytic observers, theoreticians, and analysts. Particularly crucial in this analytic review is the study of the *evolution of consciousness* from the undifferentiated matrix to the differentiation of the self from other objects in the world and the study of the cognitive mechanisms which make this and other transitions possible.

The three types of developmental psychoanalytic psychology differentially emphasize aspects of this evolving consciousness but share the basic underlying theoretical model. Self psychology (e.g., Goldberg, 1985; Kohut, 1966, 1971, 1978, 1984, 1985; Tolpin, 1983; Wolf, 1979; Wolf, Gedo, & Terman, 1972) emphasizes the development of the phenomenology of self. The object relations school (e.g., Adler, 1985; Horner, 1979; Jacobson, 1964; Kernberg, 1975, 1976; Mahler, 1969, 1972; Mahler, Pine, & Bergman, 1975; Masterson,

1976, 1981, 1985; Winnicott, 1953, 1965) focuses more on the changes in the relations of the developing person with the objects of the world, particularly other people. The ego psychologists (e.g., Beres, 1956; Blanck & Blanck, 1974, 1979; A. Freud, 1936; Hartmann, 1958) are more involved in the study of the cognitive mechanisms that make all of these changes possible. While individuals in each school might rush to differentiate their theories and results from those of the others, they have much more in common than in conflict. Their combined observations of the vicissitudes of child development and their documentation of the early environment's impact on later functioning provide an ever-expanding comprehension of the essential human condition.

I have found an extraordinary *fit* between the developmentalist's observation of early childhood issues and the strikingly similar issues of adults experiencing psychic pain. Whatever therapeutic techniques I may use, I have found the *developmental analogue* to psychopathology an invaluable explanatory tool which serves to inform and structure therapeutic intervention. All three areas of theoretical development are useful, each in its own way, with ego psychology contributing more in its emphasis on the development and fixation of ego abilities, object relations in its emphasis on the development and fixation of a person's interpersonal relations, and self psychology in its emphasis on the development and fixation of the phenomenological experience of the self.

Psychologists who insist upon a quantitative approach to research will be inclined to dismiss the insights of these schools on the basis of their nonquantitative data, the internal and nonobservable aspects of their theories, and the fact that they disagree on certain points. I think such a dismissal is extremely unfortunate and detrimental to progress in this extraordinarily important area. These researchers offer a perspective and type of research experience which is unavailable anywhere else. The longitudinal nature of both the child and adult observations is truly extraordinary. The theory, though basically psychoanalytic, has evolved and continues to evolve on the basis of observation. Finally, there is an expanding body of quantitative research supporting some of the most central developmental concepts (e.g., Emde, Gaensbauer, & Harmon, 1976; Silverman & Weinberger, 1985).

I have found a fourth school of analytic thought and practice to be essential to complete my developmental analytic understanding of patients and inform my therapeutic interventions. This is the character analytic approach, which finds its roots in classic defense analysis but incorporates a developmental view and contributes unique forms of intervention. Character analysis arises out of the original work of Reich (1949) and has been forwarded by Lowen (e.g., 1958) and his bioenergetic colleagues (e.g., Boadella, 1977; Hilton, 1980; Keleman, 1981; Muller, 1982). The main contribution of this approach is its emphasis on the types of mental frustrations that can create the developmental arrests so well documented by the others. The character analysts are unique in their incorporation of the energetic consequences of each etiological configuration and their related use of body therapy first introduced by Reich (1942). The character analytic archetypes, while not really new in psychoanalytic thought, provide a contemporary catalogue of the adult expression of core developmental issues. Though, of course, they oversimplify, they provide a useful outline for thinking about an otherwise diffuse set of phenomena.

To provide you with a synthesis of these four schools of psychoanalytic thought—self psychology, object relations, ego psychology, and character analysis—is my initial objective in this chapter.

Essentially, it is the case that a particular kind of parental frustration is either delivered or becomes salient to the child during a particular phase of development. In the earliest phases, for example, the infant appears to be aware of only the most basic elements of the environment's response to him. He requires sustenance, nurturance, and supportive handling during this period in which he is, under the best circumstances, developing a sense of security and trust. As long as these basic and simple needs are met, his development will be served. At later points in development, however, he will require more differentiated responding as he attempts to individuate, explore the environment, and express his unique individuality. In these phases, he will be far more sensitive to environmental frustrations around constriction of his individuality and movement, to disappointments in his self-expression, or to being used to gratify parental or other figures in the environment. *It is the interaction of naturally evolving developmental requirements with the inabilities of the environment to meet them which dictates the characterological issue, the arrest in ego development, and the arrest in the subjective experience of the self.*

In the first volume of this series, *Characterological Transforma-*

tion: The Hard Work Miracle, I provided a summary of those developmental phases which have been delineated by Mahler and her associates (Mahler et al., 1975). Then I provided a summary of the resulting character structures and the associated arrests in ego development for each structure. It is necessary to repeat some of this here; however, while my teaching experience indicates that such repetition is often facilitative, I am reluctant to put my readers and myself through a wholesale repetition. Instead, this chapter is devoted to a synthesis of these theories with much greater emphasis on the development of self and object relations incorporating of the insights of Heinz Kohut. In particular, Kohut's emphasis on the "experience near" description of the development of a *sense* of self is particularly useful for developing empathy and conducting psychotherapy. In addition, Kohut's perspective is particularly relevant to the primary focus of this volume—the pathologies in the formation of the self. So, this chapter will be devoted to presenting an integrated theory of how a solid sense of self is developed or arrested in an individual during the first few years of life and how that resulting sense of self is intimately related to styles of relating to others throughout life. The theory presented here is essentially the same as that presented in *Characterological Transformation*, but, bowing to Kohut, the perspective of that presentation is more emphatic, subjective, and internal than the earlier presentation. Both approaches, of course, have their advantages, with the external approach providing a more systematic, intellectually satisfying understanding and the internal approach providing a more humanistic, communication-enhancing appreciation of the client's internal state and predicament.

Autism and Psychopathy

According to our developmental theorists, the period of autism or "primary narcissism," as it is often called, encompasses approximately the first two months of life. Descriptively, the infant is extraordinarily responsive to her own inner need states during this time but relatively unresponsive to the external environment. Her behavior—or rather the lack of it—clearly indicates that she does not discriminate between external sources of gratification and has no memory for them. In this first stage in the evolution of consciousness, there is no consciousness of separation between the self and the world. This is, in a sense, the experience of oneness with the world without any awareness that there is a world. It is unconscious unitary consciousness. Presumably, all that is really required of the environment during this period is relatively immediate need gratification. The infant, existing within her "omnipotent autistic orbit" without any frustration tolerance, will begin to have this omnipotent illusion confronted by the hopefully minor delays in need gratification.

The theory suggests that massive environmental frustration at this point may result in arrested development here and that massive frustration later in development may result in a regression to this primary narcissistic state. The purest forms of psychopathy appear to qualify as examples of this kind of primary narcissistic involvement with the world. There is in this thankfully rare pathology an omnipotent orientation to the world such that its total and amoral use by the psychopath for his immediate gratification is completely accepted. It is as if at some level of awareness there is no discrimination between inside and outside and similarly no real empathy for the people in the world used to gratify needs. Similarly, there is relatively little, if any, tolerance for frustration coexisting with inability to plan ahead or anticipate future consequences. This level of consciousness, of course, represents the ultimate in primary process thinking. The individual feels that he is entitled to anything which the world might provide and responds with immediate rage to any frustration of that belief.

To illustrate this, I recall the true story of a husband and wife who returned home from an evening out to find a burglar in their home. The burglar pointed a gun at the husband and demanded his money. When the husband delivered the little money that he had on him, the burglar became enraged and said, "How do you expect me to live on ten dollars?" and shot the man in the face in a fit of narcissistic rage. Similar to the just-born infant who is his analogue, the extreme psychopath fails to learn from experience, almost as if he were living behind a "stimulus barrier." The environment barely influences his consciousness or his behavior.

In the normal development of the infant, however, the barrier does apparently lift both periodically and gradually to that marker event in which the infant smiles in *recognition* of the human face (Emde, et al., 1976; Emde & Robinson, 1978). Prior to that marker event, it is obvious that the child is soothed by human contact. Spitz's (1965) work dramatically demonstrates that human contact is extremely valuable during this period. We know that infants deprived of sufficient contact are at least less secure throughout infancy than those who receive it. The *recognition* smile is the signal of the beginning of discrimination or consciousness and, at the same time, the first discernible step in human psychological relations. We needn't reach too far to suggest that it is the repeated pairing of the human face with need gratification that, at least in part, determines the recognition of this object as the first one in the external environment and determines the nature of that response—the smile.

In some very important ways, it is even in this early and somewhat walled-off period of infancy that the child begins to develop a preliminary and probably very global sense of the quality of the experience of life itself. Here he begins to get a sense for the potential of life to provide gratification of need, the experience of life as essentially pleasurable or painful, and the role of other human beings in that basic experience.

Because of the highly global, undifferentiated, "unconscious" experience of this period, we have good reason to believe that any basic consistencies in the way the infant is handled may have pervasive effects on his future development and experience. Without knowing the exact extent of the damage, we can imagine the possible consequences to a child who is unwanted, abused, or chronically uncared for during these initial months of life. The work of Spitz (1965) and, of course, the analogous work of Harlow (e.g., Harlow & Harlow, 1966) give us some indication of the pervasiveness and severity of the effects of early contact deprivation and presumably of early abuse as well. Because such inadequate or nonempathic handling probably continues beyond the two-month period, it is difficult to know at what developmental point it exercises its determining effects. Nevertheless, the similarities between the consciousness of the infant in the primary narcissistic state and the consciousness of the extreme psychopathic character are striking. The developmental analogue fits.

Mommy and I Are One

According to Mahler, symbiosis begins at two months of age. Here there is a merged representation with the mother such that mother and child become "an omnipotent system—a dual unity with one common boundary" (Mahler et al., 1975, p. 44). This merged representation is consolidated or firmly established by the time the child is five or six months of age, and this sense of safe symbiotic unity is furthered by a mother who is exquisitely attuned to the subtle and not-so-subtle cues that her infant provides.

In some primitive cultures, this mother-child attunement is so refined that, for example, toilet training per se is never really necessary. This is true because the mother, who is in almost constant contact with her infant, knows by relatively subtle cueing when the child is preparing to eliminate. She then takes him into the bush each time he requires it and he is thereby gradually, easily, and empathically toilet trained. Like a gentle, empathic childbirth, this attuned symbiotic union cushions the child from the shock of the real world and the reality of his helpless position within it.

In the symbiotic period, the child has the beneficial illusion of control because he believes he shares or controls the mother's omnipotent power. The symbiotic illusion is an adaptive, instinctual orientation in the emergence of consciousness. To the extent that the need for such attuned symbiosis is met, the child develops a basic underlying trust in the world. He is safe, secure, and relatively invulnerable. This period of security, albeit illusory, appears necessary to produce a "confident expectation" for the confrontation of all the developmental and life challenges to follow. It is from this secure matrix of soothing, protection from overstimulation, and drive regulation initially deriving from an external source that the infant will gradually internalize capacities for self-soothing, signal anxiety, and independent drive reduction. To the extent that these important functions have not been provided by the original external source, he will retain an underlying archaic need for them and a concomitant expectation that they will never be provided in the future.

When the mothering figure fails to be "good enough" in this attunement during the symbiotic phase and the differentiation phase which follows, the child will develop the characterological patterns labeled schizoid and oral by the characterological theorists. The schizoid adaptation derives more often from chronically insufficient and cold nurturing during this period and/or from painful abuse of the child, usually by his primary caretaker. The oral pattern tends to occur as a result of a chronically unreliable nurturing environment. In this case, there may be some adequate nurturance but that adequacy varies broadly due to parental unavailability caused by depression, drug addiction, overwork, or simple parental insufficiency. The loss of a parent through death or some other serious circumstance may also produce this oral adaptation, though this more catastrophic form of abandonment is less common.

While there are important differences in the oral and schizoid adaptations, there is an essential similarity in the underlying experience of self. That essential similarity is in the level of insecurity and underlying real terror in one's experience, which is compounded by the fact that those internal structures that could be used to soothe it are either absent or insufficient. This creates a situation in which the individual is chronically dependent on external sources of soothing and yet chronically distrustful and often resentful of those upon whom he must depend. In the schizoid adaptation, there is a greater tendency toward withdrawal in this dilemma, whereas in the oral there is a greater tendency toward desperate dependency alternating with ungrounded and exaggerated independence. The first book in this series was devoted to the elucidation and treatment of these two character patterns, which essentially result from empathic failures in the first months of life.

Silverman and Weinberger (1985) have reviewed more than 40 studies in which the sentence "mommy and I are one" was subliminally projected to various groups of individuals. A number of beneficial effects of this psychoanalytically derived experiment have now been documented, leading these investigators to conclude that this unconscious reestablishment of the symbiotic state of safety and comfort is the active therapeutic agent in all these studies. To a significant degree, the schizoid client has never or rarely known this state and unconsciously continues to hunger for it, whereas the oral client has experienced it to some degree, but unreliably, or has experienced its very traumatic loss. The unfortunate result in all these cases is a chronically insecure self handicapped in all future developmental tasks and life responsibilities. Furthermore, the human relations of those of us mishandled in the first year of life are characterized by extremes of social approach and/or avoidance in dealing with the expression of human needs.

The schizoid's adaptation to an insufficiently nourishing, indeed punitive, environment is to internally migrate and in extreme cases to regress to a more autistic adaptation. The false, compensatory self of the schizoid person is characterized by distance rather than by grounded, accessible living.

The oral adaptation, by contrast, involves the repression of the primitive need together with a self-presentation of a soft, need-gratifying individual. The need gratification which the oral presents, however, is often experienced as demanding and confining because its underlying purpose is self-gratification either vicariously or through coercing nurturance from others.

In the transference of psychotherapy or the transference called up in an intimate relationship, the schizoid individual will quickly demonstrate a good deal of distrust and distancing, thereby defending against his primitive fear and need for closeness. The oral, by contrast, will be much more inclined to begin by denying his own need while meeting the needs of the other (his analyst, lover or child). Much more quickly than the schizoid, however, the oral will drop deeply into the archaic needs which have been only partially satisfied. As with all pre-oedipally derived character structures, these two will be prone to the idealization of the loved one or transference object. The content of the idealization, however, may vary somewhat, depending on the needs of the patient. To the extent that the patient is still defending against the underlying archaic needs, he will tend to idealize the other along the lines of his own ego ideal at a conscious level. Thus, the schizoid may see the therapist as providing the long-sought-after philosophical answers to life, whereas the oral may idealize her as a giving, loving person (the perfect nurturer).

Like all idealizations, these two set the stage for inevitable disillusionment; this provides the opportunity for the development of the structure of the ego and of the true experience of an enhanced and real self. Indeed, it is the frustration of unmet idealization that creates in this context the substance of the therapeutic process—the working-through.

Optimal Frustration

It is useful at this point in the presentation of the psychoanalytic developmental theory to introduce Kohut's (1971) concept of *optimal frustration*. Kohut posits that at each developmental phase the child is frustrated by a failure in the gratification of her hopes and illusions. From the very beginning, all her needs are not gratified, all of her drives are not immediately reduced, all of her expectations are not met. Yet, it is through her response to this frustration that the child begins to build *ego structure* and the *experience of self*. Although it is not the earliest example, the issue of separation anxiety and its resolution seems to be one of the clearest exemplifications of this process. Once the child develops "recognition memory" (Fraiberg, 1969), she discriminates the primary caregiver from others and begins to realize that the caregiver comes and goes. The caretaker's going away can be extremely traumatic, not only because the child is so dependent on one whom she cannot "hold" in memory, but also because the child still perceives the primary attachment figure as part of herself and is, in separation anxiety, beginning to deal with the crucial issue of separation-individuation. Consequently, each parting frustrates the symbiotic illusion and threatens security. All analytic developmental theorists seem to agree that it is during these very moments of frustration that the infant begins to build her ego and her sense of self through internalizing the caregiving and soothing functions of the external object.

Transitional objects such as blankets and teddy bears are employed in this transition from external soothing to self-soothing. Eventually, the soothing functions of both the external person and the external object are internalized to provide a more solid ego structure and a developing experience of the self. When each of these partings is *optimal*—the nature and length of the separation not too traumatic—the child repeatedly learns that the caregiver comes back. At each trial there is a little building up of that internal structure which includes the ability to self-soothe. Kohut (1971) calls this process *transmuting internalization*. Transmuting means a change from one nature, form, or substance to another. Thus, it is the repeated response to the frustration of separation that gradually transforms the dependent infant with a symbiotic illusion to the more independent child with an awareness of separateness and a feeling of wholeness in that individuation.

This process of ego building or creation of self seems to me to be analogous to the process of building strength and mass in muscular structure. In the process of "body building" we exercise a muscle to the point of some minimal tissue breakdown. Over a period of hours that tissue heals and in that healing there is an increase of mass and structure in the muscle. It is important in muscle building that the breakdown be gradual or optimal—that the muscle not be torn or injured. From the minimal and optimal breakdown, there is reformation, building, and strengthening. Muscle building, like ego building, hurts a little, and there is an intrinsic resistance to engaging in it. This is why many of us have difficulty with the self-discipline required for regular exercise and find that we need the coercion of poor health or vanity to overcome the resistance, as well as regular schedules, classes, or agreements with others to keep to a schedule.

Similarly, with ego- or self-building in the child or adult, there is often massive resistance to that process, which demands at least some frustration and pain. In the child, the coercion comes from the natural evolution of consciousness and the exigencies of life, with which the parent figures are in collaboration. The parents' role is to insist that the child confront those realities of life, while at the same time cushioning his exposure by seeing to it that the frustrations are optimal and by providing an environment of love and respect so that those frustrations may be faced with a background of security. With the adult in psychotherapy, the therapist's role is analogous to that of the parent. The setting must be safe enough for the person to face difficult and sometimes massive frustrations and powerfully archaic feelings. Simultaneously, the situation must remain frustrating enough so that those same realities of life are consistently presented.

Kohut posits that psychotherapy cures in the reenactment of this process of optimal frustration and transmuting internalization. In psychotherapy, optimal frustration occurs, for example, when the therapist fails to gratify the dependency needs, the idealizations, the narcissistic needs for attention and support, etc. Transmuting internalizations occur as the patient internalizes the acceptance, nurturance, and acknowledgment the therapist provides as well as the ego building internalization of those descriptions, interpretations, and explanatory constructs the therapist offers. As with the child, this process of frustration and transformation must be gradual and repeated for the building of ego function and the whole experience of self.

Paradise Lost

According to Mahler's system, it is at approximately six months, just as the infant consolidates the concept of symbiosis, that she begins to confront its disillusionment. The subphase of differentiation in this process of separation-individuation begins at about six months of age and extends through about ten months. Among the marker events of this era is the child's specific *smile of recognition* for the mothering figure, which indicates a specific symbiotic bonding believed to accompany that symbiotic consciousness outlined above. A second, related marker event during this period is the evidence that the child *discriminates* strangers from the mothering person (see also Emde et al., 1976; Emde & Robinson, 1979). Mahler's work indicates that children who have experienced a "good enough" symbiotic period tend to show curiosity and wonderment toward strangers, whereas children who have a less optimal symbiotic attachment show more anxiety and distress around strangers. Thus, the nature of the "eight-month anxiety" varies predictably, based on the infant's confident expectation derived out of the security of the earlier symbiotic period. It is probably necessary to highlight the fact that during the period of differentiation, and indeed for some time thereafter, the child continues to retain the illusion of symbiotic attachment. It is only during differentiation that she begins to confront that illusion and to work on the eventual awareness of separation.

"Separation anxiety" and "stranger anxiety" are the two developmental analogues for the related adult pathologies most clearly presented in this developmental period. For example, consider those extreme anxiety reactions characteristic of dependent individuals who experience mild to extreme panic when a loved one is late for an appointment, who "can't stand" to be alone or to experience the leaving of a loved one, or who experience profound and unjustified reactions of jealousy. Their developmental fixation is often found in separation anxiety. See Bowlby's (1960, 1969, 1973) work on the effects of early separation for a model of this pathology. The explanation of the required optimal frustration is frequently very therapeutic for individuals experiencing this problem. They simply need to experience again and again the separation and aloneness required in adult living and learn again and again that the loved one returns and is constant in his affection. In this way, the affected individual gradually internalizes that constancy and faith in the other required for a good adult adjustment. This rationale or "frame" on the problem in itself provides the material for a "transmuting internalization." It is a cognitively mediated, ego structuring pillar of the better functioning self. Even as it is being internalized, this idea can serve a self-soothing function during those times when an individual is lonely, anxious, or jealous. Each such experience, then, becomes a kind of ego workout which, little by little, serves to build and strengthen the structure of the ego and the experience of a cohesive and stronger self. In a very real sense, this *idea* is a transitional object which serves to soothe the individual and get her through the difficult experience of being alone and not liking it.

Where separation anxiety is a useful analogue for the oral and symbiotic character problems around aloneness, stranger anxiety is a good developmental analogue for those with a schizoid character or style. "Confident expectation" is insufficient in the schizoid. There is always a residual fear of injury from others. To a very great extent, the schizoid's withdrawal is mediated by the avoidance of anxiety associated with human contact. And, even though the level of this anxiety may be diminished by a number of therapeutic interventions, anxiety in social interactions will be retained by the schizoid individual for some time, if not indefinitely. The socially avoidant schizoid must require himself to seek out and maintain social involvement *in spite of* that persistent anxiety. He must expose himself repeatedly to the optimal frustration of social intercourse and learn repeatedly that his fears are unwarranted. He must become sensitive to the degree and length of intimacy which he is able to tolerate and, like the body builder, repeatedly extend and thereby build up his tolerance for social interchange and intimacy. He must learn slowly to trust enough to dissolve his shield so that he can take in more and more of the rewards of contact and intimacy. He must learn to tolerate not only the anxiety of social interchange but also the anxiety that will continually be brought forth by allowing more and more intimacy. The more love he allows himself to receive, the more anxiety there will be in his very real vulnerability.

This rationale or "frame" also provides self-soothing material for a transmuting internalization. It cushions and makes acceptable and understandable that bothersome anxiety and gives the hope that, through confronting it, there will eventually be diminution and even dissolution of the crippling feeling. My ski instructor used to tell me, "If you're not falling, you're not learning." In the cases of reactivated separation anxiety and stranger anxiety, this interpretation or frame for looking at it transforms the experience of anxiety to signal that maturation and growth are taking place. Additionally, it gives the person an equally useful rationale for keeping the anxiety at manageable levels, for avoiding situations that are too difficult or traumatic, and, at times, for enjoying the necessary indulgence of dependency in the one case and withdrawal in the other. This leads to an acceptance of one's problems and one's defenses, while at the same time encouraging an awareness that it is necessary to stretch one's limits and build one's self through the experience and management of anxiety. Furthermore, the good enough therapist can initially assist the client in making discriminations between what is too much and what should be attempted in spite of the fact that it creates discomfort. Then, as therapy progresses, the therapist can gradually pull back this kind of ego support and allow or demand that the client make these decisions on her own.

Let the Good Times Roll

In Mahler's model, the next subphase of separation-individuation is called *practicing*. Perhaps most important during this period is the fact that the child attains upright locomotion, seeing the world from a whole new perspective and being able to get around in a whole new way. Like the teenager with his first car, the toddler is euphoric at this and other new abilities and becomes absorbed in the exercise of these autonomous functions. During this time he is said to "have a love affair with the world" (Greenacre, 1959) and to feel that "the world is his oyster" (Mahler, 1972). So absorbed in *practicing* his many new abilities and in discovering the wonders of the world, he is relatively impervious to knocks and spills and less needy of parental attention and nurturance than he has been or soon will be again.

According to the developmental observers, the child is now grandiose, experiencing a sense of omnipotence due, in part, to the still retained belief of unity with the mother. The toddler still wishes to believe and apparently convinces himself that he owns his mother's magical powers and can have absolute control over them. He certainly must experience continual, and hopefully optimal, frustrating exceptions to that illusion. Yet, while he is building the construct of separateness, his cognitive immaturity continues to protect him from the full realization of his separateness and vulnerability. The manic high times of this period, as well as involvement in developing autonomous functions and interacting with the newly experienced world, also protect him from becoming aware of these unpleasant realities.

The grandiosity, omnipotence, euphoria, and self-involvement of this period provide the clearest developmental analogue of that grandiosity seen in the most clearly narcissistic patients. Because this grandiosity usually is to be neutralized in the next, *rapprochement*, phase, I believe that the developmental arrest of narcissism usually occurs in rapprochement. Still, since it is the failure to neutralize this grandiosity which creates the arrest, this developmental analogue of *practicing* is instructive in many ways. It helps you, the therapist, understand the truly infantile nature of all these behaviors and attitudes. To some extent, it can also help the patient understand the reasons for and nature of his immaturity in this sector of his personality. Fixated at this developmental level, the narcissistic client may feel that he is entitled to own the therapist, assuming nearly total accessibility to the therapist and the right to ask for special treatment in regard to the therapeutic relationship. When the euphoria, grandiosity, omnipotence, entitlement, and other characteristics associated with the practicing phase analogue are combined with certain tendencies toward idealization, rage at disappointment or frustration, and refusal to accept the limitations of reality characteristic of children going through the rapprochement crisis, a full and consistent developmental analogue for the various issues of narcissism is dramatically drawn.

The consciousness of the practicing subphase holds great attraction for both those damaged in the earlier periods and those damaged in later periods. For the oral client, who was insufficiently nurtured and prematurely rushed on to independent functioning, the practicing period offers a release into manic excitement and involvement in a world far more reinforcing than that of the unreliable nurturance offered earlier. Oral characters, in particular, are noted for their propensity to overextend in periods of manic excitement only to break down from that overextension into collapse, illness, or depression. In both the child and the adult, the euphoria is a release from the feelings of loss and insufficiency. Similarly, when the child is excessively frustrated during the subsequent rapprochement phase—when his need to integrate his desires for independent expression and dependent unity is badly handled and/or when his need for integrating grandiosity and vulnerability is inappropriately dealt with—refusal to accept the rapprochement with reality is often the result. Then, the infant regresses to the reassuring illusions of grandiosity and symbiotic unity and becomes fixated at this developmental level. Because the working-through of these issues is so analogous to what occurs for the optimal child in rapprochement, I will delay the discussion of its therapeutic working-through until the issues and processes of that period have been fully explored.

The Rapprochement With Reality

It is in the period which Mahler has labeled rapprochement (15 to 24 months) when the human child begins to confront for the first time life's most challenging realities. These are separateness and vulnerability. The natural evolution of consciousness in the young child demands a confrontation of these realities, while the natural defenses or instinctual vicissitudes of the organism provide consciousness cushions to the full realization of these truths. The grandiosity and elation of the practicing period provide one such natural defensive posture. This defensive stance also denies one of the primary realities to be confronted during this sensitive time—limitation.

Another naturally occurring defensive posture during this period is idealization. In the early stages of rapprochement, the child tends to couple the idealization of the other with the continuing illusion of oneness with the other. Toward the later phases of the rapprochement subphase, on the other hand, the idealized parent may be seen as separate but still retaining perfect qualities.

The third naturally occurring defensive posture appearing during this developmental phase is "splitting." When the child is unable to simultaneously hold positive and negative views of himself or another person, he will split or isolate his good and bad representations one from the other. Then, at any given time, he will be aware of only one side of the polarity, consciously experiencing the associated evaluations and affects. As the child's consciousness develops normally and optimally, he will, toward the end of rapprochement and into the next developmental phases, integrate these polarities into one ambivalent representation of himself, of his mother, and then of others.

To the extent that the issues of the rapprochement phase are not handled adequately, the individual may, in a very meaningful way, remain developmentally fixed in these patterns of archaic infantile consciousness—grandiosity, idealization, splitting the representations of self and others. Because a true sense of self comes out of the neutralization or accommodation of one's grandiosity and idealization (Kohut, 1971), there is a real impairment in the self from such developmental arrest. The individual, perhaps for an entire lifetime, continues to look for his or herself in all the wrong places—in the fulfillment of the archaic grandiosity and/or in the fulfillment of the archaic idealization. In the former case, the life theme seems to be "I am nothing unless I am perfect." In the latter, the life theme seems to be "I can be nothing without the perfect other with whom I can either merge or from whom I can derive the guidance and confirmation that will make my life meaningful." In all such cases, there tends to be some rather dramatic polarizing around the experience of a grandiose or enfeebled self, on the one hand, or the experience of perfectionistic idealization or devastating disillusionment, on the other. In both cases, the self is sought outside the self—in accomplishment or in others. More often than not, these two themes coexist in the same narcissistic person.

Two character structures appear to derive primarily from severe environmental frustration during this crucial developmental phase. These are the *symbiotic character* and the *narcissistic character*. The symbiotic character, who resembles most clearly the type of borderline individual described by Masterson (1976, 1981) suffers primarily from the failure to resolve the issue of separateness. Insufficiently individuated, the symbiotic character can feel or know herself only in immediate relation to another. Thus, she will tend to want to merge with or alternatively push away from a significant other in order to keep some continuing sense of her own existence, boundaries, or identity. Like the youngster she emulates, she will be characterized by attempts to coerce others to take care of her, respond to her, fight with her, and in all of these ways affirm her otherwise fragile existence. I have renamed this structure (from borderline to symbiotic) because I believe, along with many other theoreticians (e.g., Adler, 1985; Abend, Porder, & Willich, 1983; Chessick, 1985; Giovacchini, 1975; Grinker & Werbel, 1975; Horner, 1979), that the borderline diagnosis is primarily a descriptive and clinically useful one which cuts across a number of psychological issues. In all of my work, I have referred to borderline ego functioning as that which breaks down under stress and can be present in all pre-oedipal character structures. It has been my experience, however, that the most serious borderline cases have histories which are consistent with severe schizoid and oral etiology. The more profound borderline psychopathology always has etiological origins in the earliest developmental periods, as outlined most clearly by Adler (1985) in agreement with Horner (1979) and Giovacchini (1975).

The narcissistic character derives primarily from a failure to accommodate around the issue of grandiosity and limitation. More often a male in this culture, he finds a bulwark for his uncertain sense of self more in the pursuit of his grandiose illusion than in the pursuit of symbiotic illusion. Due to one kind of environmental frustration or another, the narcissist is arrested around the neutralization of grandiosity. His grandiose view of self has been walled off from the necessary repeated exposure to limitation. While his grandiosity may be very apparent to others, the narcissist is often largely unaware of how truly infantilely grandiose he is. Still, any threat to his false self, which is essentially an expression of that grandiosity, is experienced as a threat to his very existence.

In the diagnosis of character disorders, per se, there tends to be a very profound sex difference in the frequency of the borderline problem in women and the narcissistic problem in men. I think this trend maintains when we view more mildly disturbed people showing the symbiotic style or the narcissistic style. This is true for at least two reasons. First, there is a greater pull for the young boy to differentiate from his mother. The boy is anatomically and chemically different and, through development, identifies with his father or father figure. As a result, when the boy has a significantly impaired sense of self, he is more likely to look for himself or bolster that self through grandiosity and the continuing seeking of mirroring and approval. This biological difference is then enhanced by the influence of culture. In most contemporary cultures, the boy is more likely to be encouraged by significant others to differentiate or even rebel, while the girl is less likely to receive such encouragement and support. Girls are simply more likely to be *used* by their caretaking parents as objects to gratify the parents' continuing symbiotic needs, whereas boys are more likely to be *used* by their parents as objects of inappropriate idealization or alternatively as targets for envious attack or retaliation. It should be emphasized here that there certainly are narcissistic women and men with serious symbiotic issues. It is just that there is a relatively profound cultural trend in the observed direction.

Rapprochement is, in a sense, the first adolescence and, as in adolescence itself, it is extremely difficult to be a "good enough" parent during this time. As the adolescent is part child and part adult, the little human in rapprochement is part child and part infant, vacillating unpredictably between the two and displaying open conflict between dependency needs and the need to be independent. The evolution of the child's consciousness demands that he face limitation and separateness just as the natural desire for comfort and the vicissitudes of grandiosity and symbiotic illusion press for nonawareness.

In teaching this, I have often been reminded of my own evolution of consciousness around the issue of the existence of Santa Claus. Like many with whom I have compared notes, I had an emerging awareness that Santa did not *really* exist and that my parents were providing those extra presents on Christmas morning. Still, the pull of this idealized, omnipotent, loving, jolly old man who brought me presents was a little too good to give up. Thus, I remember suspecting that Santa Claus wasn't *real* long before giving up the belief is his existence. It is like this, I think, with the illusions of grandiosity and symbiosis—they are too comforting and functional to give up without a fight. And, it is very easy for a parent to become involved, in response to his or her own needs, in the infant's struggle over these issues. It is common, for example, for a mother who has not resolved her own symbiotic issues to fail to optimally insist on the necessary separation and to inappropriately reinforce the bids for symbiosis. In order to develop appropriately, the child needs frequent yet optimal frustration of the merger illusion. Though he expects to have his needs gratified simply by having a need or expressing it in a primitive way, it is necessary for him to be disappointed in order to develop autonomous functioning. If he is shadowed by the mother during this period and indulged at every turn, this necessary optimal frustration cannot occur. Furthermore, if this is coupled with an abandonment of maternal attention and prizing when he expresses independence, particularly during this very vulnerable phase, the issue of symbiotic attachment will not be resolved. It will be repressed, walled off, or put apart from the necessary process of feedback and correction.

With respect to the issue of grandiosity, the child needs repeated but supportive frustration of that illusion. From the practicing subphase of individuation all the way through the oedipal phase, he needs to learn repeatedly but gently that he is not omnipotent and that he cannot do or have anything he wants simply because he wants it. He needs to be optimally frustrated by failure and unrealized expectations. But, he does not need to be humiliated by harsh, continual, unnecessary, or massive exposure to his true stature. Nor does he benefit at all from the reinforcement of his illusion by a parent who, out of his or her own needs, requires the child to be more than he truly can be. Some children are doubly caught in this developmental issue when one parent needs them to be less than they are and enjoys humiliating them while the other needs them to be more than they are and continually reinforces the grandiosity. This, unfortunately, appears to be the childhood background of a number of people with the narcissistic adaptation.

Settlage (1977) has provided a useful listing of the developmental tasks of the rapprochement subphase, which also provides a list of treatment objectives for most symbiotic and narcissistic characters. They are:

> (1) mastery of the cognitively intensified separation anxiety; (2) affirmation of the sense of basic trust; (3) gradual deflation and relinquishment of the sense of omnipotence experienced in the symbiotic dual unity with the mother; (4) gradual compensation for the deflated sense of omnipotence through development of the child's burgeoning ego capacities and sense of autonomy; (5) a firming up of the core sense of self; (6) establishment of a sense of capability for ego control and modulation of strong libidinal and aggressive urges and affects (e.g., infantile rage); (7) healing the developmentally normal tendency to maintain the relation with the love object by splitting it into a "good" and "bad" object, thus also healing the corresponding intrapsychic split; and (8) supplanting the splitting defense with repression as the later defensive means of curbing unacceptable affects and impulses toward the love objects.

In psychoanalysis, these objectives are met primarily through eliciting the archaic transferences in a safe therapeutic environment which is neither infantilizing nor humiliating. While some of the archaic needs may be somewhat reluctantly gratified (Kohut, 1971), the overall objective is to optimally frustrate the archaic demands and illusions while interpreting and reconstructing their origins. The mobilization of the transference in analysis cushions the difficult task to be faced, just as the original empathic relationship with the parent could have cushioned this process in childhood. When the person is optimally frustrated, yet supported and empathically understood, he is then able to internalize, in minute proportions, those structure-building abilities that will provide a true maturation and development of self (Kohut, 1971).

In the kind of active, humanistic, psychoanalytic psychotherapy described here, this same process will be at work. In many of the cases which I describe, the issues are not as severe as those described by such writers as Kernberg, Kohut, and Masterson. Additionally, because the psychotherapy is usually on a one-hour, once-a-week basis, it does not so often pull for the kind of deep archaic transference that a three- to five-times-a-week analysis can provoke. For these reasons, it is more often necessary in this form of therapy to examine, analyze, and in other ways deal with the transference reactions that are prominent in the patient's social life. In addition, it is useful in this form of therapy, especially with higher functioning individuals, to use bioenergetic, Gestalt, and other affective treatment procedures to actively pull for such transferential archaic demands and infantile feelings. Further, it can be useful to employ hypnotic and cognitive therapy procedures which can enhance, speed up, or promote the generalization of the most important processes of internalization of function and structure. Finally, some interventions at the behavioral and social levels, through the techniques of behavior modification, family, or strategic therapy, can be used to enhance the client's social functioning or the therapeutic qualities of the social environments he constructs. By helping the client to engineer his social environment and his behavior within it, the narcissistic and symbiotic healing can be enhanced.

The greater portion of this book is devoted to the application of all of these strategies within a psychoanalytically conceived psychotherapy, enhanced by active techniques. Whereas the first volume in this series was devoted to presentation of this point of view for the oral and schizoid clients, this book is devoted to similar exposition of this strategy for the narcissistic character.

"No" and Identity Formation

During the latter stages of rapprochement and into the fourth stage of separation-individuation, which Mahler (1972) has labeled *the child on the way to object constancy* (22 to 30 months), the child establishes her identity in part by opposition. "No" becomes a favorite word because, in taking a stand opposed to the other, she establishes her separate identity. Through this nay-saying, as well as a general evolution of consciousness, the *child on the way to object constancy* achieves a more unified and realistic internal representation of both self and other. When the issues of rapprochement are well-handled, the child achieves an internalized source of comfort and love. With this internalization, the other is seen more and more as a person in his or her own right rather than as a narcissistically cathected part of the child's self. With this realistic view of the world consolidated, the child's primary anxiety will have completely shifted from the fear of the loss of the object to the fear of the loss of love of the object (Blanck & Blanck, 1974).

It is important in the child's development that she be optimally frustrated around the expression of her oppositional tendencies. That is, it is important that she lose *some* of these battles but that, once again, she lose these battles without undue humiliation or force. An important variation of the pathologies of individuation is that one termed *masochism* by Lowen and his followers. The masochistic issue is developed out of the persistent and often crushing refusal of the parent to ever allow any such oppositional behavior to be reinforced, often with a simultaneous forcing of the child to the parent's will around eating, toilet, and other behaviors, such that the child conforms to the parental schedule rather than to her own needs. This repeated forcing leads to a breaking of the will and a forced, superficial compliance with a concomitant unconsciously held spite for those who forced such unnatural accommodation. This history typically leads to an overcompliant, self-sacrificing, self-deprecating, passive individual who harbors a great deal of unexpressed spite. Often, because of the somewhat later development of masochism around issues of control and independence, there is little if any grandiosity, idealization, or splitting as seen in the symbiotic and narcissistic characters. There is more object constancy and a somewhat better formed sense of self.

There is, however, a continuing dependence on the maternal or love object along with a resistance to dependency and to identification with the love object. Internalization of the maternal functions is still incomplete, albeit somewhat more developed than in the character structures outlined thus far. Because of the great hostility toward the person on whom she depends, the masochist becomes anxious if these underlying feelings are brought out. For this reason, passive-aggressive behavior is characteristic of the masochist's social behavior.

The therapeutic task in this case involves some continued working-through of identity and object constancy. Primarily, however, in the simplest masochistic adjustment, the first objective is to reaccess and encourage the expression of the underlying hostility associated with the crushing of the person's independent will. In my experience, bioenergetic techniques are very effective with this personality type because they irresistibly pull for and assist in the expression of a number of affective states. The masochistic character has more of an unexpressed or undiscovered self than an unformed self. Thus, the masochistic character's treatment may be more accurately conceptualized in a traditionally analytic way, the task being to bring the self and its associated affects to the conscious surface for expression and resolution of conflict.

Mama's Little Man, Daddy's Little Princess

For the most part, the practitioners of ego psychology, object relations, and even self psychology do not differ very substantially from the classical Freudian position on the Oedipus complex. Let us review very briefly this classic analytic position. As differentiation is completed and individuation consolidated at about three years of age, the child becomes capable of real object love and object rivalry. With this capacity and the accompanying enhanced awareness of sexuality, the child is believed to experience the conscious wish to be not only favored by the other sex parent, but also to possess him or her sexually. Too, the child is believed to be aware of the inherent exclusiveness in the sexual relationship and aware at some level of the incest taboo. Concomitantly, there is the wish to defeat the same sex parent, who is experienced as a rival. Freud believed that this wish to defeat was literally a wish to murder. These incestuous and murderous wishes are believed to elicit certain predictable fears—the fear of retaliation by the same sex parent, the fear of rejection and loss of love of the opposite sex parent, the fear of the loss of control of these powerful impulses, etc.

As the oedipal wishes are frustrated, the child is believed to feel anger toward the opposite sex parent as well as a sense of failure and continuing sadness and yearning. Toward the rival, the child experiences anger, envy, and perhaps humiliation. Kohut (1971) refers to this classic oedipal situation as a "massive but phase appropriate" frustration. The resulting internalization is also massive according to the theory, and is the establishment of the superego—the now internal structure of the opposite sex parent as *perceived* by the ego of the child. At the point of the formation of the superego, it is hypothesized that the impulses, the associated fears, and the associated reactions to both parents are effectively repressed and thereby made unconscious.

The analysts who have concentrated on pre-oedipal development do make some unique contributions to understanding the oedipal situation. In the main, these contributions have to do with a deeper level understanding of how one with an impaired and arrested level of ego development will deal with such a difficult conflictual situation. Apart from this, however, most of these analysts essentially retain the Freudian concept of the oedipal situation.

Contrasting with this classic view is the more contemporary one in which oedipal, sexual, or neurotic issues are seen not so much as a natural consequence of the oedipal situation as they are a consequence of parental mishandling or abuse. Alice Miller (1984) is perhaps the most articulate and aggressive proponent of this view. The classic view, she feels, is unwarranted. Further, its imposition on patients in analysis has the effect of blaming and further repressing the natural child while vindicating the parents and furthering the repression of what actually happened. She states:

> I do not believe that a neurosis originates because a drive conflict has been repressed, as Freud thought, but rather because early traumatic experiences could not be articulated and therefore *had to be repressed*. . . . I cannot consider the problem of "infantile sexuality" in isolation but see it in connection with my knowledge of all the ways children can be used by their parents. I have difficulty separating what Freud interprets as libidinous desires from the child's narcissistic needs for echoing, respect, attention, mirroring, acceptance, and understanding. (1984, pp. 52-53)

This view is consistent with the characterological view as presented by Lowen (1958), Hilton (1980), and others, where the emphasis is not on drive confict but on environmental mishandling or misuse of the child. This latter view is more in line with my own conceptualization of the issue. While I am still struggling with some of the theoretical issues (e.g., the discriminability of instinctual sexual desires from the broad class of narcissistic wishes), I can say unequivocally that I have never seen a sexual, oedipal, neurotic issue that could be traced back to childhood experiences where there was not some misuse or abuse by parents or caretakers. Additionally, this view is consistent with my overall understanding of the development characterological issues: They derive from the interaction of the child's emerging developmental needs with the environment's inability to appropriately meet them.

Finally, it appears to me that Miller is correct in calling the traditional or classic view "pedagogical." The classic Freudian view is often imposed upon, rather than drawn from, the analytic patient. It seems to me that the open-minded, experimental attitude which has resulted in the "new psychoanalysis" will eventually lead to a restatement of the oedipal situation to more accurately reflect our accumulated experience. Sexual misuse/abuse of children, from the very subtle to the very profound, appears to be common—at least much more common than we had ever dreamed. This must be recognized as an extremely powerful etiological factor in the development of psychopathology. Our theories will need to be reground to accommodate that knowledge. A "remix" of that knowledge with our emerging knowledge of the formation of the ego and the self will prove to be of incalculable value in our understanding and treatment of people with relationship, sexual, and other neurotic issues. The opportunities for contribution in these areas are considerable.

It is easy to list some of the most obvious interactions in sexually related etiology. While the seductive behavior of the opposite sex parent may in some ways be desired and welcomed, particularly in an otherwise barren existence, it is also overwhelming and disorganizing. In such situations, retaliatory or rejecting behavior of either parent is often the reality and that is similarly overwhelming and disorganizing. Wherever the sexual response is split from the loving response, either in the parent's behavior or in the child's response, there will result the very common effect of such splitting in adult life. Wherever the child's primitive sexual responses are disallowed and punished, there will result a mutation, a twisting or perversion in this level of responding. And so on and on. This whole area needs extensive empirical and theoretical reevaluation. At this writing, I am able to discuss only the outline of this reevaluation. Essential in that outline, however, is the adoption of a nonpedagogical approach—indeed, an empirical approach—to the analysis of patients exhibiting these problems.

CHARACTER AND TEMPERAMENT

It is necessary in the exposition of this analytic-developmental theory, which emphasizes the interaction between the demands of the developing child and the environment's ability to meet them, to acknowledge the role of individual differences in the resulting character formation. There is sufficient evidence for the stability of individual differences in very early susceptibility to various forms of stimulation to document what is rather obvious in our experience. People differ in their genetic endowment, at least in relation to basic characteristics such as irritability, soothability, tension, and activity level (e.g., Beckwith, 1979; Birns, Barten & Bridger, 1969; Bronson, 1966; Matheny, Riese & Wilson, 1985; Thomas & Chess, 1977, 1980).

As a result of these temperament variables, as well as others which may not yet be identified, there will be individual differences in response to developmental demands and environmental realities. While these variables are not the focus of the theories integrated here, it is nevertheless important to acknowledge their importance. They figure powerfully in any individual treatment case where the objective is to assist the client in discovering, accepting, and coming to realistic terms with the realities of his or her existence. One's innate capacities and vulnerabilities are an obvious, essential part of the real self. They interact in infinite ways with developmental and environmental variables. Their significance is profound.

THE CONFLICT MODEL AND THE DEFICIT MODEL

There are a number of benefits to be derived from the integration of psychodynamic theories as presented here. Chief among them is the integration that is possible between what I've called the *conflict model* and the *deficit model*. The deficit model is that one most clearly represented in object relations, ego psychology, and self psychology. It emphasizes the view that psychopathology is a result of deficits in the formation of structure, whatever the labels for that structure may be (e.g., self, ego, superego). The conflict model is represented by the classic analytic view and, to some extent, by the character analytic view. Here, there is an emphasis on conflicting impulses, drives, or affects. Solutions to these conflict problems involve the uncovering of impulses, drives, and affects, their expression, and their eventual taming or resolution.

In my view, both levels of understanding are necessary to comprehend and treat the difficulties presented by most patients in outpatient treatment. At least to some extent, the traumas of the past have created some deficit in the psychic structures or in the sense of self. At the same time, and to a much greater extent as people are better psychologically defended, there is the problem of repressed, unconscious, conflicting drives, impulses, or affects. Bringing these to consciousness, aiming them at the appropriate targets, and eventually taming them is essential. Too much attention to structural deficit can result in too little work on affective release and eventual regulation. Too much attention to conflict, awareness, and expression can result in too little "optimal frustration" in therapy and thereby too little emphasis on the building of structure.

Finally, the deepest healing goes beyond the building of structure and the resolution of conflict. The eventual transformation is not past-oriented but present-oriented. As the structure becomes stronger and the reactions to the present become cleaner and less determined by the past, there evolves an increasingly powerful personal responsibility for creating the present. This creation, which is based not on denial of deficit or conflict (and that's the trick) becomes a well-grounded basis for human potential. This is the transformation which we seek: the establishment of solid structure, the release of and relative extinction of reactions based on past trauma, and the realistic, grounded creation of the present. All of that is what this book is about.

CHAPTER II

THE USED CHILD: *THE NARCISSISTIC EXPERIENCE*

ETIOLOGY

THE KEYS TO UNDERSTANDING narcissism are the *narcissistic injury* and the *rapprochement crisis*. Appreciating the narcissist's injury yields an understanding of his underlying emotional experience. Much, if not all, of his surface presentation, both to himself and others, is in compensation for that injury. The rapprochement crisis yields an understanding of the developmental assets, the ego resources and deficits, and thereby the nature of his object relations, defensive structure, and the experience of self.

The injury is a deep wound to the experience of the real self. In the more extreme cases of narcissistic disorder, the injury is so deep and the compensations so tight that the person has no residual experience or comprehension of the real self. In the less extreme variations of this disorder, which are endemic to the culture, there is often a veiled awareness of the real self but a concomitant rejection of it. Even though narcissism comes from the Greek myth superficially understood to represent self-love, exactly the opposite is true in the narcissistic personality disorder or narcissistic style. The narcissist has buried his true self-expression in response to early injuries and replaced it with a highly developed, compensatory false self.

Narcissistic injury can take an infinite number of specific forms, but essentially it occurs when the environment needs the individual to be something substantially different from what he or she really is. Essentially, the message to the emerging person is, "Don't be who you are, be who I need you to be. Who you are disappoints me, threatens me, angers me, overstimulates me. Be what I want and I will love you."

As outlined earlier, every characterological issue could be seen in this general way. Essentially, the schizoid is told not to exist, the oral not to need, the symbiotic not to individuate, etc. As a result, there is narcissism in every characterological adjustment, and narcissistic characteristics will be found, to a greater or lesser extent, in every character structure developed before or during rapprochement.

This is true for several reasons. First, every characterological adaptation involves the development of a compensatory false self in which there is ego investment and of which there is considerable defense. Second, the tasks of the rapprochement subphase of individuation are truly difficult ones that demand an intact ego structure and a sympathetic, understanding, respectful, mirroring, echoing environment. The environments that create the schizoid and oral structures are, by definition, far from adequate and any preexisting ego wounds can be substantial. So, a number of the difficulties in self-representation, object relations, reality relatedness, and defensive functions characteristic of the more obvious narcissistic personality will often be found in these other characterological adaptations.

Concomitantly, it is often the case that those showing the most serious narcissistic adaptations have had clearly deficient parenting in the prior periods requiring holding and nurturance. Parents who produce narcissism often cannot relate to their children as real, human, living organisms. This yields a kind of underlying schizoid unreality in object and reality relatedness—an ideal breeding ground for a highly narcissistic adaptation when the issues of self-formation are confronted. Particularly if there is then parental idealization and/or humiliation of the child as she attempts to form a self, the impetus for narcissistic resolution becomes overwhelming.

This more generalized view of narcissism is not a novel one, but is reflected in the work of Adler (1985), Blanck and Blanck (1974, 1979), Miller (1981, 1984), and Lowen (1983). A good deal of clarity has come to my own thinking about narcissism by recognizing it as a generalized difficulty that cuts across all character structures formed before or during the rapprochement subphase of individuation. Thus, I am alert to narcissistic features in other character structures, though the most important presenting life issues may not be clearly narcissistic. At the same time, I have come to see narcissism expressed in a more specific etiology and resulting in a specific characterological pattern. This "narrow narcissism" constitutes a very valuable diagnostic category. In short, individuals may be viewed as narcissistic in the narrow sense when they have had very little trauma prior to the narcissistic injury sustained in the rapprochement period. As a result, they show a pattern of adaptation in which the integrity and esteem of the self are very much at issue but in which basic security is not fundamentally a problem. I refer to this pattern as "pure" or "narrow" narcissism so as to distinguish it from narcissistic adaptations overlaying other structures.

In what follows, I will be discussing narcissism in this narrow sense for its heuristic value while realizing that narcissistic injuries and failures in self-representation and object relations cut across other categories. This is consistent with the approach of these volumes, in which character structures are viewed as expressions of central life issues. Within this framework, any given individual may manifest difficulty with any or all of these core issues. This is only more true of the narcissistic injuries and adaptations because of their position in the developmental sequence and the fact that all traumas in that sequence are ultimately to the real self.

In the narrow sense then, narcissistic pathology represents those difficulties in self-representation and object relations arising out of difficulties in the rapprochement subphase of separation-individuation. It is at this difficult juncture when the individual first fully appreciates his separation, deals emotionally with the impact of that reality, and is called upon to integrate his magnificence with his vulnerability. This rapprochement with reality represents the individual's first attempt to reconcile an idealized dream, which includes the illusions of *symbiosis* and *grandiosity*, with the realities of existence, which include *separateness* and *limitation*. If the environment can accept and nurture both sides of this polarity, love the wonders of an emerging person and the beauty of an open, dependent baby, the realness of the individual is bolstered, reinforced, and actualized. Then, the individual can be as magnificent as she was born to be and as weak and vulnerable as she was born to be. When the environment lets her be, she is, and there is no disorder of the self. But, when what you are is too much or too little, too energetic or not energetic enough, too sexual or not sexual enough, too stimulating or not stimulating enough, too precocious or too slow, too independent or not independent enough . . . , you cannot freely realize yourself. *That* is the narcissistic injury.

Your attempt to be who I need you to be is the false self. And the pathologies labeled "narcissistic" are simply the result of (1) your being who you were needed to be rather than who you really were and

(2) your developmental arrest at that point when you needed supportive mirroring to really grow to be yourself. A very significant proportion of the resulting pathology will be from your rejection of yourself. You will mirror your environment by rejecting in yourself what was rejected by others. You will try to hide that which has been rejected and you will work diligently to compensate for it. Very likely, you will shun or be angered by those who display what you have rejected in yourself.

The narcissist's object relations will consistently reflect his or her attempt to deny the rejected and suppressed reality and to achieve and present the false compensation. The pattern is most obvious in those narcissistic personalities in which there is an almost compulsive commitment to *having* the right clothes, home, car, and mate to display to the world the false self compensation. Yet, it is important to remember that compulsive forms of self-denial and self-effacement can also be narcissistic in the way we are discussing it here. When one's vulnerability or humanness was threatening that was denied; by the same token, when one's magnificence was too much, that too will have been denied. Narcissism is simply the promulgation of the false self over the expression of the real self. Successful therapy involves a resurrection and then expression of the real self.

I find it useful to think of Mahler's rapprochement subphase as the one in which two basic human polarities are first presented to the young child for eventual integration. These polarities are (1) unity-individuation and (2) grandiosity-vulnerability. Even under the best of circumstances this integration is not simple. Significant human psychopathology arises out of those familial situations in which any part of either polarity cannot be freely experienced and then integrated. Obviously, the symbiotic character arises more out of blocking the integration of the first polarity, whereas the narcissistic character arises more out of blocking the integration of the second. This dichotomy is, however, perhaps more heuristic than real, in that the narcissistic character in a sense never really individuates because he never truly becomes himself. Rather, he tries to become what the environment wants, and as a result his individuation is false. Still, he appears to be individuated and is typically capable of active, apparently individualistic, behavior in the real world.

It is particularly helpful in understanding people with narcissistic issues to remember the great vulnerability the child experiences during the rapprochement subphase. The child is threatened by his emerging awareness of his own vulnerability and powerlessness, as well as by his emerging awareness that he is separate from the mothering figure and does not own her magical powers. As he comes out of the rather manic-like practicing subphase, he requires particularly attuned understanding, sympathy, echoing, mirroring, and respect. This is the subphase in which it appears to be the most difficult to be a "good enough" mother. To be good enough means to allow the emerging individual to narcissistically cathect or use the parents in negotiating these difficult internal conflicts.

Understanding of the term *narcissistic cathexis* is necessary for true appreciation of the narcissistic development and eventual expression in adult life. An object is cathected narcissistically when it is the target of one's investment or attachment but not viewed as having its own life center or activity. Rather, it is viewed as significant only as a part of one's own life, seen as valuable only as it relates to oneself and, in a sense, expected to serve one's needs unconditionally. In other words, it is an archaic *selfobject* perceived only as one needs it to be, rather than a *real object* perceived to be as it really is.*

For the child in the rapprochement subphase, this is a legitimate developmental vicissitude. The mature parent will assist her offspring by allowing this narcissistic cathexis and permitting herself to be used by the child to define the emerging and separate self. The understanding, respect, mirroring, echoing, and love of which the analytic developmental psychologists speak are rather analogous to Carl Rogers's concepts of "prizing" and unconditional positive regard in psychotherapy. While the "good enough" parent must set limits for her child, there will be in her ministering the underlying message that the child is all right, acceptable, and lovable as she is. The unconditional positive regard will be for her essential humanness, with all of its magnificence and all its vulnerability. It is the same kind of acceptance that truly loving mates are able to give one another as adults when they attach as real object to real object and appreciate one another's magnificence while assisting one another with accepted vulnerabilities.

Alice Miller (1981) has been particularly helpful to me in my understanding of narcissism by outlining how narcissistic parents

*Kohut does not make this selfobject/real object distinction, which I believe is heuristic.

breed narcissistic children. When the parent has herself been narcissistically injured in childhood, she looks to her child to provide that narcissistic understanding and mirroring that she herself did not receive. As a result, she cannot be used by the child in negotiating the powerful issues of rapprochement; rather, she uses her child for the mirroring she still requires.

The classic archetypal mothering figure who narcissistically cathects her own child is the "stage mother." This typically pathetic character lives through the artistic expression of her offspring and loses her boundaries in that identification. Typically, the child of the stage mother is used in hope of remedying the disappointments and deficiencies in the mother's life; as a consequence, there is a desperate quality to the overseeing of the stage mother. In the film "Fame," the character Doris Finsecker is accompanied by a classic stage mother. Her mother periodically intervenes and interferes as Doris auditions for the New York School of Performing Arts. When she is later called with the audition results, the mother says anxiously, "Well, is she in or is she out?" Upon receiving the answer, she turns from the phone and says passionately, "Doris, we made it."

When the child fails to provide the necessary echoing or fails to live up to the exaggerated expectations, the mothering figure may withdraw her love or display the kinds of outbursts of temper that characterize the child's rapprochement subphase. The child, vulnerable and dependent, will then deny his real self in order to hold onto the mother. Living up to her idealized expectations and ministering to her narcissistic needs, he denies and loses himself. He invests in the idealized, false self, trying through it to regain what he lost—the love, respect, echoing, and mirroring which were required for him to discover, accept, develop, and love his true self. In this etiological formulation, the narcissistic injury exists in the parents' inability to accept, understand, and love the child with all of his real conflicts, vulnerabilities, and magnificence. To feel again that rejection of one's real self is to reexperience the very chaotic and overwhelming emotions of the rapprochement period without the necessary parental support to negotiate the crisis. A confrontation of that state, labeled "abandonment depression" by Masterson (1976), emerges in every treatment of the narcissistic issue.

There exists a related etiological picture involving a narcissistic parent who is threatened by and envies the emerging magnificence of the young child. Such a parent—usually put down and humiliated himself in early life—does not want to give his child what was denied him. Particularly where he sees the other parent idealizing the child, he will act out to humiliate the emerging individual in his child.

I have often seen the combination of these etiological factors, usually occurring along predictable sexual lines. I have often seen the case, for example, in which the mother of a male child, disappointed in her mate, idealizes her son and requires him to take care of her and live up to her idealized image. Often the mother had previously idealized the father before becoming disillusioned with him. Narcissistically cathecting her boy-child, she reinvests her idealization in him and sets the stage for a doubly painful narcissistic injury in her son. The jealous father responds by humiliating his son as the boy develops the narcissistic false self in response to the mother's cathexis. In this case, the child's real self is injured twice: first by the mother's inability to accept his vulnerabilities and idealizing him, and second by the father's need to retaliate and humiliate him.

The desperation with which the classic narcissist holds on to the promulgation of the false self can be understood if one appreciates the intense pain experienced in this dual rejection of the real self. When this side of the polarity is experienced in or out of therapy, the person experiences intense lack of support and understanding, profound worthlessness and humiliation, and a desperate need to have these overwhelming feelings stop. It is at this point that the narcissistic person may attempt to marshall every possible defense to ward off these feelings. Such defensive maneuvers include an intensified reinvestment in the false self, ungrounded grandiosity, acting-out in violence, suicide, or drug abuse, and a splitting of the external social environment such that others are seen as entirely supportive or completely threatening. It is the working-through of the abandonment depression and the eventual integration of the grandiose and vulnerable selves that will pave the way for the narcissist's characterological transformation.

Thus the narcissistic compensation is formed in response to the injury. That compensation involves an arrest in grandiosity which, because it is completely unrealistic, is extremely vulnerable. To live with this extreme vulnerability, the narcissist employs two basic strategies: (1) She tries to live up to the grandiosity by the accomplishment of perfection, and (2) she disavows and thereby renders unconscious the truly absolutistic and primitive nature of her grandiose nature. The more successful is her compromise, the more difficult it will be to ever give it up.

The child in rapprochement legitimately uses the parent in order to find himself. His identity is forged out of the symbiotic orbit as he uses the identification with and idealization of the parent figure to help define himself and discover his own identity in the mirroring which that adult provides. By contrast, the narcissistic adult uses others to bolster, fortify, and aggrandize the false self. This, unfortunately, continues the dependency because the false self can never become autonomous and self-gratifying. As we shall see in the future chapters on treatment of the narcissist, one central shift in the narcissist's healing comes when he turns to use others once again for the purpose of discovering and strengthening his real self. Initially, as with the infant, this becomes a more obviously dependent position. But as the person admits the paucity of his real self and looks to others to help him discover and nurture it, there emerge the seeds of eventual independence, because finding the real self ends the search and, with it, the desperate need for perpetual adoration. When the narcissist shifts from the use of others to perpetuate the false self to the use of others to discover the real self, he has begun the journey home.

BEHAVIOR, ATTITUDE, AND FEELING

The narcissist may be understood through the polarity he presents around the issue of grandiosity-worthlessness. While most descriptions of narcissistic personality focus on the compensated side of this polarity—his lack of humility, inability to accept failure, fear of helplessness, manipulativeness, a striving for power and a commitment to will—many a narcissistic character will display, often in the first session of therapy, the polar opposite. He will confess to his deep sense of worthlessness, his nagging sense of never being or having enough, his constant need to earn provisional worth, and his deep envy of those he perceives to be successful and healthy. In this confession, he will often admit to the feeling that he only fools others with his presentation of strength, competence, and happiness. In this state of mind, he knows that the self he presents to the world is false, that it gives him no pleasure or sustenance, and that he does not have a solid experience of himself as a real human being.

Although the compensated false self is more typical of his social functioning, he may well enter therapy when the compensation breaks down for some reason and the overpowering feelings of disintegration require him to seek out some assistance. Like the oral character in his collapsed phase, the narcissist in this crisis of existence wants something to stop the pain. Typically, he comes to therapy not for characterological transformation but for assistance in maintaining the viability of the compensation. It may be necessary to engage in therapeutic maneuvers that accomplish that goal, at least initially, because the lower functioning narcissist can be very dangerous to himself and others in the panic of decompensation. He can, for example, become very blaming of those "bad" others whom he perceives to be causing the pain, and he may act out violently against them. Alternatively, in the depth of his worthlessness, or in the realization of his falseness, he may become seriously suicidal.

Emotionally, he is at these times a 15- to 24-month-old child dealing with the crucial issues and consequent despair and tantrums of that period. Prior to the establishment of a very trusting therapeutic relationship and some critical ego-building, the narcissistic patient may be completely unable to work through this rapprochement crisis. Respect for the intense level of his pain and desperation is warranted, as is respect for how dangerous an adult can be in the throes of the rapprochement crisis. A true therapeutic transformation can be begun when there is sufficient relationship and ego strength for the narcissistic individual to experience the depth of his worthlessness, falseness, and desperation. That is the essential experience that needs to be released for the eventual transformation.

The narcissistic character in his compensated phase is a person who simply manifests those behaviors, attitudes, and affects that defend against that crisis of desperate feelings. Most typically, these include grandiosity, pride, entitlement, manipulation and objectification of others, self-involvement, and great reliance on achievement to sustain a fragile self-esteem. Although blown up in his self-presentation, he is extraordinarily dependent on external validation for the worth of his qualities and achievements. Typically, those who do not share or do not support such qualities are excessively devalued or overvalued. Any source of negative feedback can seriously reinjure and evoke rage or the defenses against it. His polarity around worthiness is mirrored in his evaluation of others. Some are seen as exceedingly worthy and are idealized in the extreme, while others are seen as exceedingly unworthy and contemptible. Paradoxically, others who approve of or buy the false self he is selling are often devalued. Because he knows at some level of awareness that his self-presentation is false, he feels he has fooled those who give him the approval he so desperately desires. Thus, he loses some respect and trust for anyone who rises to the bait of the false self he presents.

As with any person who idealizes, he also is prone to disillusionment when the idealized others fail to live up to his unrealistic expectations. This pattern of idealization and disillusionment is particularly common in the psychotherapeutic interaction. Indeed, all of the narcissist's interpersonal relations are characterized by the narcissistic cathexis of others. In other words, the narcissist sees others not as they are, but as he needs them to be. So, they are admirers, idealized models, examples of what he rejects and considers bad, etc. People are split into categories, good and bad; they are used but not related to for the people they are. Others are seen not for the gifts they have to share, the limitations they face, and the pain they experience. They are related to only in relation to the narcissist's needs. It is with the narcissist that the term *object relations* has a particular poignancy. We are objects to him, and to the extent that we are narcissistic, others are objects to us. He doesn't really see and hear and feel who we are and, to the extent that we are narcissistic, we do not really see and hear and feel the true presence of others. They, we, are objects.

If you can get how that objectification feels from both sides, the object and the objectifier, you have gotten the essence of the narcissistic experience. I am not real. You are not real. You are an object to me. I am an object to you. We use, manipulate, and play with each other. We do not connect, we do not feel, we do not love. We are machines who use each other in the mechanical process of getting through the day and night.

It is so easy in seeing the narcissist's disagreeable qualities, which he often suppresses in depression, to objectify him, to lose touch with his painful internal experience, and to forget that he is often of great service to others in his compensatory activities. In a very real sense, he has sacrificed himself for others, and he often comes close to being the hero or savior he feels he must be to be worthy. Particularly in the more prevalent cases of narcissistic style, endemic to our culture, these more grandiose and manipulative aspects are effectively disavowed and thereby largely unknown to the self and others. What remains in consciousness is only the more ego-syntonic requirement to earn worth by accomplishment. That that worth is a substitute for the love that is really wanted, that he has sacrificed himself for the booby prize, and that he is missing life in his struggle are too painful to realize.

And yet, there is that nagging sense pressing for awareness, ever-greater with age, that there is more to life than this. In those moments when the defenses are dropped, the narcissist sees that others do see and hear and feel one another—that there is real joy and love in the experience of some others—that there is realness in human experience. In that realization, and in that envy, are the seeds of the narcissistic transformation.

The narcissist's salvation is not in his accomplishments, specialness, or uniqueness. The "drama of the gifted child" (Miller, 1981) is in his discovery of his human ordinariness. In that ordinariness is his ability to feel real human feelings unaffected by his internalized parents' acceptance or rejection of his feelings. Once his ordinariness is realized, he can express his gift as just that—a gift. His gift is not who he is; his humanness is who he is.

The hard work of psychotherapy for the narcissist is to assist him in relinquishing the compromise which has often felt bad but which has provided some gratification and often looked very good. In turn he must invest in a reassertion of self which risks reinjury and brings up all the old feelings of hurt, but promises eventual fulfillment.

The narcissist can be most clearly described by his pathology in self-representation and object relations. Additionally, to distinguish him from the other character structures which contain narcissistic components, it is useful to focus on the differences in his forms of psychological defense. For these reasons, I will begin the description of behavior, attitude, and characteristic affects by using these three categories of ego functioning: object representations and relations, identity formation, and defensive functions.

Object Representations and Relations

From an object relations viewpoint, the narcissist is developmentally arrested in the rapprochement subphase of separation-individuation. As a consequence, there is a basic pathology in his being able to differentiate himself, at a psychological level, from significant others. Unlike the symbiotic character, the narcissist, as narrowly defined, differentiates himself clearly at a body level and does not have the same kind of diffuse body-ego boundaries seen in the symbiotic structure. At a psychological level, however, there is a confusion about boundaries. The extent of that confusion, and the degree to which it is perceived as ego-dystonic, represents the extent of the ego impairment. At the extreme low end of this continuum, Kohut (1971) has described the object relations as *merger through extension of the grandiose self*. In this extreme case, the client sees himself as psychologically merged, at least with significant others, and "entitled" to use them completely and exclusively.

This is the type of person who will become indignant or enraged with a therapist or spouse who is not unconditionally available for his unlimited use. He will typically be jealous of his spouse's work, hobbies, or other relationships which in any way interfere with availability. In extreme cases such a client will openly resent his therapist for seeing anyone other than himself. Further, he will expect free and unlimited access to his therapist or any significant others and be enraged by any limitations set by others to define their own boundaries. Where the arrest is this early developmentally, there will usually have been severe deficiency in the nurturing-holding functions of the parents and associated pathologies of a schizoid-oral nature.

All narcissistic characters tend to idealize, but at this extreme pole of merger the person bathes in the "narcissistic glow" of any positive attributes of the cathected other. A beautiful wife makes him more physically attractive, a brilliant therapist reflects on his brilliance, a talented son makes him similarly talented. Recall the example of the stage mother merged with her talented offspring. Frequently, the objects merged with are those that most clearly represent an aspect of the self about which there is doubt or recrimination. If I feel ugly, I will seek to merge with someone who is beautiful. If I feel stupid, I will seek to merge with someone I perceive as intelligent. If I feel boring, I will attempt to merge with someone exciting.

Although this merging transference represents the bottom of the developmental continuum in narcissistic object relations, I have experienced differences in clients' ability to employ a more or less "adult observing ego" in being aware of and syntonic or dystonic with this adaptation. In other words, some clients are able to see that they engage in more or less merging transference relationships with spouses, children, and therapists and view that as unfortunate. So, in my experience, there can be a fixation at this level of development concurrent with development of thought processes and reality relatedness which serve to inhibit the extreme manifestations of the merger transference outlined above.

Kohut (1971) posits that the "twinship" transference is somewhat more evolved developmentally than the merger transference just outlined. Here, the separateness is acknowledged but the individual assumes that he and the object have more or less identical psychologies with similar likes, dislikes, philosophies, etc. The maintenance of this illusion is necessary for the maintenance of significant relationships. The discovery that another is not "just like me" even in some insignificant respect is enough to threaten the relationship. The twinship attachment, together with its fragility, is often seen in early teenage romances, where part of the function of the attachment is the discovery of self. It is not uncommon for narcissistic characters who exhibit this form of transferential relationship to find essentially oral or symbiotic characters who will indeed fulfill this twinship expectation. The currently popular literature on "soulmates" seems to me, at times at least, to perpetuate this transferential relationship based upon the search for the perfect alter ego.

Kohut's (1971) most evolved form of narcissistic transference is the "mirror transference." In this form of relationship, the other is *used* primarily for the purpose of acknowledging or aggrandizing the false self. Here, the need for attention, "prizing," respect, and echoing is the focus of the relationship. This form of transference is more mature, in that it is directed more at the development of the separate self. In this transference, the false self has been somewhat more developed and others are narcissistically cathected to help support it. The tragedy, of course, is that others are used to aggrandize the false self rather than to help discover and accept the real self. Examples of this mirroring transference would include a client's upset at a therapist's forgetting a minor detail presented in an earlier session, a therapist's neglect to praise a current accomplishment, or a therapist's failure to remark on a new hairstyle or other significant change in personal appearance. The internal experience of this need for mirroring reduces to a more or less constant need for others to notice, confirm, and bolster the insecure self presented to the world. Narcissists with this level of development often have some insight into their narcissistic character, even though they may not know this pejorative and unfortunate label. Too, they may be much more aware of the negative and insecure polarity of their self-concept. As such, they appear more "neurotic" in the classic sense; yet, it is in their failure to negotiate the task of rapprochement and their history of *being used* that will be most helpful in engineering their therapeutic progress.

I find Kohut's categorization very useful in describing various forms of narcissistic transference both in and out of therapy. On the other hand, I have observed that all forms may be represented in the same individual. Particularly, I have seen regression to lower developmental forms of transference (i.e., merger transference) under extreme stress and milder forms of the need for mirroring when the therapeutic relationship is sound and stress is at a low level.

As is obvious from this outline of the narcissist's object relations, he is the ultimate other-directed individual. The self is defined almost entirely by the other or by the other's response to him. In the absence of the other, or in the absence of the favorable response, there is emptiness, despair, depression, or agitation, which is the narcissist's underlying emotional state. In defense of that state, the narcissistic personality will go to extreme lengths to find mirroring objects or to coerce those he has into the desired response.

The idealization of others which narcissists exhibit may be usefully conceptualized along the developmental continuum—merger, twinship, mirroring. In the merger transference, the individual will seek out and then misperceive the other as the *perfect* object with whom to merge. In ordinary life this perfection is most often sought in the *potential* mate—potential because it is nearly impossible to maintain idealization at close quarters. Where merger idealization exists there are always etiological difficulties with the nurturing-holding functions of the original caregivers. The individual is still looking for the symbiosis which was either insufficient or prematurely lost.

The perfect twinship is the idealization of the alter-ego transference, as seen in many adolescent love affairs. The perfect role model is the idealization of the mirroring transference. In this later developmental arrest, the individual needs someone to look up to, believe in, and emulate.

In each of these idealizations, the individual is looking for the self in the other. To a very real extent, this is a fruitful place to look, in that these kinds of relationships do provide the social context in which we come to know ourselves. But, unless the infantile, absolute character of the idealization is neutralized, there will be no maturation through internalization. Instead, the narcissistic person will endlessly circle from idealization to disillusionment, like the proverbial dog chasing its tail.

Identity Formation

The narcissistic etiology leads to a basic disruption in the *sense of self*, the self-*concept*, and the self-*image*. I use each of these labels deliberately to highlight the fact that the narcissist's self-representation in all three basic sensory systems (visual, auditory, and kinesthetic) will suffer some pathology. The etiological circumstances lead the person to decide, "There is something wrong with me as I am. I must be special." This basic "script decision" is similar to that of the schizoid, although it does not involve the issue of the right to exist and is not concurrent with the schizoid's extreme fear of others and terror of life itself. Rather, this decision involves more the concept of the self in all channels of representation. At the point of self-formation, the narcissist is led to reject some part of himself, to suppress the feelings of sadness and rage which accompany such rejection, and to invest his energies in the promulgation of that false self which will meet with the environment's approval. It takes the exertion of considerable will to suppress the real pleasure demands of the organism and embrace the idealized functioning demanded. Yet, the exercise of this will gives the child power in an environment that is adverse in some important respects to his real self expression. In the narcissistic situation, the normal parent-child relationship is in some important respects reversed, such that the child is used to gratify the narcissistic needs of the parent. In this reversal, the child gains considerable power to manipulate and control at a developmental period when manipulating and controlling the environment are of central importance. So, the child learns to forego the pleasures of the real self in exchange for the power and control realized by the exercise of the will required to actualize the false self demanded by the environment.

In the foregoing scenario, the child cuts himself off from a real sensory based experience of self and invests more exclusively in the self as it is seen or conceptualized (the self-image or self-concept). In other words, the self begins to be experienced not as the organismic whole it is, with the needs and pleasures it has. Rather, the self is an ideal, an image, a concept, an abstraction. The developmental arrest at grandiosity is then reinforced by the power the child experiences in meeting the parents' needs through the development of the false self. In a sense, the false self represents the ego's best shot at actualizing grandiosity in the real world. In this, the child makes the inevitable tragic decision of choosing power over pleasure. So, the self-representation at a kinesthetic level is often positively represented only by those feelings of elation and euphoria that come out of success, achievement, or the hollow joys of controlling, manipulating, or impressing others. As a result, the integrity of this "self" is extraordinarily dependent on those external sources of reassurance, yet the resulting sustenance is only temporary and unfulfilling. One is always craving more of what may taste good but is never filling or lasting.

As indicated earlier, the representation of self is far more consciously visual and conceptual than it is kinesthetic. It is more important to look good and think well of oneself than it is to feel good. In other words, "I am the one who lives up to my self-image and my self-concept." I derive good feelings only secondarily and artificially as the environment confirms the image or concept. The pride, euphoria, or elation that you see in the narcissist around his positive experience of self is often very mental and ungrounded, not truly representing a connected kinesthetic experience of pleasure in the body or even real pleasure in accomplishment. The downside of the narcissist's polarity around self-representation is far more kinesthetic in nature. When the false self fails in some way or the willpower becomes exhausted, the narcissist will collapse or compensate into ego-dystonic symptomatology.

I have found it useful to use Kohut's concept of the vertical and horizontal split to describe the three types of presentation of the self characteristic of the narcissistic patient. In Table 1, I have presented this outline using the concepts of false self, symptomatic self, and real self. The false self includes the behaviors, attitudes, and feelings of the compensation, including the developmental arrest in grandiosity with all its associated immaturity in ego functioning. The conscious awareness of the attributes of the false self by the individual is highly variable. Thus, the person may be aware that his self-esteem is very dependent on achievement or that he is perfectionistic, but he will not be aware of just how extreme these tendencies are. Similarly, he will

Table 1
THREE EXPRESSIONS OF NARCISSISM

False Self	*Symptomatic Self*
Reliance on achievement	Vulnerable to shame, humiliation
Perfectionism	Hypochondriacal, psychosomatic
Grandiosity-omnipotence	Worthlessness, self-depreciation
Pride	Isolation, loneliness
Entitlement	Depression, inertia, work inhibition
Self-involement	
Manipulation and objectification of others	

Real Self
Feelings of emptiness, void, panic with enfeeblement and fragmentation of the self
Archaic demands of rapprochement: Merger, twinship, mirror and idealization transferences
Feelings of rage and hurt at the empathic failures of the archaic demands
Searching for, discovery and development of the real self: Innate capacities, identification, ambitions, and ideals

be able to admit, at times, to the less attractive attributes of feelings of entitlement, pride, and self-involvement but will be understandably even more reluctant to admit to the true depth of these qualities. Kohut has been particularly helpful in labeling the unconsciousness of the false self as due to *disavowal*. This helps us differentiate and conceptualize its partial and variable conscious awareness. Also it assists us in understanding how the narcissist's self-involvement may be so obvious to us yet so apparently invisible to him.

This highly fragile compensation is difficult to sustain, and its breakdown will result in symptomatology represented on the right side of the vertical split. In this state, the person is extremely sensitive to slight or criticism, prone to depression and hypochondria, bothered by thoughts of worthlessness, imperfections, etc. These symptoms are conscious but their relation to archaic grandiosity is largely unknown.

These symptomatic defenses are usually polar opposites of those qualities that produce the elation, euphoria, and pride in the false self. If the compensation is bolstered by a beautiful self-image, the narcissist feels ugly in the extreme. If intelligence is the bulwark of the false self, she feels incredibly stupid. If energetic strength is the compensatory quality, he becomes weak. If material possessions provide the necessary positive projective identification, those possessions become hollow or inadequate.

The well-defended narcissist will spend his time primarily on the left side of this vertical split, but with dim awareness of its true depth and falseness, actively engaged with life in a frenetic attempt to keep this active-disavowing defense structure in place. As long as this ego-syntonic compensation is working, there is really no reason to seek out any therapeutic intervention; indeed, if he ever does, he will be interested in therapy only to reinstate that compensatory state. The less well-defended narcissistic character will spend more of his time on the right side of the vertical split in a chronic state of self-absorption, which may be cognitive and/or physical in nature, or in the crisis which occurs when all defenses fail. This, of course, is the condition in which most patients with a narcissistic style or character disorder will present themselves for treatment. Almost all seek the alleviation of these symptoms; only a few have a dim view of the underlying emotional reality which exists in the unconscious, below the horizontal line. This reality, which anyone would certainly avoid, includes the archaic crises of the rapprochement subphase and the affects associated with the failure of their resolution. Included here are the injury and rage of legitimate narcissistic demands chronically unmet and, perhaps most frightening, the sense of void in the experience of any real self.

The vertical split then relates to the experience of the polarity around self-worth. The characteristics outlined above the horizontal line describe what you will see in the narcissist. Some of the characteristics of the false self will be consciously and ego-syntonically experienced but most will be at least partially disavowed. The horizontal split covers the underlying unconscious demands and feelings and the essential absence of self. Perhaps the most difficult aspect of psychotherapy with all character problems involves the fact that it results in the very uncomfortable experience of the underlying emotional reality on the road to characterological transformation. The experience of that reality is quite understandably resisted, often at an unconscious, body level, making the discovery process long and painful.

Because the pure narcissist is generally better defended than the character structures developed earlier in the developmental process, it often takes massive, cumulative failure coupled with supportive therapeutic intervention to pull her toward that most uncomfortable underlying emotional reality. The key to any successful treatment of this tragic personality is in accessing whatever real self there is and furthering the development of self from arrest to transformation. As the compensations, both syntonic and dystonic, are dissolved, the person will begin to experience that very primitive and vulnerable self, subject to overwhelming affective states. As outlined in Table 1, the person may experience those extremely aversive feelings of panic, emptiness, and void associated with feeling there is no substance to the self. This direct experience of nothingness, of enfeeblement and fragmentation, is probably the most overwhelming affective experience and, for those narcissists who have any propensity to act out, the most dangerous.

Particularly at the lower or borderline end of the continuum, these feelings will be accompanied by deep experiences of rage and injury, demanding current empathic perfection to immediately gratify the archaic demands of the original rapprochement subphase—the need to merge with the perfect idealized other, the need to be attached in an experience of symbiotic twinship, the need for constant and perfect mirroring.

These patients may at these times launch vociferous attacks on the therapist and significant others in the environment. There is a very real danger of violence either to the self or others.

At the higher end of the continuum—the narcissistic style—there may very well be some rather extreme experiences of panic, void, and emptiness, together with a more controlled experience of those archaic demands and the associated narcissistic rage and injury. In other words, the higher functioning narcissist may experience but still be in wonderment at the extent to which he seems to want idealization or mirroring, and he may become alarmed at the depth of his hurt and rage. While he is easier to manage clinically because of the strength of his observing ego, the depth of his affective experience must be appreciated.

The silver lining in these very dark clouds is the beginning of the experience of reality. In the higher-functioning narcissist, there may even be expressions of relief and gratitude at the profundity of the reality of this experience. Even though it is bad, it is real, and that realness is to the higher-functioning person encouraging and, in a way, enlivening. It really requires this deep emotional experience to actualize the crucial shift from the *use of others to aggrandize and support the false self* to the *use of others to find and nurture the real self*. When that shift is made, the person can then devote his energy to that mission, which is at once human and heroic, simple and grand.

For me, it is the polarity around the self-representation in the vertical split that is clinically most definitional of the narcissistic presentation. But, it is the individual client's *particular* collapse into the underlying emotional reality that reveals the nature of early developmental injuries and resulting characterological issues. The false self compensation is the ego's best adaptation at the time of original injury to survive, maintain contact, retain love, and formulate the self. When the compensation fails and symptomatic defenses dissolve, the primary anxiety of the developmental period at which the false self was begun will resurface.

For the schizoid character, this will be the literal fear of annihilation. For the schizoid, if the false self dies, the being will die or be killed. The schizoid individual who has achieved a moderate level of observing adult ego abilities will experience the irrationality of this fear. Yet, she will still experience the extreme threat to survival and frequently have conceptual and imaginal experiences of actual annihilation when the false self is threatened. By contrast, the oral character will, in periods of severe depression, experience himself as extremely needy, weak, and distasteful and fear the desertion of any attachment objects that are significant for him. The collapse of the false self compensation will lead to the core fear of the loss of the object.

For the symbiotic character, the collapse of the false self will trigger similar fears of the loss of the object and, concomitantly and frighteningly, the loss of the emerging self. The symbiotic character knows who she is only in relation to the attachment object, so the loss of the object triggers the fear of the loss of the emerging self. In the narcissistic character, where the self-object discrimination is further along, the primary anxiety triggered is the loss of the love of the object. But since the love of the object is still intimately related to the existence of the self, that very existence is similarly threatened. Furthermore, for the narcissist the loss of the false self amounts to the loss of the ability to manipulate the environment and be in control. So, this loss also brings up the fear of being manipulated, humiliated, and used again. As a consequence, the "pure narcissist" (one who suffers from relatively little injury in prior phases) is more concerned with the loss of self-esteem and power to control the environment than all other character structures.

The characterological transformation of any pre-oedipal structure will involve this collapse into archaic, often overwhelming, feelings. In his treatment of the borderline and narcissistic character disorders, Masterson (e.g., 1976, 1981, 1985) has referred to this as the *abandonment* depression. Adler (1985), on the other hand, has emphasized the seeming threats of *annihilation* which come up for borderline patients. In his theoretical structure, these are the most essential core issues having to do with developmental arrest in the nurturing-holding phases of growth. Masterson sees borderline and narcissistic pathology as primarily coming out of developmental arrest in the individuation subphases, due to abandonment for individuation, whereas Adler and others see *borderline* pathology, particularly, as coming more out of failures in the parental nurturing-holding functions in the earlier developmental periods. I tend to agree with Adler's concepualization with respect to the more serious manifestations of *borderline* pathology, although I acknowledge, with him, that the late abandonment for individuation issues are also often present in borderline individuals. Similarly, the earlier issues of nurturing and holding are very often present in individuals with narcissistic pathology.

I think, however, that the "depression" label is somewhat of a misnomer when applied to these archaic, chaotic feelings. Though there are often depressive features in this reactivation of infantile feelings, and people certainly don't feel very good when they experience them, there is a good deal of creative expression in these times of emotional crisis. This expression may be shut down by depression, but depression is not the essence of the experience, but rather a defense against it. For all of these reasons, I will henceforth label this most critical therapeutic step for all pre-oedipal characterological transformations the *annihilation-abandonment crisis.* This label acknowledges the dual and often mixed role of the activated fears of annihilation on the one hand and abandonment for individuation on the other. In addition, it highlights the essence of the experience—a crisis—a healing crisis which may be either resisted or worked through.

The narcissist will be more easily reachable and treatable to the extent that he possesses an adult observing ego and to the extent that he has some ability to identify with the real self. That real self exists in the person's real feelings in the abandonment of depression, in any vestiges of natural human pleasure, and in the positive feelings of relatedness that derive from constructive past relationships.

As the real self is developed in the course of psychotherapy, both extremes of feeling will be tapped. Often, the pleasure is more difficult to reach than the pain, because the experience of real body pleasure elicits guilt and fear and the experience of relatedness elicits the fear of humiliation and the realization of all the human contact that has been lost. The fear involves letting go of the false security provided by the false self and embracing the life in the body, which is relatively unknown and is therefore anxiety-provoking.

Accessing the real self through pleasure and relatedness opens the person to accessing the pain of the annihilation-abandonment crisis. Still, many narcissists will remember or appreciate simple good feelings that can come from the ordinary experiences of life. These are the vestiges of the real self and represent the eventual rewards of finding that reality. Thankfully, the exaggerated forms of the narcissistic character presented in textbooks are rare. Most individuals with narcissistic issues can at least remember real pleasure and relatedness and either spontaneously or through therapeutic intervention be led to experience real pain. Both are necessary for the discovery and development of the real self.

The Nature of Real Self Formation

This search, discovery, and development mission cannot be done solo. Rather, it must be done in a social context in which the input and support of others are authentically used to form a better reality experience of the self. Though the transition from symbiosis to individuation has its very real difficulties, there is in the human being an innate push to differentiation, autonomy, and individual self-expression. In the unspoiled condition, the most natural self-expression exists in the realization of those innate capacities which develop spontaneously. We do not know how specific those innate capacities are, but we can be sure from observation of children that they at least include such variables as activity level, strength, and intelligence. At least a part of what Kohut has termed the "nuclear self" or what we may call the "real self" is the unfettered realization of these innate capacities.

At the same time, that expression of real self needs to be contextualized within the culture which surrounds and shapes the individual. It is clear from the observation of children that they seek to identify with and mimic the significant others in their environment and begin the creation of a unique self in this early identification. Furthermore, Kohut has offered the interpretation that the self is also the ultimate product of the child's natural and healthy grandiosity, which ultimately matures into ambition, and natural and healthy idealization, which matures to the formation of guiding ideals and admiration of idealizable figures. Thus, for me, the true or nuclear or real self is an amalgam of the expression of innate capacity, the fine-tuning and maturation of identification, the neutralization of grandiosity to the expression of ambition, and the maturation over an entire life span of values which are arrived at by a functioning self within a social context.

The reader familiar with Kohut will see the profound influence of his thought in this conceptualization, though there are some subtle differences of language and model. There is in this conceptualization a treatment of both the lower and higher selves, although it is often difficult to know exactly where one leaves off and the other begins. The "self" is a complex construct on the one hand and a simple experience on the other. It is the experience of self which is ultimately most important to the individual, but it is the integration of lower and higher elements that makes that experience whole. At the "lower" level, it is an experience of wholeness in the body, groundedness in one's reality, continuity over time, and cohesiveness. At the "higher" level, it is the experience of integrity, meaningfulness, and purpose in the context of a lifetime. Thus, in a sense, the experience of a whole self integrates the body-mind duality and, though we can have words for that duality, the *experience* of self in its most complete form is not dualistic, but unitary.

As Kohut has so poignantly pointed out, we live in a time in which that unity or wholeness is rare and difficult to achieve. The tragedy of Kohut's "tragic man" is the conscious experience of the lack of wholeness and unity, indeed the experience of fragmentation, enfeeblement, and unrealized potential. The depression of tragic man is the awareness of *what could have been* with the achievement of wholeness compared with *what is* in the reality of his experience of fragmentation and enfeeblement. The compensation for this tragedy, which is tragic itself, is narcissism.

Defensive Functions

A useful paradigm for understanding the narcissistic character was offered by Werner Erhard in his *est* training. I paraphrase this presentation to be more consistent with the present object relations metaphor for understanding narcissistic behavior. The essential proposition is that, for the narcissist, the ego creates the false self to meet the needs of the real being as well as they possibly can be met under the circumstances. In this creation, however, the ego begins to mistake the false self for the real self. Thus, any threat to the false self is responded to as if it were a threat to the real self—a threat to the integrity of the being. A threat to the false self threatens annihilation-abandonment and the associated anxieties of any prior developmental phase in which there was trauma. This state of extreme alarm automatically calls up defensive maneuvers available to the individual. In the case of the "pure narcissist," all psychological defenses are available from the earliest developmental periods (e.g., denial, introjection, projection, reversal), as well as the more developed defenses of the rapprochement period (e.g., splitting, coercion, and other forms of acting-out). In its often frantic attempts to save the false self, the ego will marshall all defenses, even to the point of destroying the *life* of the real human being. So, for the narcissist, if you threaten his self-image or self-concept, it is as if you are threatening his very being. This, in part, explains the intensity of the annihilation-abandonment crisis and the extremity of the defensive maneuvers to which the narcissistic individual may resort for self-protection.

It is very easy to conceptualize the defensive functioning of the false self because its reliance on achievement, perfectionism, grandiosity, pride, and manipulation all obviously serve to protect the individual from the confrontation of the basic injury and the continuing reality of archaic demands and their disappointments. The functions of the symptomatic self are less obvious and therefore deserve further elaboration. I view the characteristics of the symptomatic self as being both symptomatic of the underlying characteristics of the real self *and* symptomatic of the breakdown of the false self compromise. The symptoms are really the battleground for the struggle between the demands of the real self with its painful emotional reality and the valiant attempts of the compromised false self to avoid that pain and maintain functioning.

The propensity to shame and humiliation, for example, at once signals the "press from below" of the basic narcissistic injury, the enfeeblement of the real self, and the associated archaic demand for mirroring. Concomitantly, it signals the unrealistic, grandiose demands imposed by the infantile false self with its arrest in grandiosity. The extremity of the feelings of worthlessness, humiliation, and shame associated with any failure or embarrassment is symptomatic of the refusal to relinquish the grandiose self-concept which allows no human fallibility.

To the extent that the blows of failure or disappointment can be cushioned, the frustration can be made "optimal" and result in a gradual accommodation of the false grandiosity. Otherwise, the propensity to shame or humiliation persists as a casualty of the battle between the demands of the real self and the equally archaic and arrested demands of the false self. This same dynamic explains the feelings of worthlessness and the propensity to self-depreciation whenever there is a failure or embarrassment.

Psychosomatic illness and hypochondriacal preoccupation are similarly casualties of the battleground. The psychosomatic illness can often be a symptom of the tension created by this epic conflict. Further, the illness may be maintained by the function it serves in releasing the patient from the unrealistic and grandiose demands of the false self. The hypochondriacal overinvolvement with the body may usefully be conceptualized as an example of isolation of concern with the self. Since the body is the concrete manifestation of the self, a preoccupation with its enfeeblement may be defensively isolated in a body part or specific illness (Kohut, 1971). This maneuver defends against the real affective experience of such enfeeblement at a more psychological level.

Depression may represent a real deadening of the organism so as to avoid the underlying feelings of void, panic, and fragmentation when the false self compromise has failed and the underlying emotional reality of the real self threatens to become overwhelming. I view true depression as a deadening rather than experiencing of affect and, as such, a defensive maneuver. Like illness, depression also serves to protect the grandiose-omnipotent expectations of the false self ("I could do it if I weren't so depressed/ill."). The inertia and work inhibition frequently seen in narcissistic individuals relate to this defensive posture. In the full flower of his grandiosity, the narcissist believes that he should be able to achieve great things with little or no effort. Thus, even outstanding achievement may not be very rewarding if it has to be earned by hard work.

Finally, the isolation to which the narcissist usually subjects himself is in part the result of his grandiosity and associated perfectionism for others. No one is really good enough when known well—the narcissist's social distance defends the breakdown of idealization. In addition, the isolation really protects the individual from intimacy, which would trigger the threatening archaic demands of the real self, as well as challenge the perfectionism that the narcissist retains about his potential interpersonal relations. The loneliness which can result from this isolation is primarily symptomatic of the push from below—the needs of the real self. Such demands are very threatening to the false self; this, in part, explains why many a narcissistic individual will suffer loneliness rather than use it as a signal to reach out.

Thus, the qualities of the symptomatic self are the result of the intense pressure and resulting conflict with the false and real self. The symptoms are, in part, compromises in this struggle which protect from awareness the grandiose elements of the false self as well as the affective demands of the real self. The symptoms are at once signals of the underlying demands and defensive compromises which protect from awareness what they are signaling. The crucial therapeutic task is to help the individual discover and identify with what the symptoms are signaling, while simultaneously defusing the defensive use of those symptoms. Psychotherapy is a tricky business.

Energetic Expression

In understanding and utilizing the present character typology, it is important to remember that the narcissistic character will show greater diversity in all forms of expression than those structures outlined earlier in the developmental sequence. This fact follows the developmental theoretical model in that the etiology of narcissism, in the narrow sense, is later in the developmental sequence. At this time, the child possesses a relatively larger number of resources and defensive capabilities. In addition, and perhaps more importantly, there is greater variability concerning which parts of the real self are unwelcome in the environment. Because of the variability in the type of frustration experienced, there will be greater variability in the characterological expression at all levels. To complicate things even further in the actual clinical situation, narrow narcissism per se probably never occurs singularly, without any other forms of earlier character pathology. In other words, every narcissist I have seen has demonstrated aspects of schizoid, oral, or symbiotic characteristics. In spite of all this complexity, however, I still find the archetypal guidelines useful.

In orienting to the understanding of the energetic expression of the narcissistic character, it is useful to remember that energetic distortions are primarily the result of the self-negation process in character formation. In other words, we develop energetic blocks in the body to restrain or render unconscious those impulses and reactions that are unacceptable or punished. To a lesser extent, the bodily expressions of character can reflect the ego ideal or the false self presented to the world in compensation for the original injury. In the narcissistic character, both etiological factors are operative on the body level.

In their discussion of the "psychopathic" character (which I believe is better named narcissistic), the bioenergetic analysts have distinguished two types of bodily expression, emphasizing one or the other of these basic processes. The "upward displaced psychopath" is characterized by underdevelopment or weakness in the lower half of the body with accompanying overdevelopment—a sort of a "puffed up" appearance—in the upper half of the body. This body type is thought to reflect that narcissistic development in which there is an ungrounded and weak base supporting exaggerated power, willfulness, and achievement. The "chameleon psychopath," on the other hand, shows no obvious distortions in the body; rather, a false self mask is presented to the world.

In either case, however, there are blocks in the body that prohibit a full feeling awareness of all or part of the real self. Because the body is the real self and the feelings that it signals, both types can share rigidity and constriction in those areas that block that natural flow.

Since the parental using or restriction of the narcissistic patient often involves the sexual realm, the narcissistic client often shows a pelvis that is rigidly held, the tension therein blocking the awareness and release in the sexual charge. Together with this, there is often a block or constriction at the waistline that further inhibits the awareness of sexual impulse. In the upwardly displaced narcissist, this break also inhibits the awareness of the ungroundedness or weakness in the lower half of the body.

Moving up the body, the narcissistic character often also shows a tightness and constriction in the diaphragm, inhibiting full body breathing and often yielding shallow chest breathing that inhibits full awareness of the body and its feeling. Symbolic of the narcissistic "rising to the occasion" of parental manipulation and expectation, the narcissist often shows raised shoulders with a good deal of tightness across the shoulders. There is often tightness in the narrows of the neck region, inhibiting the flow of feelings between body and head, a constriction that is also seen in schizoid and oral structures.

Similarly, and in common with the schizoid structure, the narcissist often has a severe block in the muscles at the base of the skull or the "ocular segment." This block is, among other things, the "one-yard line" through which bodily feelings might break through to awareness. In addition, that block is often associated by the bioenergetic therapists with the narcissist's unwillingness to see the reality of his family situation. In a more contemporary sense, the eye block also prevents him from really seeing others as real human beings and allows him to dissociate, seeing others as objects for his gratification and manipulation.

Not surprisingly, many bioenergetic analysts have reported noticing the eyes of the narcissistic character to display suspicion and/or charm and beguiling qualities. Both are consistent with the narcissist's concern about being used and his adaptation of using others to prevent this dreaded result.

Though the upwardly displaced narcissistic character with all of these energy blocks is the easiest to spot in clinical practice, many truly narcissistic characters will share an energetic block in at least some of these areas. The chameleon character is often harder to spot from the energetic point of view. In this case, there can sometimes be a more truly psychopathic character disorder that represents injury at a far earlier etiological base. The slipperiness and smooth manipulativeness of this person may warn of a more truly dangerous character pathology.

THERAPEUTIC OBJECTIVES

At all levels, the therapy for the narcissistic person must be consistently devoted to the discovery and enhancement of natural self-expression. The narcissist, for good reason, has martyred himself and reinvested depleted energy in egocentric pursuits. To regain his life, he must become aware of this martyrdom, feel how he has sacrificed and is continuing to sacrifice himself, and mourn the irretrievable losses in that historical and continuing death. Eventually, he must rediscover his own deeply buried needs and, however clumsily and tentatively at first, meet them. This is a person who, however glamorous and successful he may appear, is *bereft in his internal experience*. Often obsessed with success, he is a failure by the criterion of the very experience of life itself. The affective and cognitive awareness of this fact is necessary to initiate any change.

Cognitive Objectives

An organizing therapeutic objective with the narcissistic person is to enhance self-awareness—awareness of the grandiose false self, the dystonic symptomatic self, and the underlying, if enfeebled, real self. I will begin this discourse with cognitive objectives because it is often easier for a person to discover who he is trying to be, who he hates being, and ultimately who he really is at a more cognitive level. Of course, a cognitive understanding of this alone is totally insufficient, but it is a beginning and one which often triggers the more central underlying feelings. In a very real sense, the intelligent narcissist may need to fill in his own "three faces of narcissism" as listed in Table 1 to fully understand himself.

The overall therapeutic objectives with the narcissistic patient are (1) to erode the compensations to the experience of reality whether they are ego-syntonic or -dystonic, (2) to assist and pace the patient in experiencing the painful but real underlying realities of the self, and (3) to support and nurture the discovery and development of the real self. Successful therapy with the narcissist must set the wheels in motion toward what Kohut has called the "transformation of narcissism," which involves a deep maturation of the human being and results in the development of creativity, acceptance of transience, the capacity for empathy, a sense of humor, and wisdom. To cure the narcissist is to effect at least the beginnings of a real "growing up" of the individual – often from a quite immature little boy or girl to a very wise man or woman capable of living at once in the body and in the expression of ideals. This, of course, is an ideal, but not a bad one by which to be pulled.

Because most narcissists will begin psychotherapy with symptomatic expression, it is often possible to begin movement in treatment with the therapist's empathic experiencing of the client's pain. This gives the patient an experience of empathic regard, provides an appropriately idealizable model of this natural human capacity, and begins the creation of a safe place in which many painful experiences will be confronted.

A very therapeutic interpretation or reframe of the symptomatic self is this: The pain of the symptoms is a signal from the denied real self that its needs are not being met. The worthlessness and self-depreciation are signs of the underlying injury; depression or inertia a signal of unwillingness to martyr the real person for the nonsustaining nutriment which the false compensation provides; the loneliness a signal of the deprivation which occurred earlier and which persists now as a result of the narcissist's objectification, manipulation, and rejection of others. Physical pain is a direct signal of psychic pain – a result of the chronic holding back of impulses in defensive preoccupations which prevents the experience of that self and real underlying emptiness, injury, and rage. The pain of the symptomatic self is at once real and bogus. The patient hurts, but the hurt is only an approximation, a signal, a defense against a deeper level of pain and an acquired inability to deal with it.

A detailed analysis of how each symptom may be defensive to the underlying pathology will, especially at first, be experienced as a narcissistic reinjury. Such premature analyses can usually be experienced only cognitively, yet have the unwanted affective result of causing people to feel guilty and overwhelmed. They encourage a migration of conscious awareness to the head, resulting in fruitless obsession. The overall reframe, *pain is a signal*, however, can be very empathically delivered and facilitate turning attention to where it belongs. The reframe also provides the rationale for techniques that open the person to greater awareness of the psychic reality of the real self. There can then be the self-exploration of the psychic and historical meaning of those peculiar vulnerabilities to criticism and shame and those persistent feelings of worthlessness. Similarly, the reframe can pave the way for an internal search, using numerous therapeutic methods, for the meanings of the signaling function of depression, inertia, loneliness, and physical symptoms. In that process, it will then be useful to access in some detail the self-statements which accompany dysphoria.

It will be very therapeutic for the narcissistic client to fully access, explore, expand upon, and find the exact language for the uncomfortable states which she experiences. Perhaps even more important, it will be therapeutic for her to have this understood and fed back to her in an empathic and caring way. A narcissistic individual will often express surprise that another person is genuinely interested and caring and, after that surprise, will begin to experience the extraordinary longing that she has always had for such concern. In this process, the focus on cognitive content will naturally lead to the important affective experiences surrounding these issues and ultimately lead to the deeper affective experiences of the real self.

Once some of this affective experience has been accomplished and trust has been built, it will be more possible to move on to at least a cognitive understanding of the compensatory grandiosity of the false self. Here it is important for the person to realize the very real and infantile extent of his grandiosity, reliance on achievement, pride, and his attitudes of entitlement, manipulation, and objectification. At the lower or borderline end of the continuum, the individual will, at least initially, be more likely to experience these tendencies as ego-syntonic. He may, for example, be angry with others for not recognizing his special status which entitles him to be the center of other people's universe. Even here, however, the repeated verbalization of these attitudes to a therapist who is empathic, yet not fully indulgent of these beliefs, will begin the growth and the healing process. Fortunately, this extremely low level of functioning is relatively rare and most patients who present themselves for outpatient care will have less conscious access to these more infantile attitudes and will experience some surprise, embarrassment, and even disbelief at uncovering them in a safe therapeutic context. In these more common cases, their repeated accessing and verbalization will more quickly establish greater ego control over these tendencies and thereby pave the way for the emerging awareness of the underlying real self with its painful but real emotional experiences.

When one gets to this point in the therapeutic process, a cognitive exploration of the defensive functions of the compensatory false self is usually possible without serious narcissistic reinjury. When such explanations or interpretations are provided or when they are elicited from the client herself, they give a very real hope for significant change. Even though there is a good deal of negativity as these disagreeable qualities are brought to awareness, the insights regarding them have the same results as other insights—they provide a kind of cohesion to the self in their offering self-understanding and providing historical comprehension. In addition, this kind of self-understanding is self-supportive because of the very significant use of the self's intellectual and rational functions in achieving it.

As the compensatory qualities are revealed, understood, and dissolved, more and more of the underlying emotional reality—the real self—is brought up for examination. Though much of the initial work at that level will be of an affective nature, the organization I have imposed on this presentation calls for elucidating the work at a cognitive level. Here the primary work is one of explanation, reconstruction, and interpretation which relates the current disappointments, injuries, and rage to the earlier failures of the environment to meet legitimate child demands. Further, the resulting emptiness, void, panic, and fragmentation are the result of a self that has been undernourished, unsupported, and undeveloped in certain crucial areas of functioning.

Although it is important in this discourse to emphasize that not all of the work at this level will be of a cognitive nature, the cognitive work has largely to do with the person's understanding of who he is currently and achieving a cognitive history of the self so that he understands how he got here. Furthermore, this cognitive work will then lead to presentation of a road map for the client in his work of self-discovery and self-development. The therapeutic work will involve a good deal of support for his innate capacities, his right to live out his mature ambitions, and his need to identify his values and live consistently with them.

Through all of this, the therapist will repeatedly encourage and support a realistic assessment of the client's abilities, resources, and achievements, while at the same time encouraging a realistic assessment of his limitations, weaknesses, and vulnerabilities. This work, then, is really a rapprochement between the three selves heretofore isolated. Cure is a rapprochement and acceptance of one's abilities, achievements, and ambitions with one's vulnerabilities and weaknesses in the context of achieving an expression of one's innate true self within the larger context of an imperfect world.

In list form, then, here are the cognitive objectives for the treatment of the narcissistic client:

1. Access self-statements of worthlessness, distrust, self-criticism, inertia, depression, loneliness, etc.
2. Access the self-statements of reliance on achievement, grandiosity, pride, entitlement, manipulation, and the rationalization of such qualities.
3. Access the defensive functions of the false and symptomatic selves.
4. Assist the client in developing a historical and dynamic understanding of himself with regard to his feelings of emptiness, void, fragmentation of the self, his archaic demands of others and life itself, and his feelings of rage and deep hurt.
5. Assist the client in establishing an understanding of the process of discovery and development of the real self through the expression of his innate capacities, ambitions, and ideals.
6. Assist the client toward an integrated and ambivalent experience of the self and others.
7. Support a realistic assessment of the client's abilities, resources, and achievements.
8. Support a realistic assessment of the client's limitations, weaknesses, and vulnerabilities.
9. Assist the client in an integration and acceptance of all the above qualities of self.

Affective Objectives

The essential affective objectives with the narcissistic person are to mourn the injury and the loss of self and to then build a true sense of self. Additionally, in the course of the therapeutic process, the person will need to expose the disavowed parts of his grandiose false self, including the feelings of superiority, entitlement, pride, disgust with others, etc. Then, as the grandiose elements of the false self are exposed, the patient will need to be assisted in dealing with the terror that arises when the compromises of the false self are seen for the failures they are and relinquished. If I am not my accomplishments, my beauty, or the other false, grandiose symbols which have heretofore defined me, then who am I? As that question is posed, the terror of the void arises. To face this, of course, requires courage and a therapeutic relationship of considerable trust.

To surrender / to the Self / to the Void / to Christ

The building of such trust will be necessary in implementing all objectives, but particularly the affective ones. The narcissist needs above all else to be understood. There is a great propensity to shame in revealing the exaggerated claims of the grandiose false self, the human failings of the symptomatic self, and the intense archaic demands and feelings of the real self. It is very therapeutic for the narcissistic client simply to show his vulnerability and confess his grandiosity in a setting where he can be empathically understood. Whichever side of the polarity he begins with (false or symptomatic self), he will typically oscillate between the two throughout much of the initial phases of the therapeutic work. The therapist's deep understanding of the "phase appropriateness" of his grandiosity on the one hand and his vulnerability on the other will assist the therapist in giving the kind of empathic response required. Often, little more than this ever needs to be done.

I have found that the more purely narcissistic the individual, the less I have to rely on any "technique" to bring up the affective realities. If you provide empathic understanding, you will, often without any further probing, go deeper into the levels of the false self and eventually to the archaic demands and affects of the real self. Techniques are differentially more useful, in my experience, as the client is less obviously narcissistic, better defended, and thereby more functional—the narcissistic style. Whether more obvious techniques are used or not, it will be the client's life and current level of awareness that will dictate the order in which his affective realities—either in the grandiose false self or in the repressed real self—will be brought to awareness. In many cases, to simply own the disavowed grandiose aspects of the false self is adequate to begin their frustration and maturation.

In working with the affects of the real self, it is often the feeling of injury at the empathic failures which most needs to be accessed. That accessing of injury will also lead to the fears of reinjury which underlie the suspicion, distrust, and even paranoia of the narcissistic person. Further, this distrust is a very close cousin to that disappointment experienced around the failures of idealized others in the past. In all of this, underneath the feeling of injury are the repressed needs for merger, twinship, and/or mirroring. And, underneath the feelings of disappointment are the repressed needs for idealization.

Mixed in among all of this, of course, is the well-known narcissistic rage, which can be of overwhelming proportions. Particularly in the more borderline narcissist, it is wise to be careful in accessing this rage and to manage its resurrection at tolerable levels throughout the treatment course. As these more negative affects are handled, it begins to become more and more possible to transform them into their more mature counterparts and to nurture the narcissist's abilities toward empathy and love. As structure is formed and made more solid, the narcissistic person is in an ever-better position to open himself to these softer feelings with the knowledge that he can protect himself and survive any future disappointments. Here, in list form, are the affective objectives with the narcissistic patient.

1. Access the injuries caused by empathic failures in response to the needs for merger, twinship, and mirroring.
2. Access the injuries of disappointment at the failures of idealized others.
3. Access the fear of reinjury—the suspicion, distrust, and paranoia.
4. Access the narcissistic rage in response to injury and disappointment.
5. Access the continuing need for merger, idealization, twinship, and mirroring and assist in the differentiation and maturation of these needs.
6. Access all affective elements of the grandiose compensatory self—grandiosity, entitlement, pride, etc.
7. Access the feelings of emptiness, void, fragmentation, and discontinuity of the real self.
8. Nurture, support, and effect internalization of empathy and love for others.

9. Establish trust in the real self and trust for others.
10. Transform the grandiose false self into the "normal narcissism" of true self-love.
11. Transform the injury to vulnerability and the accepted limitations of the self, others, and life itself.

Behavioral-Social Objectives

In a general way, the behavioral-social objectives for the narcissistic client are the same as for all other pre-oedipal characters. It is important to support those behavioral strategies and social support resources that will sustain the client through the hard work of a very basic and therefore very threatening change in his way of being. Anything that supports the viability of existing resources will be important. A number of techniques can be employed to enhance the value of already existing resources. Where strategies exist to combat work inhibitions, for example, they can be acknowledged and supported. Where such strategies do not exist, they may be taught and then supported. In a very meaningful way, psychotherapy for the narcissist is disorganizing. Yet, compensatory and consciously applied strategies for organization may be very therapeutic in preventing very real ego breakdowns, which can reach dangerous proportions when the affects of the underlying real self become overwhelming.

Most narcissistic individuals are in some very meaningful way isolated. However active their social life, there is an isolation from real contact with a real human community. A great deal of the narcissist's treatment will involve accessing his real need for others and assisting him in getting his needs met. Both directly and indirectly, this will involve training in becoming a more social being—one who is able to initiate and sustain empathy, regard, and understanding of others. This behavioral-social work is so interwoven with the affective and cognitive work that it is difficult to separate. Still, it is possible, in some very meaningful ways, to directly retrain the narcissist in open communication through the use of modeling, practice, and reinforcement. He may be taught active listening skills or empathic responding and asked to participate in exercises that directly teach him how to receive the caring responses of others.

Perhaps the most important work with the narcissist on the behavioral-social level is to assist him in finding and then sustaining a support system that really helps him find himself, rather than one that merely mirrors his grandiose, false self with its associated achievements and symbols. If he can find, and then sustain, a social system that gives him the support and understanding he needs to really find and develop himself, he is on the road to that outcome. If he can find people who really like *him*, who can accurately see and accept his virtues and vulnerabilities, who can lend him the support he needs, give him the acceptance and understanding he needs, and provide for him the role models and realistically idealizable figures he needs, he will get better. To do this, of course, he will have to accept his need for others and accept a level of humanity and fallibility in others which he probably has heretofore rejected. To a very great extent, it will be his confrontation with the void and its associated panic that will motivate him in this direction.

A significant amount of failure and frustration appears to be necessary for the narcissist to get on the right track in terms of his own maturation and healing. Once he does, however, the system may provide the increasingly mature levels of acceptance and frustration he requires to effect the internalization of resources, resulting in real autonomy in the context of greater real support. While a good deal of understanding, release, forgiveness, and growth can occur in psychotherapy, the narcissist really requires a functioning social system in which to mature and transform his narcissism. Without that functioning social system, the therapeutic gains of the narcissistic client will be severely limited. Here, in list form, are the behavioral-social objectives:

1. Support or teach those ego-organizational abilities which will counteract fragmentation of the self in response to the therapeutic process.
2. Support realistic achievement and assertiveness in the client's life.
3. Support the client's social resources and assist him in using them as fully as possible.
4. Directly instruct the client in social behaviors that communicate empathy, regard, and understanding of others. Teach him to "let in" the warmth and human caring that others can provide.

5. Assist the client in the development of a self-discovering and self-sustaining support system which incorporates others for merger, mirroring, twinship, and idealization. The goal of such a system is to provide internalization of resources resulting in greater autonomy in the context of greater support.

The healing of narcissism, like all characterological healing, involves, at core, the *decision to grow up*—a decision to mature with respect to those infantile issues at which one is quite literally *arrested*. The decision to grow up is a decision to finally give up the infantile hopes of magical fulfillment—fulfillment without effort, without compromise, without limitation—without a rapprochement with reality. My way, right or wrong, is the infantile demand. It is hard to give up, and the elaborate unconscious maneuvers reflective of this refusal are truly impressive. The objective of therapy is to defeat those maneuvers but, particularly in the narcissist's case, that defeat must be gentle—neither humiliating nor destructive of the human spirit. The narcissistic person, no matter how disagreeable he may be initially or from time to time, deserves love like all other human beings. The task of growing up which he faces is formidable and other human beings who can love will be willing to help. In accepting such help, the narcissist accepts his essential humanity, begins his rapprochement, and finally lets in what he has always wanted, the love and acceptance which only other people can provide.

CHAPTER III

TREATMENT OF THE SYMPTOMATIC SELF

THE THERAPEUTIC SET AND COUNTERTRANSFERENCE

WHEN YOU ARE ONE-TO-ONE with a narcissistic patient, there is only one person in the room capable of any real love and recognition for the true self of the narcissist—you. Such true love and recognition are the narcissist's deepest longing and most long-forsaken hope. The gratification of this wish does not share the pitfalls of many other forms of indulgence in the therapeutic setting, for this is not the kind of gratification that the narcissist consciously demands. Indeed, such love and recognition are often threatening and frustrating and, in the right doses, optimally so. The child in the adult, the real self buried beneath the symptoms or a well-polished front, needs an advocate. In the successful therapy of the narcissistic person, you will be that advocate. Through your attention, understanding, patience, prizing, compassion, and yes, even love, your client will learn that he is worthy and lovable.

The narcissist's long and ultimately self-denying attachment to his grandiose false self merely represents a deeply injured person's attempt to hang onto some semblance of self-acceptance. It was his only choice in an environment that did not really recognize *him* and/or sadistically humiliated him for his very humanity, as represented by his needs and vulnerabilities. Mirroring his early environment, the narcissist now persists in doing this to himself—even as he struts in his self-pride or complains in his pain. While your work with him may at times be difficult and complex, your guiding principle is very simple—to discover, understand, accept, and support that real human being who wants only what human beings have always wanted. To remember this set and behave consistently with it will avoid many therapeutic errors, which come from countertransference reactions, overemphasis on technique, or overinvestment in results.

In the early stages of therapy, this can mean simply understanding, or "getting" the phenomenological reality of a client. It is very useful with this kind of person to initially do this and nothing more—to avoid embellishing, interpreting, explaining, or intervening, at least for a while. Many such interventions are unwelcome to the narcissistic patient, and, indeed, are experienced as a narcissistic injury in one form or another—an implication that she is flawed, too stupid to figure things out for herself, in need of support, etc. Even though the client with a narcissistic style is not nearly so sensitive, she will typically very much appreciate and code as *different* this experience of being listened to and simply understood. Most of us value such an experience, but the narcissistic person, with her archaic needs for mirroring, will treasure it. This initial care and understanding will provide a bond between you and the client's real self, which will help sustain both of you through the frustrations and crises which are inevitable in a characterological treatment. The narcissistic person has really sold herself out, either out of the need to live up to others' expectations or because of the need to protect herself from intolerable injuries, or both. She now continues to do what was done to her—idealize herself and expect far too much of herself while concomitantly punishing herself and disparaging her worth because of failure to measure up to these unrealistic demands. She needs someone to listen to and understand *her*, to mirror, prize, and value *her*, and to demand that she fulfill her potential to meet her real human needs. This is what her parents could not adequately do for her but what you and others can do for her now, so that, over time, she will transform through internalization and maturation.

As with most characterological problems, the primary block to your offering this kind of care is your own narcissism. To the extent that your issues are narcissistic, you will be inclined to narcissistically cathect the client and unconsciously resent giving her what you yourself have not received. Though you may very much wish to fulfill the therapeutic role, you will tend to unconsciously resent being an advocate for someone else's real self when you desperately need this for yourself. There will be a tendency to resent giving another this kind of echoing and mirroring and, particularly in the early stages, allowing yourself to be *used* simply as a mirror or sounding board. You will want to do more—to intervene, create, experience, change, transform. And, to the extent that you do this, the client will once again have a set of expectations to live up to. She will try to be your best patient. You may find her ever so ready to convert to whatever brand of psychological intervention you are selling and aggrandize your false, grandiose self by exemplifying the success of your efforts.

Though I think there are many valuable ideas and strategies provided by the transformational psychology movement, I think that it is particularly prone to this form of error. Its ideology and claims for instant success are often characterized by grandiosity, and its participants sometimes appear to be great exemplars of "transference cures" based upon an unintegrated identification with an idealized charismatic leader. Here there is a collusion of the narcissistic idealization transference of the client with the narcissistic need for mirroring transference in the leader or therapist. Since both are thereby bolstered in their false, grandiose compensatory selves, there is nowhere a push for resolution of the transference.

In transformational movements, the client is often further *used* to promulgate the transformational message to others. The quality of his transformation is then evaluated by the success of such promulgation. This unfortunate scenario is not limited to those more obvious examples, but can occur for any therapist or leader whose narcissistic issues are both unconscious and unresolved. The "quiet competence" (Kohut, 1984) of a therapeutic program which consistently pursues the discovery and expression of the person's own true self within realistic limits and through inevitable frustrations will ultimately succeed. The other alternative only compounds the original injury.

The other pole or risk in the countertransference with the narcissistic client is to buy the rather polished package he may be selling, to idealize him, and to miss the truly impoverished real self that exists beneath the surface. While this is a far less likely outcome in most cases, those very effective narcissists who may enter treatment ancillary to the therapy of their spouse or family may be the most likely to succeed in pulling the wool over the therapist's eyes. Particularly when the therapist may be prone to envy this often more active and successful individual, there is the risk of such countertransferential reaction. While this kind of client is difficult to manage and may never really see his own personal difficulties, he certainly is not helped any by recruiting another member for his fan club. Though his compromises may appear to be working, he too has sold himself out and is usually getting very little real nurturance and pleasure in life.

The cardinal principle of characterological therapy is to avoid repetition of the original injury and to allow some gratification of the natural human needs that were not gratified originally. In the narcissist's case, these principles are followed by constructing a therapeutic relationship in which there is some degree of basic trust, genuineness, and conscious avoidance of false promises or manipulation. The narcissist's history is one of use and/or humiliation in close interpersonal relationships, so in the therapeutic close encounter it is important to avoid this kind of relationship and to repair it immediately whenever there is a slip in that direction. Because the narcissistic character, like all others, tends to recreate the original trauma, it is not unlikely that the drama will be played out, if only in some small way, in the therapeutic relationship. Even when the therapist behaves perfectly, the narcissistic client will tend to project reasons for mistrust, manipulation, and ingenuineness.

In building this trustful and genuine relationship, it may be necessary to allow some of the client's idealization of the therapist in cases where the client needs to work through this transference notion. Still, it is important for the therapist to have a realistic perception of himself, his abilities and limitations. It is important to avoid promises of success, as well as techniques that in any way manipulate. Doing, believing, manipulating, and living up to expectations are the fortes of the false self. The narcissist can perform, but he cannot be himself. Gaining the ability to be himself will be the objective of the psychotherapy. So it is important for the therapist to *be himself* in the most genuine and realistic manner. In this way, the therapist produces the optimal condition for the client's trust. This does not mean that it is necessary for you to share all of the details of your life or disabuse your client of any necessary projections or idealizations. Quite the contrary; it means only be genuine and trustworthy.

I recall one humiliating example in which I made a breach of trust and then had to repair it before the therapeutic process could continue. I was seeing a narcissistic client with whom I had some limited outside committee involvement. He asked me in front of another committee member the time of our next meeting. I, misunderstanding him, responded with the time of our next session rather than the time of the next committee meeting. Whether or not the third party caught the significance of this slip, it was a definite, if unconscious, breach of confidentiality. The incident still makes me uncomfortable in that I most definitely erred and the unconscious motivation may well have been to aggrandize myself by revealing the relationship.

In a postmortem of the incident with the client, I apologized for the error and used the opportunity to explain to the client why it was such a serious error in relation to his own history. At the same time, it was an error with tremendous therapeutic potential in that its repair, which resulted in a restoration of trust in the relationship, is precisely the kind of repair that ultimately needs to be accomplished. We do not live in a perfect world and, to the extent that we are looking for and setting up our original injuries, we can find just the imperfections in others that are needed to justify distrust. Working this through by repairing incidents of relationship breakdown can be a most critical part of a narcissist's treatment.

I always feel better about myself if the breach in trust has more to do with projection than in the previous example. Still, it is in the interest of repairing the therapeutic relationship that a therapist must take responsibility for her part in the difficulty. I have had narcissistic clients, for example, pick up on those instances when I am even slightly less available or present than usual and use this variation to justify a serious breach of therapeutic trust. In these cases, it is important for me to take responsibility for the lapse in my own behavior and to acknowledge my own limitations. While perfection as a therapist may be a laudable goal, perfectionism around obtaining it is a narcissistic adaptation. To model reality for the narcissistic client, one must model acceptance of one's limitations and forgiveness of one's errors. When you do that, you are being real and genuine; more importantly, you're acting healthy and allowing yourself to learn from your mistakes. The narcissistic position often results in a very real learning disability, for if you must hold to the perception of perfection in yourself, you cannot learn from the feedback provided by your errors.

The second derivative prescription from the basic orientation outlined here is the following: Be on the lookout for and avoid or repair situations in which the client illegitimately uses or manipulates you. The narcissistic person is often an expert at manipulation; in addition, he has a powerful need to be "special" to you. He is more likely than other clients, for example, to attempt to get you to alter your basic ground rules for psychotherapy. He will try to *use* you to support and aggrandize his false self by getting you to treat him as a special case in some way or by using you merely as another high status member of his fan club. If you allow him to use you in these ways, he cannot use you in the way that is really necessary: to find, in his relationship with you, his real self.

The narcissistic client will be among the most likely to try to serve you or take care of you in some way. I have had these patients offer me theater tickets, access to word processors, business and financial advancement, and other things which I would very much appreciate and enjoy. In the context of psychotherapy, it is my job to refuse these offers by the narcissistic client to be used again. Each provides a beautiful opportunity to interpret and work through the original narcissistic injury.

So, in sum, the prescription of therapeutic elements to be attended to most judiciously are as follows: Build a therapeutic relationship of trust in which you, the therapist, are honest, genuine, and nonmanipulative. Avoid being manipulated yourself, and avoid using the client to serve you. Most important, when you fail in achieving this ideal goal, confess it, repair it, and get on with it.

COUNTERTRANSFERENCE AND THE REAL SELF

The countertransference problems presented thus far will be in response to the narcissist's presentation of his false self. The countertransference pull of the patient's real self represents a far different and, in many cases, more formidable challenge. The dismantling of the grandiose false self and the ego-dystonic symptomatic self results in the release of the archaic demands and affects buried in the undeveloped real self. When this happens, the narcissistic patient becomes more or less "borderline" and has to cope with powerful infantile emotions. This can get scary for the most mature and experienced of therapists, but becomes particularly threatening to any therapist who harbors a fear of such affects or of archaic enmeshment. Here, the therapist will be threatened by the demands for merger, the displays of hostility, which may be only barely within the grasp of the patient's observing ego, or the splitting, which may include extreme examples of primitive idealization, etc. At these times, the threatened therapist may resort to any number of inappropriate interventions aimed at stopping those behaviors and affects which threaten her. In such cases, the therapist will often fail to empathically grasp the experience of the client and may respond by overintellectualized interpretations or explanations, subtly or not-so-subtly conveying disapproval of the infantile affects. Alternatively, she may disrupt the necessary transference relationship by becoming herself too frightened of these extreme affective states.

The therapist willing to take on characterological issues must be willing to not only tolerate but also actively welcome the activation of rather primitive demands and affects as a signal of characterological healing. Not only that, but she must also be willing to serve the patient by being the target of such demands and feelings. It is not necessary, however, for the therapist to be impervious to the real threats of such patient regression or even to the countertransferential reactions which such regressions can engender. Rather, it is only our responsibility to be aware of our countertransference reactions, to obtain supervision or psychotherapy to deal with them, and to use all our resources to maintain as solid a reality orientation as is humanly possible. When we fail in either major or minor ways, it is important and therapeutic to admit to such failure and thereby repair the very kinds of narcissistic wounds that torment our patients.

The treatment of truly borderline and narcissistically disordered clients is very hard work. It requires an understanding and tolerance of high levels of interpersonal stress which, though they may be diminished by our understanding, are still real and can still deeply affect us. These patients, perhaps more than others, confront us with our limitations. Dealing with that confrontation furthers our own development and the development of the people we treat. As we more realistically handle the tremendous emotional upheavels that our clients present, we build increasingly mature structure in ourselves and model such structure for our clients, so that they, in turn, may internalize these capabilities. This treatment is a study in maturity, integration of limitation, development of possibility, and ultimately, integration of our magnificence on the one hand with our humility on the other.

This attitude of tolerance and welcoming acceptance is particularly important both for the archaic demands of grandiosity and for the archaic demands and affects of the underlying real self. The patient himself is almost always insufficiently tolerant of these more or less unconscious drives. To access them is the first step in their maturation and transformation. Some strain in this process is inevitable, because for therapy to work the therapist must remain empathic, and to remain empathic she must remain affected. Psychotherapy surpasses all forms of psychotropic or mechanical intervention currently or potentially available solely on the basis of this empathic human connection. Essentially, it is the failure of empathic human connection that we are treating and we can treat it only by maintaining it ourselves. Even if we therapists were enlightened, there would still be emotion in this process; short of enlightenment, there will always be some strain. To make it otherwise is to subvert the essential nature of psychotherapy.

WORTHLESSNESS, GRANDIOSITY, AND THE NARCISSISTIC INJURY

Narcissistic individuals, particularly those who have suffered the more humiliating etiology, frequently complain of feelings of worthlessness. Worthlessness is not for me a primary feeling. Rather, it is derivative and, though it may have its affective components, it is primarily a cognitive event. It is a decision, conclusion, or judgment. The underlying feelings are really of two kinds, each relating to the pressures of either the false self or the real self. From the false self, the feeling is one of fear as the grandiose beliefs are threatened. From the real self, the feeling is one of hurt at the original narcissistic injury. The feeling of being injured can be incredibly deep and the narcissist is profoundly motivated to avoid it. His continuous attempts to prove himself worthy are essentially misguided, in that they never put the injury to rest. One cannot remedy the deep underlying hurt, sadness, and grief by doing worthwhile things. The worth issue is essentially bogus and neverending. The essential answer for the narcissist is to feel himself and then to eventually discover those thoughts, events, behaviors, and other people which will make him feel good.

Before the patient knows what will make him feel good, he must feel. When the narcissist truly begins to feel, among his first feelings will be that injury, that hurt, that humiliation, which drives the grandiose false self in its quest to prove self-worth. Once these deep negative feelings are experienced and at least begun to be worked through, the person may then become open to feeling enough of himself to begin to discover who and what makes him feel good. A very useful cognitive intervention is to label this issue of worthiness as a bogus, largely cognitive issue which creates the pointless merry-go-round of worthlessness motivated acts of worth that are never worthy. Among other things, the individual may be encouraged to repeatedly remind himself of the fruitlessness of pursuing worth and the necessity to feel himself. The narcissist does not really feel worthless. The narcissist feels threatened and hurt. When that can be felt, expressed, and shared with another human being, one has begun to find the real self.

PSYCHOSOMATIC ILLNESS AND HYPOCHONDRIASIS

For a number of narcissistic individuals, the collapse into the symptomatic self is somatic. The secondary gains or payoffs of a somatic collapse are numerous for the narcissistic person, though an awareness of them is typically not useful until well into the therapeutic process. Even then, awareness typically accomplishes much less than real experience of the underlying emotions, which is the ultimate therapeutic objective. Still, it is useful for the therapist to be aware of the dynamics of somatic conversions.

The psychosomatic and hypochondriacal concerns give the individual a reason for collapse and to be needy. They provide a cognitive focus for obsessive activity, thereby avoiding the underlying demands and affects of the real self. In addition, the somatic difficulties protect the perfectionism by giving an acceptable excuse for achieving less than perfection. Finally, the somatic distress provides a focus that denies the underlying demands and feelings of psychic pain by conversion of affect to isolated physical discomfort.

In dealing with these difficulties, I have often found it facilitative to avoid entering into the debate that is typically going on all about the client concerning the cause of her somatic problems. I typically turn a sympathetic ear to the complaints she has about all the psychological interpretations she has received, their frustrating and unhelpful nature, and her desire to see the symptoms as purely physical. Like all secondary gain interpretations, those which attribute somatic difficulties to psychic origins do very little good early in therapy and can do a great deal of harm. They represent another narcissistic injury and typically leave the client feeling helpless. I simply tell clients that they will probably feel better all around with greater self-awareness, self-expression, self-acceptance, and an enhanced interpersonal life, all of which successful psychotherapy can achieve. Then, beyond sympathetically acknowledging the physical symptoms and pain, I focus on history, family, feelings, current relationships, work, and other typical psychotherapy issues, as in other cases.

There is one exception to this strategy, when the somatic versus psychic battle is prominent. Then it is often therapeutic to focus attention on the overdetermined quality that the somatic patient has concerning the psychic versus somatic origin of his symptoms. You can often learn and teach a lot by getting the patient to engage in an inquiry about the overdetermined intensity of his often expressed need to *prove* that his symptoms are somatic in origin. Frequently, you will find that that debate reflects the basic doubt of his own self-worth. If the illness is psychosomatic or hypochondriacal, this means he is bad and to blame. However, if the illness is of a somatic origin, this means he is still all right and not to blame. This battle over self-worth is then externalized in his arguments with family, friends, and physicians. These battles preoccupy his consciousness and further isolate him from confronting the other psychic issues. An inquiry into the intensity of this battle often begins to reveal, in a more benign context, those psychic issues with which he is loathe to deal.

The analysis or active bioenergetic work will eventually bear fruit in the client's enhanced awareness of his own somatic patterns. At times, especially in body work, the client will begin to see that his somatic difficulties come out of contractions against self-expression and aliveness. At other times, he will begin to become aware of the conversion of feelings to body symptoms or obsessions. In other cases, the client will become aware of the somaticization of his fears of actual disintegration during an annihilation-abandonment crisis. With others, there will be a beginning of awareness of secondary gains. When any of these patterns occur, I gently assist the client in developing these insights. More importantly, I begin to focus the client's attention on his *willingness* to be free of the somatic complaint. I ask the client to seriously and repeatedly ask himself, "Am I willing to give this up?" and, "What would I lose and what would I gain if the symptoms should disappear?" With this orientation, I focus not on the client's being responsible for his symptomatic picture and its disappearance, but only on his *willingness* to have a symptom-free life. This focus elicits the secondary gains in a more positive context and brings forth the resistance to change in a more affirmative context of enhanced therapeutic alliance.

It is also useful when one begins dealing with physical symptoms directly to help the client differentiate between the disability or pain that she experiences in her body and the disability that that disability creates in her life. While she may feel legitimately helpless in eliminating the disability, she is usually not so helpless in working to minimize the disability that the symptoms create in her life. Frequently, of course, the disabilities created in life represent the secondary gains. To the extent that she is willing to work on eliminating these often well-established payoffs, she becomes willing to do whatever is possible to eliminate the somatic symptoms. Thus, for example, the chronic pain patient who will curb her tendency toward social isolation or her obsessive, self-involved "pain talk," will treat the disability created in life and may then be more amenable to whatever strategies can be really effective in healing the somatic difficulties.

To the extent that the somatic problems occur from the restraint of the expression of the real self, however primitive that may be, a consistent program of real self-acceptance and expression will slowly remedy these difficulties. This is particularly true to the extent that the client is willing to face the feelings that will result from the loss of the somatic compromise and achieve *primarily* the gains that have thus far been achieved only secondarily. To be ultimately healed, a somaticizing narcissist must give himself permission to be needy, to fail, to feel a host of vulnerable and often infantile feelings, to relinquish his grandiose false self, and to work through these most archaic demands and affects of the real self. Even then, some of the accumulated somatic damage of a psychosomatic adaptation may never be fully corrected. In most cases, then, the somatic healing really requires a fairly complete characterological transformation and much patience is required in the treatment of these psychologically based somatic ailments. Eventually, the client must express directly what the symptom blocks, ask directly for the gratifications that the symptom demands, and face head-on the threatening feelings and memories that the symptom protects.

CHARACTER STYLE AND CHARACTER DISORDER

In conceptualizing client problems and their treatment, I believe it is extraordinarily useful to employ a continuum based on the level of ego functioning. On one end of this continuum exists the narcissistic structure with borderline features, where the defensive and other ego functions are marginal, unreliable, and liable to break down under stress (borderline narcissist). At the other end of this continuum is the more highly defended individual; although he has the same potential for characterological issues, these issues are covered by a more reliable defensive structure (narcissistic style). Often, but not always, the characterological issues are less serious and the developmental history less traumatic in cases of character style. Because this continuum will be an organizing principle around which much of the forthcoming therapeutic material will be organized, it will be useful to elaborate on the characteristics of individuals at each end of this continuum.

The borderline narcissist is distinguished by the fact that the archaic demands and affects of the real self, as well as the archaic demands of the grandiose false self, are more available and overwhelming. At the same time, the more borderline individual will possess an observing ego less attuned to reality, so that he is more likely to be caught up and really believe in his grandiosity or feelings of entitlement, on the one hand, or in his feelings of intense need or rage, on the other. As a result, he is more inclined to act out these demands or affects in the more disorganized symptomatology of the borderline, including acts of violence to himself or others. He is more difficult to live with, being demanding, obviously manipulative, and prone to uncontrolled emotionality. Similarly, he will develop more exaggerated transference reactions with less ability to perceive them as overdetermined by the past. Relative to the individual exhibiting a narcissistic style, he will show more impulsivity, inappropriate and exaggerated emotionality, unstable and intense relationships, and a greater propensity to self-damaging acts. In general, his false self adaptation will be less successful and always less reliable. The psychotherapy for the borderline narcissist involves much greater need for support, ego-building, and working-through of the transference reactions to the therapist. Developing trust in the therapist and accepting help are among the most common initial therapeutic problems. There is greater need for learning affective containment than affective release. Often, evocative techniques are not only unnecessary, but inappropriate and even dangerous for individuals at the more borderline end of this continuum in ego and defensive functioning.

It is useful to develop an understanding of the rationale for the prescribed care and perhaps even prohibition of using evocative techniques (e.g., Gestalt, bioenergetic, or hypnotic therapy) with patients at the borderline end of the narcissistic continuum. The individuals at this end possess a less reliably constituted self with less reliable relationships with reality and less reliable self-other boundaries. Kohut (1971, pp. 210–212) likens the process of analytic therapy, which involves the accessing of archaic demands and affects, as analogous to one's experiences when going to the theater or the movies. When we involve ourselves in these make-believe artistic realities, we participate fully only by temporarily leaving ourselves and becoming involved through emotional participation in the lives of the characters on the stage or screen. We can then, with or for the actors, become angry, afraid, or gripped by despair, without fear of losing our own reality of self in the process. We can, to the extent that our ego or self is solid, give in to this experience. We know that it is not real, but in some very meaningful sense we allow ourselves to forget that unreality. We can lower the boundaries of self to pretend that the reality in front of us is real and respond accordingly. At the end of the play or movie, we can then reconstitute our boundaries and ourselves without carrying the emotions and conflicts of the "story" out into our own lives.

A similar relaxation of ego boundaries also occurs in sexual experience and in falling asleep. All such experiences require at least a minimal level of self-formation or ego strength. In the regressive states which occur in much analytic psychotherapy, there is the same kind of emotional participation in a situation which is, to some significant degree, unreal, like our experience in the theater. The client's participation in transference reactions is the primary example, and that participation requires the client to reconstitute after such an experience and to eventually "work through" the transference. This latter requirement demands that the client can, sooner or later, acknowledge that his reactions are indeed transferential.

The borderline narcissist has all he can do to live up to these requirements in the context of face-to-face interaction with the therapist, which is in most respects "real." The more evocative techniques encourage, and on occasion even demand, a kind of unreal dissolution of boundaries and contemporary reality relatedness, and an emotional participation which is often regressive. This kind of participation is usually too much for the more fragilely constituted and more profoundly arrested self at the borderline end of the continuum. This becomes less true, of course, as a successful therapeutic course is realized, but then these less defended individuals will usually not require special techniques to access the useful regressive states.

When they are able to tolerate them, most borderline clients can benefit from bioenergetic, hypnotic, or Gestalt procedures to the extent that they are ego-building or self-enhancing. Additionally, it may be useful for such an individual, toward the end of his or her work, to simply experience the kinds of altered states of consciousness which can be achieved through hypnosis or bioenergetics in the safe setting of psychotherapy. As a result, the experience of relaxing boundaries can then be generalized to other similar experiences, such as sexual experiences or artistic participation. The greater need for these techniques in the more defended and usually more well-constituted individual derives from the fact that he or she needs a hand in relaxing the defensive structure and accessing the underlying emotional reality.

It is quite possible in considering this continuum from character style to character disorder to be confused by those individuals who have a usually more rigid and brittle defensive structure overlaying a very fragile structure. This configuration often is detected by experienced clinicians in the rather simplistic and inflexible quality of the defense or in a very exaggerated response to a therapeutic maneuver. In these cases, it is equally important to go slow, to build the therapeutic relationship, and to engage in ego-building therapeutic procedures. Though some evocative procedures may be necessary later in the course of therapy, one is still safer utilizing strategies of a more ordinary nature, such as confrontation or interpretation.

At the other end of the continuum, the individual exhibiting a narcissistic style has less access to the archaic demands of either the real or the false selves and comes off as a much more reasonable and more easily understood individual. This person is not necessarily better functioning, but is better defended. While there is usually more accomplishment in this type, it often comes with a great deal of pain, symptomatic interference, and limited joy. While there is more ego strength, there is often also more chronic depression, pain, illness, or other symptoms which appear "neurotic" in the everyday sense of that word. While there is less awareness of the extreme grandiosity and entitlement of the false self, there is more awareness of "obligation" or "duty," together with a disavowal of the true depth of even these compensatory feelings. The individual with a narcissistic style is not just unaware of the archaic demands and affects of the real self; rather, he is expert at avoiding such awareness. Usually, there are very effective unconscious energetic defenses, as well as the usual cognitive and interpersonal defenses against such forbidden awareness.

Obviously, the individual with a narcissistic style is unlikely to act out, less prone to transference reactions, and more aware of or open to genetic interpretations concerning such reactions. These individuals are far more accommodating both in life and therapy, are ostensibly easier to work with, and are far less obviously egocentric. If, however, the treatment is successful in accessing the archaic demands and affects of the real self, there can then result some very extreme reactions to these intense emotions. Again, however, the person with a narcissistic style is much more likely to simply become depressed in defense of these feelings and, if he acts out at all, is more likely to do so in self-destructive ways, either actively or passively.

In the treatment of the narcissistic style there is, then, obviously much less need for support or ego-building and more need for direct, evocative techniques such as bioenergetic, Gestalt, or hypnotic procedures, which pull for the unconscious elements of both the false and real selves. Transference reactions also need to be more actively evoked and the therapist often needs to be more deliberate in his pursuit of these issues. Concomitantly, there is much greater need for affective expression than for containment. The therapeutic task can be summarized as one of pulling for unconscious affective experience while building greater and greater tolerance and ability to be aware of and feel archaic reactions which have been disavowed or repressed.

In spite of their differences, the individuals even at the extreme ends of this continuum are similar in being most accurately understood through the concepts which delineate narcissism, including the narcissistic injury, the ego functioning and issues of rapprochement, and the resulting loss of the real, organic self. At the lower end of the continuum, the borderline narcissistic individual is differentiated from other character disorders by the nature of the characterological issue, the defenses used to deal with it and the reliance on the grandiose false self. For me, individuals who are more purely borderline have much greater difficulty with issues labeled schizoid, oral, or symbiotic and do not promulgate a grandiose false self in defense. It is more as if they are actively struggling with the terror of having no real self. At the upper end of the continuum, the narcissistic style can be differentiated from the more neurotic or phallic character structures on the basis of greater development of the ego and associated object relations in the latter. The neurotic character has far greater access to and comfort with who he really is but is still plagued by issues in the arena of love and sex.

At both ends of the narcissistic continuum, the central therapeutic goal remains the same. It is the achievement of peace, indulgence, and maturation in the expression of the real self. The experience of individuals at both ends of the continuum is often extremely painful, whether characterized by instability and affective extremity or simply by chronic depression, pain, or illness. While one condition appears far more serious than the other, this is often only a surface impression. Beneath the differences lies the essential similarity of the original betrayal of the natural child and a continuation of this betrayal by the contemporary adult.

At both ends of the narcissistic continuum, psychotherapy is generally initiated when the breakdown of functioning is relatively severe. In my experience, such a breakdown almost always contains a heavy loading on depression. The narcissistic individual is typically very reluctant to ask for help. The breakdown itself and the need to ask for assistance are all experienced as humiliating. Because the depression experience is an almost universal aspect of the initial referral problem, it seems a good place to begin our discussion of actual treatment. To assist in this exposition, I will present two case studies in their initial treatment period, one exemplifying the narcissistic character disorder, the other the narcissistic style.

Daniel: Character Style and Depression

Daniel, a successful professional man in his late thirties, entered therapy with problems of chronic pain and acute depression. Though he had suffered episodes of such depression previously, as well as three years of psychotherapy from another therapist, this episode was as bad as any he could remember and was exacerbated by the painful effects of a skiing accident that had occurred nine months previously. He was also distraught by the fact that he was seriously blocked in his creative artistic work and could not get on with a project that was intimately related to his assessment of self-worth. The vulnerabilities triggered by the physical pain and the block in artistic productivity—

the main bulwark of the client's relatively effective false self—were a threat of the first magnitude. I conceptualized the presenting depression as primarily frozen fear in response to the failure to live up to the expectations of the grandiose false self, on the one hand, and the fear of awakening the vulnerable archaic demands for acceptance and love when helpless, on the other.

For the more highly defended narcissistic person, the organizing principle of life demands continual proving of worthiness and earning of affirmation. While there is often an unconscious belief that that accomplishment should come without effort, the individual with the narcissistic style is usually more willing to work for accomplishment than is the narcissist with a less developed ego structure. But, when the person can no longer earn self-worth through external accomplishment, the sense of self is seriously jeopardized and the individual is threatened with experiencing that void and fragmentation that are more characteristic of those at the borderline end of the continuum. A complete deadening of the organism in depression and/or hypochondriacal preoccupation can be an effective, if equally painful, defensive solution. This was what was happening to Daniel. In this case, ego strength was high, social support was adequate, and the therapeutic relationship was good enough early on to warrant early use of more evocative techniques. This assessment was further enhanced by the fact that a good deal of Daniel's earlier therapy involved these procedures.

Daniel's is the type of case in which the patient needs to be brought back to life. This "bringing back to life" means reestablishment of the energetic flow of the organism—an opening of the breathing and the associated relaxation of the energetic blocks, muscular spasms, or character armor. Without this kind of life in the body, it is not really possible to achieve any emotional reality or therapeutic regression to the split-off aspects of either the real or grandiose false selves. There is, rather, only the possibility of a similarly split-off insight which, though it may give a name to the problem, will not in any meaningful way complete or heal it. While I believe it is possible to get to this necessary emotional reality in an intense several-times-a-week analytic process, this alternative is slower and much more expensive than the possibility I am about to present.

In any case of organismic deadening, the initial body work must involve bringing the client back to his body through a deepening of the breathing, a loosening of the spasms and blocks, and enhancing awareness of the body. Basic bioenergetic procedures for these purposes are outlined in detail in *Characterological Transformation: The Hard Work Miracle* (Johnson, 1985) and will be easily comprehended by anyone familiar with the basics of this discipline. The basic outline of these procedures may also be found in Lowen and Lowen (1977) and Lowen (1967). In addition, samples of these exercises for grounding, breathing, stretching, and muscle relaxation are presented in the appendix.

In Daniel's case, techniques that deepened the breathing in both the chest and abdominal regions were critical. In addition, we established greater grounding through the use of numerous procedures designed to bring flow and charge to the feet and legs, including work in the forward position, walking on the dowel, and exercises for the legs and ankles. The bioenergetic stool was used frequently both to deepen breathing and to open blocks in the chest, abdomen, and lower back. Additionally, direct manipulation of the shoulders, neck, and jaw was employed to release blocks in these areas.

Sometimes, even these very "soft" bioenergetic exercises, aimed primarily at achieving body awareness and relaxation, can result in the calling up of underlying emotions. This tends to be more true as one moves toward the borderline end of the continuum or during the latter stages of therapy with the more defended structures. Those bioenergetic exercises in the second group devoted to *building an energy charge* in the body are somewhat more likely to pull for underlying emotions, although frequently, and particularly with the more well-defended structures, they simply serve to increase respiration, circulation, and movement.

In Daniel's case, these *awareness-relaxation exercises* and those exercises used for *building an energy charge* did not in themselves produce any emotion; rather, it was necessary in his case, as with most well-defended individuals, to move to the third group of bioenergetic methods, which are primarily devoted to pulling for a *discharge* of energy or affect. These more evocative and often "noisy" procedures are those which are more dramatic and unusual. They are the procedures by which bioenergetics is more superficially known by both the lay and professional communities and for which it is most often superficially dismissed. Yet, these are the very procedures that are required when we deal with an energetically well-defended individual. The essential strategy in selecting these exercises is to pick from an available repertoire or create new processes which pull for the split-off or repressed feelings.

In selecting such evocative techniques, one pays attention to the specific issues evolving out of the specific history and to the nature of the energetic defenses or character armor. Briefly, Daniel's narcissistic issue may be summarized as follows: He was worshiped rather than loved. His okayness was provisional, depending on display of qualities or accomplishments admired by his parents. He was *used* to make them happy, to fulfill their dreams and wishes, to make their lives worthwhile. His injury existed in an unconscious realization of this fact, as well as from episodes of negative evaluation, occasionally accompanied by parental rage and humiliation at times of weakness or vulnerability. It is significant to note that, prior to his previous therapy, Daniel had been unable to cry and, while he had liberated this response to some extent, he was still unable to sob. In his earlier therapy, he had recovered an early adolescent scene of humiliation around crying in which he had "decided" never to cry again, never to expose himself to such shame. There were still some unresolved issues around nurturance-holding. These were in the foreground during his earlier therapy, but were now secondary to the narcissistic issues.

Two bioenergetic postures, both of which create charge and pull for discharge, were especially useful in his treatment. The first, labeled the *reaching squat*, requires the client to stand with feet spread to shoulder width. Then the client is asked to squat such that the knees are deeply bent with the thighs parallel to the floor. From this position, the client is then asked to look up and reach out toward the therapist, who stands several feet in front of him. In some cases, it is more useful to ask the client to imagine a parental or other figure in the therapist's position. This posture is maintained as long as possible and, in the resulting stress and pain, the client is encouraged to vocalize and free associate. The vocalization will eventually involve screaming and the free association may bring up particularly relevant phrases, the repetition of which is often useful.

In Daniel's case, this posture accessed the rage at being strained and used. The simple phrase "I hate you" further deepened this experience. The posture also brought up the longing and need for acceptance and unconditional support, along with the simple phrase, "Help me." Though these sessions were painful both physically and emotionally, Daniel reliably left the therapy session feeling much better than when he had entered it and this immediate effect would usually last at least a day or two. The cumulative effect was a gradual lessening of the deadening depression, together with reexperiencing the archaic feelings and the situations that evoked them.

Daniel has become increasingly aware of the profound life-and-death quality of the feeling that surrounds his artistic work. He remembers the intense feelings of insecurity, fear, and psychic pain involving the completion of other similar projects and increasingly sees how he was killing both the pleasure and growth of his real self in the tense survival-oriented approach to his work. He is still working on letting go of the desperate need to produce in order to feel adequate. As he does so, he paradoxically becomes more productive while less driven. In the process, he has also uncovered, with some surprise, the archaic beliefs within the grandiose false self. He has, for example, become aware of how perfectionistic he is, even around the smallest matters, requiring himself to do everything perfectly the first time. He has become aware of each failure to do so as a reenactment of the earlier narcissistic injury. While such reactions still occur, they are at once diminished and a source of humorous observation rather than psychic pain. In other words, Daniel is less at the mercy of these reactions and more in observation of them.

We now move to the other end of the continuum to consider the treatment of depression in a more borderline narcissistic case.

John: Character Disorder and Depression

John was a young man, 28, who was a college student and who, for the previous ten years, had bounced around from college to college and job to job. He had had three intimate relationships in his adult life, though much of his time had been spent alone. His coming to therapy was occasioned by separation from his latest girl friend, who had had an affair while living with John. This was one in a series of betrayals which accessed overwhelming injury. John had sought me out, however, on his girl friend's recommendation. She had participated in one of my graduate seminars years before. These facts are particularly important because, during the course of therapy, John would persist, with some very limited, periodic insight, in merging me with his former girl friend because I had known her. Further, he resented me for being inept and uncaring because I had refused to call her and urge her to participate in couples counseling.

These issues made up only a part of the massive negative transference, barely and unreliably recognized, which became an important part of the therapy. Indeed, in John's case, much of the therapeutic process involved the working-through of negative transference with the disappointment of archaic merger and mirror demands on the one hand and disappointment of the idealization transference on the other. In this biweekly therapeutic contact, supplemented by weekly group treatment, the therapeutic relationship itself provided much of the "heat" in the work.

There was never a need for evocative techniques. Indeed, on several occasions the failures of containment and propensity to act out became very serious considerations. While in Daniel's case it was often difficult to even produce transference, and when it was produced it was always recognized, in John's case the transference reactions frequently threatened to be overwhelming.

In contrast to Daniel's "dead" depression, John's "depression" was highly agitated and affective. His was the annihilation-abandonment crisis. Indeed, John attempted to deaden his feelings by overconsumption of alcohol and through driven one-night-stand promiscuity. Following these episodes, there would be immense shame and self-recrimination. Only at these times did he appear to be depressed in the usual sense. At other times, John would act out by appearing unannounced at his former girl friend's apartment and, on one occasion, at my home. At these times, John would drop into overwhelming dependency on me, accompanied by frequent and desperate telephoning.

During times of breakdown, he would abandon the aloofness otherwise shown to members of the group and reach out to them as well. At these times, too, he would telephone his parents, often with combinations of despair and recrimination. He would feel at least somewhat better when in contact, but this improvement would last only as long as he could maintain the contact. The benefits of this support were, however, very minimal in John's eyes. No one was anywhere near *enough*, with the possible exception of his former girl friend when she responded sympathetically to his plight. At these times, he would become significantly buoyed and hopeful and be extraordinarily appreciative of her past and present contributions to him.

On several occasions John threatened to drop out of school and leave town in pursuit of some other educational experience or employment. Each time, the feedback of others, most notably other members of the therapy group, encouraged him to stick with his schooling, therapy, and pursuit of relationships in the current setting. I, too, advised this course, though always repeating the reality that John had to make his own decision. I assured him that he would have my support whatever he decided to do. The circumstances of one such occasion are diagnostically noteworthy. In response to one of the more alarming calls home, one of his brothers flew from some considerable distance to support him and assist him in an anticipated move. Almost as soon as his brother arrived, John became very encouraged at his situation, changed his mind about moving, mobilized to find a full-time job to support his college education, and moved to drop out of psychotherapy. Subsequent to this visit, he did obtain a well-paying manual job, but quit after one grueling week's work. This was not a bad decision in view of the excessive demands of both school and full-time hard labor, but the incident most dramatically illustrates the pattern.

As described above, the periods of breakdown were juxtaposed with episodes of mobilization of the grandiose, false self. The intermittent decisions to move, drop out of school, and discontinue therapy were a part of this mobilization. At these times, as well as others, John became highly negative about his school, the faculty, other students, myself, and other members of the therapy group. At these times, no one was experienced positively, though he did hold out great respect, admiration, and even love for a deceased uncle with whom he had had a positive relationship. On these occasions, his positiveness would also extend to himself, particularly toward his *potential* for becoming a successful, recognized, and morally superior person. At these times, as well, he would fantasize about using his power to retaliate against evil people in the world. On some occasions, he would allow himself to be carried away with these fantasies and the demands of the grandiose false self, to the point of accessing his overwhelming hostility in fantasies to "crush, smash, and destroy" others. Then he would become aware of the pathological depths of this hatred and his need to get even.

As might be expected, John maintained a life of extreme isolation because no one was really good enough, yet he suffered the excruciating pain of archaic needs unmet. During periods of mobilization, he could be tremendously productive in either work or school, but during periods of collapse there was almost total inertia. On several occasions, he attempted to quietly drop out of the therapy group, but when gently prodded to share his plans with those who had helped him in his periods of crisis, John would begin to reveal the great depths of his hatred and then the great depths of his despair. Whenever this occurred, John would receive massive support and recognition from the group members. He was even able to let a very little of this support in and, over the course of therapy, he became increasingly more able to feel and acknowledge such support.

Typically, too, he evidenced a good deal of splitting in relation to himself and others. At times, for example, he expressed a great deal of gratitude to me for my caring and constancy in relation to him, yet at other times he would become vicious in his criticisms of me as uncaring and untrustworthy. In one session, during a later and relatively mild crisis period, John was able to experience a great deal of his negative transference, articulate it, and yet see its transferential nature. This was another session in which I wasn't completely accepting of some of the accusations he was making about his former girl friend. He asked me why I persisted in questioning his word. I replied that I had observed that he was very suspicious of others in many contexts and that I wanted to question whether he was seeing things clearly in this case. At this he shot back:

John: Now, I have every right in the world to be suspicious after how I've been treated in my life.

Therapist: I agree.

John: So, I don't really consider it being suspicious. I consider it smart to not let that shit happen to me again. So, I'm extremely cautious, and I will not trust anyone 'til that person is beyond doubting. And, I don't want to change that. I really don't want to change that, Steve. And you'll never convince me—and nobody'll ever convince me—to let go of that. 'Cause every time I let go of that, I get hurt.

Therapist: Listen to what you just said.

John: I know what I just said.

Therapist: Feel it. See if you can just feel it.

John: There's a great deal of anger behind it.

Therapist: Just feel what's there.

John: I know what's there.

Therapist: Feel it.

John: Well, I don't feel safe with you right now. And what I feel is a lot of pain and agony. And I don't want to share that with you because I'm afraid you'll belittle me with it—you'll hold it against me. And I won't give you that chance.

Therapist: Feel as much as you can of what you just said.

John: I just told you, I will not do it because I'm not gonna share it with you right now. Don't ask me again, please, because I'm not going to . . . I'm very upset that you would defend that woman. . . . What it feels like is you're putting her over me—saying I'm the one in the wrong and she was right. And . . . I'm very upset about that.

Therapist: Feel it.

John: I am. If I thought it was absolutely the truth, I wouldn't be here.

Therapist: I know.

John: But that's the feeling I have. And that's why I'm very cautious with you. 'Cause I can't prove it. But, if I ever do prove it, I'll . . . I'll . . . I don't know what I would do. I don't know what I'd have a right to do. But I would definitely have a tool.

Therapist: Proof?

John: That you were in cahoots with her against me. And I can feel it. And it's something I know I can't put down on paper. It may be on celluloid, but it's not evidence in court.

Therapist: But it is in your feelings, and I'm just encouraging your feelings.

John: I go through oscillations about your trust. Sometimes I trust you and I feel like you're more honest with me. Sometimes I am a million miles away from you and it's like I almost beg you to give me any kind of provocation just—actually, come attack me, Steve—physically try to attack me. And it's like, I feel this vengefulness right now. I could just build that up and build it to a rage and I'd just yell at you. I'd say "Come on. Come on." And I would just—I'd fucking want to kill you. If you tried to attack me I'd have every right in the world—to defend myself. And it's kind of weird, 'cause when I get this way—get angry like this—my vision becomes very tunneled, very focused. And it's almost like a smile comes on my face because I have an opportunity to vent a whole lot of anger. And it's a very destructive kind of thing.

The intervention initially demonstrated here—the instruction to focus inward and *feel* the affect—is a very useful one for accessing the affects which require working-through. It is most productive with patients exhibiting the narcissistic style or with narcissistic character disorders when one has reached that stage in treatment where the transference is more fully acknowledged than in the present case. More often, an interpretation of the transference elicited above would be the intervention of choice in such borderline cases. In this case, however, that interpretation had been repeatedly given and was acknowledged, at least superficially. As a consequence of this, I opted for the intervention of calling for feelings, knowing that it would either elicit these underlying feelings or further elicit the resistance, which also required working-through.

The persistent call for feelings led to the mobilization of the resistance and the narcissistic rage tempered by insight: "If I believed that were true I wouldn't be here." This led to some working-through of the rage and paranoia and eventually to a strengthening of the therapeutic alliance and an enhancement of trust.

Group therapy was often very useful in dealing with the splitting because John could often find someone in the group whom he experienced as caring, trustworthy, and helpful to him, while seeing me as opposite to this. This same polarization around the experience of self has already been alluded to. His self-hatred was highest around episodes of dependency on alcohol and promiscuity, and his self-concept was highest when he saw himself, aligned with his uncle, as being superior to most of the world and holding out for the one-and-only merger object who would be as good as himself. In one direct, poignant session in which he was capturing a good deal of useful insight, John described his pattern with women as follows: "I pick women who think they are the very best and present themselves that way. I present myself to them that way, too, but when they really get to know me they get disgusted and can't handle my real, demanding nature. They're afraid of me because they're afraid too—of themselves. So they leave me and look for someone else who is as good as they think they are. I see that they're not perfect either, but I always want to stay together—to work it out. If someone really loves you they should be able to hang in there with you. I'm beginning to see that I just ask for too much."

In many ways, the person I am describing here is classically borderline. While it is crucial to take that into account, John is, for me, better understood in his three expressions of narcissism. On the one hand, he relies a good deal on the false self with its associated grandiosity, omnipotence, entitlement, pride, perfectionism, and reliance on achievement. In periods of breakdown, he moves to the symptomatic self, primarily in worthlessness, self-depreciation, and vulnerability to shame and humiliation. At these times, he feels his isolation and loneliness and experiences an agitated annihilation-abandonment crisis. When mobilizing to fight that off, he jumps back to the false self and, from a position of power and superiority, rejects everyone and everything in his life. In either expression, however, he often falls into the archaic demands and affects of the real self and ultimately finds there the possibility of self-discovery and self-development. He is better understood through the concept of mobilization of the grandiose false self than through the conceptualization of the absent self (the symbiotic character).

Relative to Daniel, John's archaic demands and affects are far more accessible, obvious, even conscious, but his cohesion of self or strength of ego is correspondingly diminished. The therapeutic task, therefore, is much more characterized by the building of ego resources and the development of a sense of cohesive self. The therapeutic task must be far more supportive and, at times, even "reluctantly indulgent" (Kohut, 1984). The problem is more one of keeping the archaic demands and affects within manageable limits and increasing ego strength or self-cohesion through self-maintaining activities or relationships (including the therapeutic one) and through any direct therapeutic techniques that enhance functioning or the building of personal resources.

In both cases, there are similarities in the narcissistic structure and in the underlying realities of the real self. And certainly the ultimate objective for both is the same. But the roads to getting there are quite different. In a sense, Daniel gets better as he gets more borderline, for then he has more access to the archaic demands and affects of both the false and real selves. Such affective awareness is necessary before he can graduate from his painful compensation. John, on the other hand, gets better as he gets more cohesiveness of self, so that he can tolerate and then work through these feelings, which are more readily available at the outset. Part of this strength will come from an ability to employ better defenses; in this sense, John will get better as he becomes better defended. The more he can handle, the more he can work through. What is called for, then, in this and similar cases of borderline narcissistic depression is an essentially supportive, ego-building therapy, which enhances the patient's capacity to deal with and work through the issues of narcissism and eventually to discover and develop the real self.

For purposes of explication, let us consider the treatment of John's annihilation-abandonment crisis—those episodes in which he fell into the overwhelming archaic demands and affects of the arrested real self. Kohut (1971, pp. 152–153) helps us understand the painful realities of this "crisis" state in the following words:

> The central anxiety encountered in the analysis of narcissistic personality disorders is not castration anxiety but the fear of the de-differentiating intrusion of the narcissistic structures and their energies into the ego. These intrusions are fear of loss of the reality self through ecstatic merger with the idealized parent imago, or through the quasi-religious regressions toward a merger with God or with the universe; fear of loss of contact with reality and fear of permanent isolation through the experience of unrealistic grandiosity; frightening experience of shame and self-consciousness through the intrusion of exhibitionistic libido; and hypochondriacal worries about physical or mental illness due to the hypercathexis of disconnected aspects of the body and the mind.

Often, an individual experiencing the terrifying breakthrough of these de-differentiating fearful experiences cannot be very articulate about them because of their singularly primitive, affective, and overwhelming nature. The patient often only knows that he feels terrible, threatened, and motivated above all else to terminate this state. Frequently, he will desire to be understood and soothed perfectly and be impatient with any request to specify the nature of his problem. He can be greatly assisted by your articulation of the overwhelming feelings he experiences. Though this articulation will be imperfect and inaccurate, it will be therapeutic as it is empathic and displays a *desire* to understand. Further, even its "missing the mark" will be therapeutic insofar as it provides an optimal frustration. It will be particularly so as it demands the client to provide clarification to another who is trying and succeeding in an attempt to comprehend this overpowering state.

The experience of being *finally understood*, particularly when the client himself works to accomplish that understanding, is at once gratifying and self-building. Such dialogue communicates to the patient that his real self is eminently worth understanding and soothing, and such therapist activity models the attempt to understand and accept the underlying real emotions, primitive as they may be. It is in such an interchange that the narcissistic person can experience "that great relief of having someone to talk to" (John Sebastian).* It is, however, critical in order to avoid both the inappropriate gratification of merger and its associated anxieties that the patient be required to actively participate, even in a very limited way, in this dialogue and experience the associated optimal frustration. The ego or self is thus built through this exercise of function. The optimal interventions for the patient in these periods of annihilation-abandonment crisis are those which simultaneously provide the soothing which is so desperately sought after and the building of self which is the ultimate objective of the therapeutic process. This requires a balance in the selected interventions, such that there is the optimal combination of reliance on others and reliance on self.

As the real self develops, there can be a progressive shift to greater and greater reliance on the self without, of course, encouraging the grandiose illusion of complete self-reliance. I have, for example, used the therapy group to provide differing levels of support to an individual member in the throes of the narcissistic crisis. When the individual is at his lowest level of functioning, I have asked group members to agree to telephone and check in on him for various reasons. At intermediate levels of functioning, I have gotten the individual to agree to a schedule of telephoning or contacting group members. With functioning at a higher level of independence, I have simply suggested that the client contact and receive support from other unspecified members of the group. Even where the level of ego functioning is at its lowest, however, I have been careful to require *something* of the client in crisis. Thus, for example, I might get the client to agree to some activity that would enhance his ego functioning or experience of self and then have the group members telephone him, partly to monitor his keeping of the agreement.

In John's case, as well as in every other case of annihilation-abandonment crisis, the provision of empathic understanding and support is the first and primary task of the therapist. From that base, the therapist may then suggest and encourage the client to seek out this same kind of empathy and support from others in his environment

*From "Darling, Be Home Soon."

who are able to deliver it. Using others in this way is truly legitimate for the narcissistic patient in crisis because it is in the support of the discovery and development of the real self. In the therapeutic context, this connection or reliance then makes possible the client's constructive use of any explanations, reconstructions, or interpretations that you, the therapist, wish to deliver. Prior to the establishment of such an empathic connection, the patient is interested only in relief and will often experience such interventions as compounding narcissistic injuries.

For John, the most successful sessions from an analytic point of view came at times when he could "discover" that his relationship with his girl friend and his current annihilation-abandonment crisis with its exaggerated desperate dependency were reenactments of his incomplete relationship with his mother and, to a lesser extent, his father. He was helped by the developmental analogue interpretation that his feelings were those of a child needing a completely attuned and dedicated nurturing parent. During each such crisis, with the accompanying insight, he would experience some of the necessary learning of this forever-lost experience. In each crisis, he would give up a little on the unrealistic hope of achieving this infantile symbiotic nirvana. In each case, he was healing, maturing, and neutralizing the archaic need for merger and the merger idealization.

On such occasions, when John was exceedingly real and poignantly insightful, I deliberately let him experience my admiration and respect. At first, this was exceedingly difficult for him to take in, but over time he became more and more able to register that which he had longed for most. The same phenomenon occurred in the group, and John was progressively able to accept more and more genuine positive appreciation from an increasing number of people. I believe that this kind of gratification or reinforcement of the real self is essential to the healing of any narcissistic person.

As Kohut has eloquently argued, the narcissistic needs really never disappear. Instead, they mature so that the real self can enjoy the gratifications in relationships that provide opportunities for merger, twinship, mirroring, and idealization in adult life. The crux of the issue is not gratification. Rather, it is what is gratified. The therapist must be careful to avoid gratifying and therefore reinforcing the grandiose false self and the defensive symptomatic self. While it is essential to monitor what you gratify, it is equally essential to gratify the maturation and development of the self. Over time, the explanations, reconstructions, and interpretations of the historical antecedents of the annihilation-abandonment crisis serve the transmuting internalization function.

Even though John continued to have these disorganizing experiences, they became briefer and less intense. In part, this therapeutic change was due to the fact that he could attribute them to the historical issue and stop his unrealistic quest for that idealized other who would undo it. Each episode became a signal of more and deeper mourning and the relinquishing of archaic demands. In short, each episode became more of an optimal than overwhelming frustration. The insights, explanations, reconstructions, and interpretations served as transitional soothing objects during this process. Finally, during each episode, John looked more and more to others in the current environment for the provision of "imperfect," yet self-sustaining, support. As treatment progressed, he became more and more able to ask for and really feel such support. For illustration of this, see Chapter VI, where this process is documented with transcriptions of John's work in both group and individual sessions.

The intensity of the annihilation-abandonment crisis, the client's intolerance of this uncomfortable state, and the often real danger of the client's acting-out in this condition all cry out for the therapist to *do something*. While it is often useful to do something, it is important to act with a theoretical understanding which contextualizes what you are doing and gives a purpose to your actions, minimizing the risk of *over*doing it. Apart from preventing any dangerous acting-out, the purpose of any activity during the crisis must continue to be the overall building of the ego and self. Such activity must be guided by the principle of "guardianship of autonomy" (Greenacre, 1959). So, although your therapeutic activities may very well include using yourself to serve as the patient's "auxiliary ego" (Mahler et al., 1975), and while you may gratify the patient's needs for a caring, knowledgeable, and active other, all of that should be done with this overall objective in mind.

Too much activity or reliance on technique at this very vulnerable and potentially productive period risks the fostering of dependency and the furthering of the client's inappropriate idealization of and wholesale identification with the therapist, his theories or techniques. This danger is very greatly increased when the therapist needs his therapy to produce cure, transformation, or optimum functioning. In these cases particularly, the narcissistic needs of the therapist are being played out at the expense of the realistic evolution of the patient's damaged self. Ultimately, neither the therapist nor the client is being truly served.

Whenever John's depressive episodes were overwhelming, I would actively remind him of the types of activities that provided support, soothing, and self-sustenance. Whenever there is a breakdown of self, any intense physical or mental activity will tend to mobilize organization. John was a very good athlete, although he had taken little pleasure in his athletic abilities prior to therapy and had used them as a bulwark of the grandiose false self. Nonetheless, running and various competitive sports served a self-mobilizing function. I encouraged him to engage in such activities. Once again, the availability of other group members to participate with him during such times was particularly fortunate. With these fellow travelers in the therapeutic process, John did not have to hide the reality of his depressive state, yet he could participate with others in these self-mobilizing activities. In this case, of course, it was not only the activity but also the meaningful contact that served a self-enhancing function.

John was also intelligent and quite capable of high levels of academic performance. This, too, had been a bulwark of the false self, but he had experienced very little pleasure either in study itself or in the resulting accomplishments. As he improved, he discovered himself in his academic work and found that, particularly with some subjects, he enjoyed the learning process. He also found that he did not, and indeed did not have to, like every subject. In this, he discovered himself by discovering his likes and dislikes. This element of the self-discovery process is present in every narcissistic healing. Another client told me poignantly that it was not until he was 35 years old, when someone asked him what he liked to do, that he realized he had never meaningfully asked himself that question. Narcissists, all along the continuum of ego development, ask what they have to do to please others or to prove themselves. Deeply felt personal pleasure is not relevant. During therapy, John delightfully and naively discovered, "I don't have to like everyone; I don't have to please everyone; I don't have to prove to everyone I'm all right." The discovery of discrimination based on organismically felt sensations of approach or avoidance is uniquely pleasurable for the narcissist. It is almost an altered state of consciousness and a signal of what is possible in real living.

It is during the annihilation-abandonment crisis that any narcissistic client will require permission to be vulnerable, imperfect, or lost and need encouragement to engage in activities which are self-soothing. These may include meditation, self-hypnosis, mild bioenergetic exercises, yoga, warm baths, walks in the woods, etc. The therapeutic role of "child advocate" can help clients care for their real selves by understanding, nurturing, and protecting the child within them. Eventually, we wish patients to become their own child advocate. Internalization of this attitude and the abilities that accompany it constitutes one important objective of the treatment. Borderline narcissists, particularly during periods of crisis, will usually be unable to engage in the kinds of active reparenting processes which I will outline later in this volume. They will, however, be acutely aware of and able to begin to internalize a good parental model. Your repeated and consistent insistence on putting the child in the patient first, your inquiring into and respecting her wishes, and your empathically "reading" her will slowly revive that denied "child" and eventually provide her with the internalized caring she requires. In this revival, the internalization occurs in part because it is impossible for you, the therapist, to ever really provide all the acceptance and nurturance which that denied child craves. Your inability to do this creates the optimal frustration required for internalization of this new attitude, which then accomplishes the self-soothing and motivates and legitimizes the reaching out for the needed external soothing.

Like many narcissistic individuals, John became aware of his resistance to engaging in those self-soothing, self-sustaining, and self-building activities that would actively bring him out of the crisis. It was particularly fruitful to explore this resistance during those episodes in which the therapeutic alliance was strong and ego-functioning was basically intact. The methods of focusing (Gendlin, 1978) and reframing (Bandler & Grinder, 1979, 1982) were useful for this exploration process. Both of these processes were discussed at length in *Characterological Transformation* and are presented once again in the appendix to this volume.

With these methods, John discovered the underlying emotional determinants for the resistance. Essentially, what he discovered was this: The resistance to engage in those activities was in part due to a continuing need to punish himself for his imperfection and worthlessness. He had, in effect, internalized the punishment he had either received or felt for being less than the perfect son his parents wanted. The punishment of the depression was thus "deserved" and he did not deserve to terminate it by getting the support, soothing, and self-organization that was possible for him. His discovery and working-through of deeper and deeper levels of the need to self-punish was therapeutic.

Like many narcissists, John was ashamed of his need for soothing and would resist it until the pressure became overwhelming. At that point, he would lose control and engage in self-destructive behaviors of excessive drinking and promiscuity. During therapy, John rediscovered a long-neglected ability to play the guitar. He found this activity to be progressively more soothing as therapy developed and I reminded him of its soothing function when necessary.

As part and parcel of the working-through process, John was progressively able to internalize alternative orientations from me, the group, and eventually significant others in his environment. He internalized the right to be soothed, the right to feel good, the right to be weak and ask for support, the right to pursue activities that he enjoyed, the right to refuse activities or relationships that were not productive, etc. This is the kind of "parent transplant" that occurs in all successful characterological treatment and does, indeed, rely on the people in the external environment for its realization.

In the treatment of all narcissistic characters, I actively encourage the discovery and development of social support systems that will enhance this internalization process. This part of the recommended treatment is essentially behavioral in that it focuses on the patient's external environment and his behavior within it. At the same time, its focus is internal in that the intention is the internalization of the more beneficent attitudes toward the client of his supportive, even loving, social system. It is important to note, especially for the narcissistic individual who is prone to grandiosity, that even with such internalization he will continue to have legitimate adult needs for such a supportive and self-enhancing social environment. As narcissistic individuals improve, they very noticeably enhance their social environment, leaving those individuals or systems that do violence to their real self and embracing individuals and systems that nurture and support it. I have found it very helpful to repetitively outline in some detail this process. The appreciation for this element of the treatment of the narcissist is perhaps Kohut's most important contribution to my understanding and treatment of individuals with this issue.

Like all individuals experiencing any intense dysphoric crisis, John wanted to escape it. Alcohol abuse and promiscuity represented attempts at escape, but most profound was his repeated threat to repeat the old pattern of quitting school and leaving town. At these times, it proved important to give John what he had never had but longed for from his parents: a solid, consistent personal stance regarding the issue. I avoided ordering him to stay, but made it abundantly clear that his flight was a significant part of the repetitive life pattern that hadn't worked. I insisted that it was important for him to stay in school and to stay with therapy with either myself or someone else. Additionally, I indicated that I felt it was important to maintain contact with the same person and therefore stay with me, but indicated that I would support whatever choice he made in this regard. In short, I tried to be clear about what I thought he should do without telling him what to do.

I recall one powerful session around the issue of his continuance in therapy which proved to be a turning point in his development. This was a session in which he again expressed a great deal of disappointment in me as therapist because he perceived me as uncaring. It is important to note that this discussion did not include the possibility of his dropping out of school or moving to another area. It is also important to note that this session took place after more than a year of therapeutic work in both individual and group contexts. I reviewed for John, quite nondefensively I believe, the kinds of interpretations we had been over many times before, both in group and individual treatment. I conceptualized his feelings about me as (1) transferential and (2) defensive in character. His seeing me as uncaring kept me at a distance and kept the threatening archaic fantasies of merger impossible. Everyone in the therapy group and in his current social environment was 'spoiled" in some way to prevent him from getting too close and confronting his archaic merger wishes. In each of his three romantic relationships he had merged with an idealized other and fallen into the bottomless hole of archaic merger dependency. On each occasion, he had been too much for the other in the intense symbiotic relationship that they developed together. He had then been rejected and forced to feel not only the current rejection, but all the archaic rage and injury of the past. He reserved his deepest trust and longing for a potential mate—a relationship in which he believed the wished-for symbiotic merger to be possible. He was unwilling to let anyone else really matter because, at an unconscious level, he knew he would then have to face inevitable frustration. He knew that a therapist or male friend, for example, could not possibly give him all the dependency gratification that he desired.

Though the content outlined above is important for our purposes here and served an essential purpose in John's overall treatment and in that memorable session, it was not the crucial therapeutic element in that breakthrough contact. What was essential, I think, was my own self-exploration around this issue of caring, which I shared with John. I "looked inside" myself for any reason for which I might be withholding the kind of caring that I provided to others. What I found and admitted was some fear that, if John were to trust me as much as he wished to and if he accepted that I cared for him as much as he wanted, he would collapse into a catastrophic dependency, would confront me with more demands than I could possibly meet, and would confront both of us with his overwhelming regressive feelings, which could prompt suicidal or other dangerous acting-out, require hospitalization, etc. While I told him I couldn't determine the extent to which this had inhibited my caring, I was sure I experienced the fear and wondered aloud whether he, too, experienced such apprehension. We had been through enough episodes of his annihilation-abandonment crisis to warrant such concern.

Additionally, I confessed to John that I was probably not the most compassionate, attuned, empathic therapist that he might find. My own characterological issues produced some limitations in these areas. Furthermore, I said that some client-therapist relationships just work better than others due to many unknown reasons, as is true in all interpersonal relationships. Still, and most importantly, I told John that what he was getting from me was all I had to give and that his recurring feelings of disappointment, while necessary to the treatment, would not change my abilities. With whomever he worked, it was the essential purpose of therapy to mourn the loss of the caring and nurturance which he desired and to then accept the contact and support that were, in fact, available. Finally, I told him that while I would accept and understand whatever decision he came to regarding further contact with me, I felt it essential for him to continue therapy in the group for the support and contact he had been able to find there.

In this session, and others reminiscent of it, I believe a critical therapeutic component is the self-exploration and confrontation of limitation that are expressed and modeled. Transference explanations are immeasurably enhanced, particularly with narcissistic individuals, when they are accompanied by the therapist's attempt to own his or her contribution to whatever interactional difficulties are being experienced in therapy. This humanistic and self-disclosing stance makes this kind of analytic psychotherapy more difficult for the therapist than the more traditional approach, in which the analyst more rigidly adheres to a set of rules prohibiting self-disclosure. However, it provides an extraordinarily reparative experience for the client who has usually been subject to parents who were never wrong and who always blamed the child.

This kind of session makes possible a real human-to-human therapeutic alliance that pulls the client toward an adult-adult relationship. Subsequent to this session, John not only stayed in therapy, but also obviously committed himself much more fully to the process. In the following group session, he was more real, insightful, contactful, and committed to furthering his own growth than I had ever witnessed. Further, this proved to be a watershed point in his therapeutic progress, with enhanced interpersonal trust and personal responsibility.

Finally, a useful theme for intervention with the annihilation-abandonment crisis is psychological defense building. The borderline narcissist in particular can be assisted in getting through crisis episodes by using new defensive strategies or self-consciously using old ones. It would be fortunate if the borderline narcissist were amenable during his annihilation-abandonment crisis to learning techniques which are known to serve a resource building or even defense building function. It has been my experience, however, that the borderline narcissist is simply too agitated during crisis periods for this to be very productive. While the person with the narcissistic style may benefit from such strategies during a crisis, the borderline narcissist usually needs to learn them when he is a bit more tightly wrapped than in the crisis situation. Then, when he falls into crisis, he can at least be reminded of these strategies.

For the most part, however, the borderline narcissist needs to use the live interpersonal contact with the therapist to work through and eventually resolve the archaic issues and feelings so powerfully accessed during the crisis periods. For this reason, I will delay my presentation of such strategies derived from hypnosis and neurolinguistic programming (resource accessing, strategy analysis, and reparenting processes) until the discussion of the treatment of the annihilation-abandonment crisis in the patient with a narcissistic style (Chapter V).

CHAPTER IV

TREATMENT OF THE FALSE SELF

> To search for perfection is all very well,
> But to look for heaven is to live here in hell.
>
> – Sting

CHARACTEROLOGICAL PSYCHOTHERAPY unfolds in a series of "rounds," in which the client's basic issues are brought forth and worked through again and again. The second round in the therapy of the narcissistic character disorder or narcissistic style usually involves the treatment of the remobilized, grandiose, false self. When the depression or crisis passes and the person begins to function at least adequately again, she will almost certainly revert back to false self functioning. For one with a narcissistic style, this usually means a return to overactivity of some kind, usually overwork. In this common form of "child abuse," the individual throws herself back into a pattern of overwork and excessive reliance on achievement to obtain self-esteem. This kind of narcissistic compensation is illustrated very well in the Bob Fosse film, "All That Jazz," in which Joe Gidion drives himself to death in the futile attempt to prove that he is enough: "Nothing I ever do is good enough. It's not beautiful enough; it's not funny enough; it's not deep enough; it's not anything enough."

Seeing this addictive, self-destructive behavior accompanied by the denial of its inevitable consequences, like alcoholism, typically drives friends, family, and therapists alike to urge restraint. Often, however, this oft-heard plea to cut down is merely reinforcing to the grandiosity which drives the pattern. By acknowledging his often superhuman stamina and abilities, these remarks often serve more as medals on the inflated chest of the aspiring hero. While a well-timed, dramatic or mobilized set of confrontations may well have a therapeutic effect, the constant urging of restraint which occurs in the lives of such workaholic narcissists is counterproductive. Ultimately, it is necessary for the narcissistic person to really experience the pain and destruction which he is visiting on himself. Often he needs to be hammered into the ground by suffering before he can begin to give up the patterns that create it. For this reason, it is often necessary for the narcissistic individual to experience a very traumatic crisis or series of crises before he will very reluctantly choose to embrace the extraordinarily threatening archaic feelings and demands of the real self.

The "successful" narcissistic person makes a very stubborn client in that his compromise almost works, or it used to work, or it sometimes works, or it works for a while. He often gets a lot of attention or even adoration, makes a lot of money, and is able to procure whatever other gratifications are available. As long as this gratification maintains, he is able to keep the repressed demands and feelings of the real self at bay. In confronting this situation, the therapist's task is to erode the defensive compromise by whatever methods are effective, while supportively bringing to awareness and nurturing the legitimate claims of the real self. The individual with a narcissistic style stays in therapy for this threatening process because (1) in spite of the denial, he experiences enough of the pain to keep him coming and (2) he is capable of a therapeutic alliance and trusts the therapist's judgment. But, much more than the borderline narcissist, this is an individual who can "forget" his pain and *real* self-denial in the press of the demands and successes of day-to-day living. It often takes many rounds and much recurring pain before this type of patient will decide to give up the pattern to which he is addicted and decide to try to begin living for himself. I say *try to begin* because the narcissistic person facing this decision knows very little about what he will have to encounter in this process of self-discovery and self-love. In effect, he will be asked to let go of a painful pattern which nevertheless almost works to face the void and pain of an injured and undeveloped self. Some choice. Our compassion is not wasted on him, nor is it unjustified. Compassion is one of the essential aspects of our work with narcissistic clients.

The mobilization of the grandiose false self reinstates the narcissistic inability to accept and live within limitation. In some individuals, this may develop into a very exaggerated, manic, ungrounded activity, while other individuals may be able to sustain a fairly realistic existence but push themselves to dangerous, self-denying extremes.

Because nothing is ever really enough, the person with a narcissistic style will push herself beyond whatever her real limits are. If she can sustain a 12-hour workday six days a week, she will move to a 16-hour day, etc. Where you have a patient with a very strong genetic and characterological structure, you will probably have to face your own limits around any attempts to curb the activity and simply wait for the inevitable collapse or crisis. With very strong individuals, the spouse or family will often be the ones to cause enough difficulty to force the patient to see some realistic limitations.

All the considerations listed above are relevant in underlining the great desirability of group treatment for narcissistic individuals. Typically, they can develop much greater insight and compassion for others exhibiting this pattern than they can for themselves. Denial and habit collude to prevent full *self*-awareness, but the repeated confrontation with others like themselves and the compassion and recognition which this stimulates has a cumulative curative effect. Like everyone else, they are quick to persuade fellow travelers on this self-destructive journey to stop, slow down, change. Often, in the group therapy context, their persuasion has more effect on themselves than on the target of that persuasion. When this is coupled with a therapy process which encourages and then supports true self-expression, the group provides an invaluable adjunct to individual work. Often, I think, group work is virtually necessary to effect any lasting change in the patient with the narcissistic style.

UNDOING

The analysis of most narcissistic compromises will invariably lead to *undoing* as a central unconscious motivation of the defensive patterns. The unconscious hope is that the original injury can somehow be reversed, the lost love regained, the wasted years brought back and relived. Ultimate change is resisted in part because it requires such mourning, not only of the original loss, but all those subsequent ones set in motion by it. Giving up the compromise means that all the efforts and all the time devoted to undoing it have in some meaningful way been wasted. I have often heard clients say, "I feel if I could only hold out a little longer, achieve a little more, do just a little better, that I could make it all work out." And, typically, the more successful the compromise, the more stubborn this hopeful illusion.

The unconscious motive of *undoing* is more or less universal in the compromise behaviors of the character disorders and character styles. It is particularly obvious in unconsciously determined mate selection, wherein the person selects a mate who is reminiscent of the parent who was most injurious. Then the person attempts to change the mate in order to undo the original injury. Each reinjury in the present accesses the accumulation of similar injuries and each failure to change the other accesses the despair of the original situation until a recommitment to the compromise is realized. Often, people go from mate to mate in serial attempts to maintain the denial of the original injury by repeated attempts to undo it. For numerous examples of one expression of this universal pattern, see Robin Norwood's (1985) *Women Who Love Too Much*.

The unconscious motive of undoing is also frequently apparent in one's work, particularly where that work is clearly overdetermined. I particularly recall Mary, a 39-year-old social worker who dealt in child welfare cases. She worked extraordinarily long hours in this demanding job and handled most of her work very well. However, whenever she dealt with any case of sexual child abuse, she would become very anxious, overwork compulsively, and be unable to sleep. She would become overinvolved in the legal prosecution of the offender. In therapy, she confessed that the possible acquittal of the perpetrator terrified her. She was understandably concerned about the offender's return to the home in which he had committed the offense, but her reaction went to catastrophic proportions and activated her extremely rigid and compulsive defense structure. The working-through of the sexual abuse she experienced as a child led to her awareness of the unconscious motivation in these cases to undo, thereby keeping active the denial of her own painful history.

Like many clients with this unfortunate history, Mary vacillated between accurately remembering the incidence of abuse and questioning or disallowing those memories. Her own recognition of the overdetermined quality of her work with sexually abused clients increased the plausibility of the memories she recovered. Still, my assurance, as well as the assurance of all the members of her therapy group, regarding the validity of these early memories was necessary to bolster her confidence. Finally, she accidently saw the movie "Sybil," in which the same kind of sexual abuse visited upon her was portrayed in graphic detail. Simultaneously, a sibling confirmed the reality of her memories of such abuse. These instances capped a number of very dramatic individual and group therapy sessions in which she worked through the memories and denial of these early terrors. As this was completed, Mary experienced a dramatic breakthrough in her therapeutic work, realizing that she was not responsible for saving all the abused children of the world. Subsequently, her work with cases of sexual child abuse did not disorganize her.

In working through Mary's early sexual abuse, I was again reminded of why we maintain such massive levels of denial, retain obviously overdetermined patterns of undoing, and resist in the most elaborate ways the remembering and feeling-through of our original losses. During the working-through process, Mary would become terrified, feel numb all over, seriously question her sanity, and become transiently withdrawn and suicidal. Particularly when she was remembering the sexual abuse and yet refusing to believe her memories, she questioned her sanity. At one point she said, "I wonder if whoever came up with the idea of denial knew it like this." For her, that simultaneous awareness and denial were insane.

At these times I would attempt to get Mary to understand that the denial had saved her sanity. Still, the extreme psychic pain and actual threat to survival that this pain engendered made me once again understand the extreme lengths to which we will go to avoid reexperiencing the truth of our lives. At the same time, this expression gave me great respect for those of us who have the courage to continue on this course and renewed my ability to support all those who give me the privilege of accompanying them. When Mary had finally worked through her own early sexual child abuse and was ready to let go of her compensatory saving behaviors, she said, "I just have to remember that this is God's universe. It is not my job to make it all work."

Letting go of the responsibility to "make it all work" represents a relinquishing of the grandiose hope that this is single-handedly possible. Relinquishing this specialness and accepting one's reality represents another loss, which must also be mourned. In all cases of narcissism, it is not only the original and subsequent losses that must be acknowledged and grieved, but also the final loss of the residual grandiose belief that I *can* undo it and reclaim the lost life. This very popular illusory belief is nicely demonstrated in two contemporary films: "Superman II" and "Back to the Future." In both cases, the reality of the past is, through magical action, changed to effect a new reality in the present. Though I have used and endorse most of the procedures of neurolinguistic programming, I have typically eschewed the full use of the procedure labeled *change history* because it, too, gives some support to this illusory possibility of actually changing the past to effect a change in the present.

The variety of these undoing scenarios is virtually endless. Joe, for example, tried to recapture his lost adolescence by devoting his life to the creation and maintenance of an adolescent care center where he specialized in treating drug and alcohol abuse—the very things that robbed him of a normal adolescence. His only other devotion was the hobby of motorcycling, which he embraced with an adolescent frenzy, driving himself and his machines beyond all limits. A serious accident, which could have been fatal for him and his girl friend, eventually brought him to the realization of these patterns, the relinquishing of which was accompanied with great sadness and loss.

Often, the undoing patterns are not quite so apparent at first blush. Arthur, for example, was one of those children who was taken into his mother's bed at a very early age when his father was in military service. When the father returned, some two years later, Arthur was suddenly displaced. Though it was by no means his major problem, it was curious that in numerous situations, Arthur became involved in profound conflicts over keeping his place. On more than one occasion, he got into physical fights over his retention of an airline seat, a theater seat, or a place in line. The frequency and intensity of these episodes signaled their overdetermined quality and led to useful insights concerning the undoing process.

The interpretation of undoing usually has the greatest therapeutic utility in the middle to latter phases of the therapeutic process, when the person has some idea of what it is she needs to work through and relinquish and some idea of what this process involves. It is often helpful if she has seen another person go through it in group work or, better yet, if she has gone through it herself in some other area. Given too early, the undoing interpretation can precipitate another narcissistic injury, make the client feel stupid, and engender further defensive undoing. The effects are much like a premature interpretation of secondary gain, in which one experiences being told that she *likes* being depressed or *manipulates* with her somatic illnesses. Even if she experiences that interpretation to be correct, it leaves her nowhere to go, nothing to do. However, once the working-through process has begun, she knows what she must do and can understand the resistance to doing it.

Given a timely presentation, the *undoing* interpretation undermines this unconscious defensive strategy and pulls the patient inexorably toward the underlying feelings that are being resisted. It confronts the sacrifice of self and life in the pursuit of specialness and illusion. A dramatic confrontation of undoing is often necessary to move the patient to the necessary pain of relinquishing and working through the inevitable feelings. A therapist's confrontive skills are particularly demanded with this kind of interpretation, together with a therapeutic neutrality. The neutrality required is not one of unemotionality. Rather, it is one of disengagement from the outcome, such that the client is not pushed to change or to serve, please or be used by the therapist; rather, she is faced with the tragedy of her life lost to false pursuits. The therapist needs to be like a tennis player caught up in and impassioned by the game, who always knows he is playing a game. Such a therapist realizes that the patient's life is ultimately in the patient's hands. He does his job, plays the game, but leaves its outcome open. He knows the game well enough to know when he has played it well and is disengaged enough to receive feedback, positive or negative. This ideal is, of course, only approximated by most of us, but, again, it is not a bad one by which to be pulled.

I am somewhat enamored of the undoing interpretation because of its relative universality and its therapeutic potential. It is, I believe, one of the few interventions which can sometimes prevent or minimize the massive failure of the narcissist's compromises that is often necessary before change is undertaken. If one can see one's failure to undo in the ways outlined above, it is just possible that one may not have to reach the depths in a current failure (e.g., bankruptcy, divorce, or serious illness) in order to motivate the necessary pain of working-through and relinquishing. Such insight can often be facilitated by a therapist who has mastered the timing and passion of an enlightened confrontation.

ENERGETIC INTERVENTIONS

Whenever I find myself struggling with the question of how to help bring my narcissistic patients back from their compulsively driven, life-denying, and often "workaholic" behavior, I am helped by what

I've learned from my bioenergetic colleagues. They assert that we are all ultimately rescued from our characterological compromises by our biological reality. Only if we can be brought back to the reality of our physical existence will there be enough force to challenge and ultimately renounce the grandiose, false self compromises which remain so seductive.

I conceptualize this reconnection of the self with one's biological reality in five steps. The first step is grounding. This work involves anything which anchors one in current direct kinesthetic experience and brings one down—down to one's self, one's body, and one's earthly existence with connectedness to the ground. At the most minimal level of intervention, this grounding will involve some simple breathing exercises, meditative procedures, or hypnotic induction strategies. One of my favorites for this purpose is the "I am" meditation in which the client is simply asked to say to herself repeatedly, "I am . . ." and fill in the blank with whatever body sensation becomes apparent. Three to ten minutes of this meditative procedure will often have a centering, relaxing, and even humbling effect. Slightly more intrusive interventions involve those body therapy procedures which enhance grounding, breathing, and body awareness. A selection of these procedures is presented in the appendix.

The second step involves the opening of the pelvis and chest so that the natural flow of the body's energy can be felt and released there. Where there is the firmly held narcissistic upward displacement in the body, it is often useful to work directly on it to relax the mobilized false self. One initially effective procedure involves literally forcing the patient to drop his shoulders. To achieve this, simply stand behind the patient, usually on a chair, and place your forearms on the fleshy part of the patient's shoulders. Then shift the appropriate amount of your body weight onto his shoulders, forcing them downward. Maintaining this posture for one to four minutes often results in considerable relaxation of the upward displacement while enhancing grounding.

Where there is armoring in an artificially extended or "puffed up" chest, you may make headway by encouraging or forcing a collapse in this area. I recall the case of one borderline narcissistic individual who could be very quickly brought back to himself by simply encouraging deep belly breathing together with an instruction to simply collapse the artificially extended chest. The better defended patient with a narcissistic style will typically need more active work in this area. A collapse of this kind can be prompted more forcefully by applying considerable pressure to the upper chest region as the client exhales. This is often most efficiently done with the client lying on his back on the floor, but can also be accomplished with the client sitting up or done even more forcefully with the client extended backward over the bioenergetic stool (see appendix). The stool is perhaps the most universal bioenergetic tool for work on the chest, abdomen, and back.

Whatever the exercise, you look for movement and color in the upper chest to signal opening in this area. Over the stool, get the client to drop his hips to pull for release. Subtle movement in the hip area often signals a release of the block there. In this position, or in others, it is useful to call for movement in the hips and eventually to achieve connection with experiencing pleasure in such movement. To accomplish this, you might ask the client to lie on his back on the floor with his knees up and his feet flat on the floor. Then, call for anything from subtle hip movement to thrusting, exaggerated hip movements. For greater release, ask the client to lift his hips off the ground an inch or two and then drop them. Repetition of this procedure can further loosen the muscles of the lower back and ultimately result in pleasurable movement there. Obviously, this kind of movement carries strong, though not exclusive, sexual and aggressive components. This kind of active intervention should, of course, be delayed until one has a good developmental diagnostic picture of the client and a firm therapeutic alliance has been established. The chest, abdomen, and lower back are among the most sensitive and vulnerable energetic areas and should be approached with caution.

The next step involves the movement of energetic flow through the neck and into vocalization. Here exercises that open the throat and release sound will be useful. One of these simply involves asking the client to open his mouth wide and extend his tongue out and down toward his chin as far as possible. This posture can lead to choking, which itself can have a releasing effect. To mitigate the choking response, ask the client to extend his head forward a bit and look down. Light massage of the throat on either side of the Adam's apple can also be facilitative, as can vocalization in any of the foregoing exercises.

With these channels open, you then move to connection with and release through the eyes. Here again, a number of exercises are applicable to release in this area. It is often necessary, particularly with more schizoid individuals, to do a good deal of work on the eyes before a connection at this level can be accomplished (see *Characterological Transformation* for eye exercises). Alternatively, in the work with a more highly functioning "narrow" narcissist, you may be able to simply ask the client to soften her eyes and attend to what she is feeling.

The extensiveness of the necessary body work will vary greatly. The less well-defended patient, or the one who has been in treatment for some time, may require very little of it to bring him back to himself and enable him to move on with the more critical psychological work. The very well defended client or one who has not been in therapy for long may require 30 to 60 minutes of body work before beginning to achieve some sense of real self.

It is not necessary to be particularly clever or bioenergetically innovative in doing this work. Simple repetition of the exercises given here and in the appendix or others of which you may be aware is usually quite adequate. You simply watch and feel with the patient until he "softens" to the reality of his physical existence. At that point, you will discover what a drop into that bodily reality means for him. Sometimes, the relaxation will be experienced as a relief and the individual will be reintroduced to what he has been missing. On other occasions, this energetic drop into the real self will engender fear—fear of punishment, fear of not being enough, fear of disapproved impulses, etc. On still other occasions, or with other individuals, this energetic drop will result in grief, despair, or sadness associated with current or past injuries and losses. On still other occasions, the client will hit his real exhaustion, which has been buried under the manic narcissistic activity. Whatever the result, both you and the client will once again be in touch with the client's real self. When the biological reality is grounded and flowing through the midsection and upper body, and when it is available for expression through the voice and eyes, you have the physical experience and expression of the real self.

Now you are ready for the communication of the patient's real self to the therapist and the firming of an *empathic connection* between the two. *It is the experience of the real self with empathic connection to others that is the essence of the narcissistic healing*. It will need to be achieved again and again, but each experience is a sampling of profound intimacy—an experience for which the patient longs. The longing is denied in the narcissistic states and resisted with a vengeance because it leads to the affects of the narcissistic injury—the disappointment, shame, humiliation, and anger originally experienced. If, however, there is a therapeutic relationship of sufficient empathic trust, and if the energetic cognitive and behavioral defenses can be relaxed, the client *may* have the courage to stick with his biological reality and experience his real self.

Fortunately, not every experience of the real self brings up negative emotion, particularly as therapy progresses. As stated earlier, this collapse into the reality of the self can often be very pleasurable. The maintenance of a grounded, energetic flow in the body, with its expression through the voice and eyes, can feel extraordinarily right. Its pairing with intimacy with the therapist makes it even more profound and sustainable. As this experience is extended out into the client's real life, there is the narcissistic "cure."

In this kind of bioenergetic psychotherapy, it is important that the client *feel* the grounding, the movement, and then the connection. Throughout the work, it is important to call for movement and to direct the client's attention when necessary to *experiencing* that *movement*. As he feels movement in the hips and in the chest, and as he feels the movement of expression through the voice, he feels *self* and the real affects that are pushing for expression and awareness. There is in this movement the hurt, the longing, the pleasure, and the completion of his connection with another and with the process of life itself.

So, in requesting those movements that bring charge to the legs, movement to the hips and chest, and expression in the voice and eyes, you are not doing calisthenics or merely training in self-expressive abilities. Rather, you are helping a person connect with his own biological and psychological reality. The methods may be specialized, seemingly intrusive and bizarre, but they are designed to assist the irresistible life force in breaking through the immovable object of archaic resistance. These are not, I would maintain, human potential tricks of the '60s for which we are too sophisticated today. Rather, they are procedures that tap into the natural biological-psychological structure of the organism buried beneath an entrenched resistance. Our supposed sophistication, as well as that of our clients, is often just another bulwark of that life-denying resistance.

Because of such resistance, bioenergetic work is not, usually smooth or easily completed. The negative affects are threatening and automatically pull for an energetic contraction which stifles them. At each point in the sequence, the bioenergetic therapist's job is to keep an eye out for such contractions and take one of two courses of action in response. The first course is to engage in exercises or direct "hands on" work to relax the contraction. The second course is to encourage the individual to identify with the resistance, owning it and verbalizing it.

Among the most powerful feelings to be accessed in this process is the need for the empathic understanding and help of the other. Characterologically, however, the narcissist resists such need and continually pursues the illusion of doing it all alone. She desperately needs and desperately hates to need. Many sessions will be devoted to the swings from one side of this polarity to the other. When she is in resistance, it is useful to help her discover the depths of the hatred of her own need ("I refuse to need. I will do it all myself."). As this is worked through, she will come to experience the archaic absoluteness of her refusal to give in to her longing. As the infantile grandiosity meets the reality of her human need, the patient will experience the irresistible force meeting the immovable object. She has survived for years without moving, without giving in, and she knows she can continue to so survive. But that survival is at great cost. With age, accumulated pain, and the therapeutic process, the reality of that pain becomes increasingly undeniable. And, there are those experiences, even if fleeting, of pleasure, realness, intimacy, and even love. With all of this, the pressure to move becomes more irresistible. With movement there is progressively less denial, more pleasure and intimacy, and the momentum of real change. For a long time, and perhaps for life, there will be the temptation, often automatic and unconscious, to fall back to the old ways. But, as therapy and life progress, there is increased awareness of the real pain and loss of life which this course demands and there is an increased intolerance to accept it.

The other very related issue is the persistent grandiosity of false self accomplishment, which may also be indulged and exaggerated. In some cases, for example, the more sophisticated client will be aware of and somewhat embarrassed by the grandiosity he exhibits. His mere confession of grandiose ideas, fantasies, and feelings will be therapeutic, as he exposes them to the light of day with a witness, as well as to his own observing ego. Sometimes, all one needs to do is be a sounding board for the self-recognized grandiosity and its expressions (e.g., entitlement, pride, objectification and manipulation of others, etc.). Where this process needs an added boost, I have found two simple processes to be facilitative.

In the first of these exercises on grandiosity, I simply ask the client to stand and strut back and forth in the therapy room while bragging about his or her accomplishments, attractiveness, positive qualities, social position, etc. It is important that the therapeutic alliance be strong for this procedure, as it is meant to be embarrassing and humorous but must not be humiliating. If you suspect that you are prompted to do this exercise out of any countertransferential hostility toward the client, don't do it!

The second technique involves the coupling of one of the more difficult grounding postures with some verbalizations. I ask the client to put all of his weight on one leg and bend deeply at the knee over some pillows. Within a minute or so, this posture will begin to produce a painful strain and burning in the leg. At this point, I again ask the client to brag, often to his father, boss, or other authority figure, about his accomplishments and about how hard he is working. When the patient has endured all of this he can stand, I ask him to fall forward on the pillows in front of him, saying, "I give up." In contrast to the former exercise, this one tends to pull for feelings of exhaustion, pain, and the awareness of being used and sacrificed. It demands collapse. While both procedures aim at the erosion of the grandiose false self and are similar in content, they pull for somewhat different affective experiences and forms of resolution.

When the grandiose, false self is remobilized, therapeutic procedures that encourage the patient to identify with and verbalize it are called for. As therapy progresses, these procedures are increasingly effective in helping the client feel the pain and loss that the false self perpetuates. They increasingly require the client to feel the depths of his hatred of being needy and fallibly human. With these feelings in the open, they can be worked through.

Another useful approach to the resistance of the false self is the oldest "exercise" of them all—free association. I have very productively used free association as one procedure among several, particularly when dealing with the polished, well-defended client early in therapy. When the client's usual and somewhat overly smooth social behavior interferes with his or her accessing relevant material and where "things are going pretty well and there's not much to talk about," this procedure has proved invaluable. It puts the responsibility for eliciting material where it belongs and mildly reduces defensive maneuvers, just as Freud said; yet, it does not demand exposure, as do some of the potentially embarrassing procedures of Gestalt or bioenergetic therapy. By no means do I reserve it only for situations of false self mobilization, but it is useful in response to this constellation and may well provide a jumping off place for any number of other interventions. There is no valid justification for viewing free association as a sacrosanct procedure which cannot be varied nor for throwing out such a valuable tool because it is reminiscent of classic analysis and so many cartoons in *New Yorker* magazine.

Particularly during periods of false self mobilization, which include manic, compulsive, and overextending behaviors, it is often important to recommend procedures or exercises outside of therapy that will interfere with this destructive pattern and bring forth the pleasures and vulnerabilities of the real self. This is a good time to suggest and get commitment for such procedures as meditation, self-hypnosis, yoga or bioenergetic exercises, or for unstructured time. A walk in the woods, listening to music, or taking a hot bath are all things that may be welcomed or which may make the narcissitic individual anxious and challenged. Even when these activities are somewhat forced, they can still serve a very therapeutic function.

I have often found it helpful to get such self-soothing, slow-down commitments from a person in the context of building more appropriate "self-parenting." I employ the useful Gestalt therapy fiction of separating one into "parts" and help the patient see how his current "parenting" of his "child" is demanding, unforgiving, and destructive. Then, as a part of Gestalt role-play or other internal process, I ask the client to adopt the position of parent and talk to his "child" as a nurturing helpful parent who commits to be kind, to spend time with the child, and to give the child plenty of opportunities for rest, relaxation, and play. In this way, I begin to take myself out of the parenting role and get the client to play it.

It is particularly important in structuring extratherapy behavior to avoid an authoritative role that will pull for power struggles and noncompliance in the interest of self-assertion. The procedures which gently and cooperatively shift the self-caring, parental role to the patient will assist in "guardianship of autonomy" rather than threaten such maturation.

When resistance is not overpowering, the therapy session can be an opportunity for the expression and sharing of real life. At these times, I am reminded why I signed on for this occupation of psychotherapist. The client discovers himself, expresses himself, strengthens himself, and firms his trust in his own nature, sharing all of this magnanimously. When this occurs, it is our job to be present, but primarily quiet. In our enthusiasm for our patient's much awaited movement, it is important that we not snatch it away. It is important to communicate your enthusiastic support but avoid drowning the client in it. Go tell your colleagues or write up a case report, but let your client own his victory in this epic struggle.

There is more to say about the content of these sessions in which the real self is expressed. There is also more to say about therapeutic strategies that encourage the necessary awareness and expression once the defenses have been relaxed. All this will be discussed in the next chapter on the discovery and enhancement of the real self.

FALSE SELF-REAL SELF DIALOGUE

In every case of treating the narcissistic style, I attempt to establish and encourage a running dialogue between the grandiose, false self and the real self. In this Gestalt-inspired exercise, I typically identify the real self as the "child" in the person and the grandiose false self as that part of the patient who drives him, disapproves of him, and expects a great deal of him. In this exercise, it is common for the patient to access the real depth of hatred that exists for the real vulnerabilities, archaic demands, and feelings of that "child." Often, the grandiose, false self is analogous to that overdemanding, unempathic, critical parent who literally hates her child for his weaknesses and failure to live up to expectations.

The child, cowed and intimidated by this powerful rejecting figure, seems helpless but in reality is able to bring the other down by continual frustration. The hidden and unconscious spite in the child, which often results in depression, illness, or work inhibition, can be accessed in an artful Gestalt process. Indeed, the archaic and exaggerated demands of both sides of this polarity can be accessed and deepened throughout the course of therapy as this technique is employed again and again.

It is then useful to call up a "third part," which is more adult, wise, and disengaged from the struggle. This part can be asked to referee, balance, or assist in negotiation so that the necessary maturation of the arrested parts is furthered. Done often enough, this process will lead the client to engage in variations of it outside the therapeutic context. This, in turn, will lead to realistic compromises regarding activities, work, and relationships, such that the real needs of the child are both met and optimally frustrated. Similarly, the grandiose needs of the false self are frustrated optimally and the demands of grandiosity are ultimately neutralized.

It may be important to emphasize to the client that the child is not always right and the press from the false self not always wrong or vice versa. Rather, both sides are arrested and immature, requiring a sympathetic reparenting so that they can both mature. The grandiosity needs to be tamed to a healthy narcissism and the needs of the real self (the child) need to be acknowledged, met insofar as realistically possible, but frustrated by the very nature of life itself. In this continuing, repetitive process there is maturation, and the fiction of separating the individual into "parts" is merely useful in effecting that.

Many sessions with a narcissistic client may be productively devoted to this simple Gestalt "two-chair" procedure. Among other things, the client may have occasions for insight into the creation of symptoms as the result of conflict between the demands of grandiosity and the archaic demands of the real child. In this simple repeated process, then, the client can be made aware in concrete terms of these four essential parts—the grandiose false self, the archaic real self, the symtomatic self that results from conflict between these two, and the conscious adult self, which is evolving from the neutralization of the arrested selves.

Case Example: Phil

The "parts" dialogue described above provided one central intervention model for part of the long-term therapy of Phil, a 38-year-old man who initiated therapy with severe depression, long-standing alcoholism, and chronic pain. His four-year therapeutic course included a period of residential treatment in an alcohol treatment center with follow-up group support and nine months of Reichian breathing work which helped him get in touch with his extreme terror and despair. On entering therapy, Phil's functioning was intermediate between the clear-cut cases of borderline narcissism and the clear-cut cases of narcissistic style presented in this book. While the quality of his paranoid perceptions and hostile reactions could reach borderline proportions at times, he had been able to sustain a long-term marriage, employment, and commitment to artistic self-expression. Additionally, his transference reactions in therapy were not exaggerated as in the clear-cut borderline cases, and he always recognized these reactions as transferential.

The etiology of Phil's narcissism was, as far as we could determine, exclusively of the humiliating-shaming variety. He grew up in a home with an alcoholic, abusive father and a mother who joined the father in his drinking and failed to resist him in the abuse of his children. Phil's older brother passed down the humiliation and shame which he received so that Phil was consistently the most helpless target of both males' spiteful talionic impulses, with little or no protection from the mother. Upon entering therapy, Phil could be described as a highly paranoid and pained person who was quick to take offense and strike out, particularly in the family setting. He would engage in periodic episodes of alcoholic bingeing, during which he would disappear for days at a time. He was extremely self-recriminating; this was, of course, greatly intensified during and immediately after the alcoholic binges.

Once Phil's alcoholism was brought under control, he was able to experience repeated rounds of feeling through the archaic demands and affects, which included the terror and grief associated with the history just outlined. After much of this *necessary* negative affect was worked through, however, it became clear that Phil was continuing to experience the *unnecessary*, bogus affect of cognitively mediated worthlessness. To address this unnecessary negative affect, we embarked on a course of more cognitive intervention which employed the useful fiction of the Gestalt "parts" model. Through this work, Phil began to identify his internalized self-punitive part as "Bobby," his humiliating father. Further, he developed a very comprehensive understanding of his process of projecting that internalized punishing figure onto others and became progressively more adept at talking himself down from episodes of paranoia and self-denigration. The final seven months of his therapy were almost exclusively devoted to this kind of Gestalt-cognitive intervention. His therapy was brought to an end by my moving to another area, but it appeared to be very well along at the time of this forced termination.

This case represents my most successful experience with a cognitive intervention in a stubborn, long-term therapy, though I believe this is so because of the prior energetic work in the affective realm. As Phil and I were reviewing and refining this cognitive work, the following dialogue was captured on an audiotape recording. This small excerpt of therapy demonstrates many things, including Phil's poignant outline of his cognitive processes, his self-acknowledgment concerning his own therapeutic strategy, and my deliberate attempts to be enthusiastically supportive. The supporting and praiseful comments, which I made in this particular interaction, not only reflected my genuine enthusiasm for his progress but were also informed by what I perceived to be his need for a prizing, self-building other who could be available for internalization. Though I laid on this prizing and praising somewhat more heavily in this session than in prior ones, I had consistently tried to serve Phil by providing this kind of self-sustaining support for maturation. The interaction begins with my delivery of such praise.

Therapist: Do you know how much better you are?

Phil: I'm so much better that everything should be wonderful by now. But it's not.

Therapist: Well, you're not that much better . . .

Phil: [laughs]

Therapist: You're at least 40 percent just watching it. You're also reacting in the old ways some, but you're also watching it.

Phil: I'm watching me react.

Therapist: You're not fully buying it, you're also not fully not buying it, at times. But that's the direction you're going—keep observing, keep observing, keep observing—even to the point of "I'm doing it and I'm reacting to it, and I'm pissed off at myself for doing it and believing it . . ."

Phil: And that's okay too.

Therapist: Yeah. It's like, you're not a bad person no matter how many regressions you go through, no matter how many awarenesses of awarenesses . . .

Phil: As long as I end up . . . saying, "but be compassionate 'cause this is you."

Therapist: Right.

Phil: And if I end up the one that says "and you're fucking it all up and you'll be crazy forever!!" then I gotta step back and say, "but that's you and it's okay." It's almost like every time I get to Bobby I remember to step back to that, to the compassion.

Therapist: How do you do that?

Phil: I don't know; I was using some sort of little mechanism about being scared of people that went: "I just can't afford to care, it's just too much trouble to care. I can't be scared of everyone that's out there. So, I just sorta go, 'Well, I'll worry about what they think about me some other time.'" I consciously don't speculate, I consciously don't do any of that. I shut down all of the old shit, and I do that to everyone outside, and I do that to the guy inside. So, it's like a twofold little step. It's just a little step with me now. It's just shut that down, shut this down. And then, we were talking about buttons and stuff—and I just sort of use that same kind of feeling. When I feel that I just shut it down.

Therapist: Shut it down?

Phil: Shut that down. When I get to Bobby, I just step back—to compassion, 'cause it's real close. I just stuck it right behind Bobby, so it'd be there. So, when I get to Bobby, I just step back one more step. I try to make that automatic.

Therapist: Very good.

Phil: It seems to work.

Therapist: It works—not because it works, but because you have worked on it, worked on it, worked on it, worked on it.

Phil: Yeah . . . because the automatic steps back to Bobby were so fucking automatic, I just had to . . . it seemed reasonable to stick one more step 'cause I was already real good at this.

Therapist: See, what I'm trying to acknowledge is that this stuff is in all the books—certain psychology books. A lot of people have read them and know it—a lot of people have taken consciousness trainings—they know it, but they don't necessarily do it. Doing it means doing it and doing it and doing it and doing it, and not letting up. You let up from time to time, but basically you don't let up, you just keep doing it. And that's why it's worked for you.

Phil: Yeah, I think I could read about it forever.

Therapist: So, I just want to say contratulations for all you've done,—you've taken on an awful lot. You have had a heavy load—a real heavy load. You were a pretty messed up guy.

Phil: Yeah.

Therapist: And that was not your fault, but that was the hand you got dealt, and you played the hand remarkably—awfully, awfully well. And I just respect you for that.

Phil: Now I feel like I gotta do it right—for you . . .

Therapist: NO, no, no, no.

Phil: I do! That's the first thing—I can't disappoint you. [Here's the major transference-countertransference risk of this kind of support.]

Therapist: Watch *that*.

Phil: Yeah, I was, that's just what I was lookin' at . . . I have found something recently—and I guess it's the product of all this work. I've always been real intense and real . . . it's like . . . there's something happening sometimes and it's like I'm in a situation and I don't need to have everyone in that situation impressed one way or another anymore. I can sit there and be whoever I am.

Therapist: Right. You like you better.

Phil: And that's a new thing. I'm not busy slamming myself . . .

Therapist: And then compensating by proving . . . trying to get everybody else to say that you're wonderful or okay or super-okay when you don't think you are. That's how it used to work. Once you get that you are okay, which is also hard work because you can't just read it or say it to yourself once, you've gotta keep . . . going to compassion.

Phil: Yes, going to compassion.

Therapist: And letting in the acknowledgment when people tell you things like I just did, and that can flip you right back to irrational thinking. And then there's more work to do. When you begin to really like yourself—which you are—then you don't have to do all that defending and proving yourself. And, I'm still working at that. This is really true for sure: You are a model for me in a very important way . . . because of the distance you've come.

Phil: Great.

Okay, so maybe I laid it on a little too heavily. Maybe not. In any case, an awareness of that *maybe*—an awareness of the risks and potential benefits of this kind of support—will allow a therapist to realize those benefits without realizing the potential damage because there is a knowledge of that potential and a vigilance concerning it. We needn't be perfect; we need only be good enough. To be good enough, we need only be open to the process of therapeutic expression, feedback, and correction. The creative dialogue that is psychotherapy must be informed by knowledge and theory. But knowledge and theory must not be allowed to destroy the spontaneous authenticity of the human interchange which is itself so curative.

NECESSARY VERSUS UNNECESSARY PAIN

It might be useful at this point to distinguish between that necessary emotional pain which requires a release and working-through from that unnecessary emotional pain which can most profitably be attacked by dealing with what maintains it, as just illustrated in Phil's case. Necessary emotional pain is that which is a natural organismic outgrowth of a life circumstance. In a contemporary sense, this may mean mourning the death of the spouse or child, feeling the betrayal of a friend or feeling anger when seriously frustrated. In psychotherapy, the necessary pain to be felt is often not current, but historical and often archaic. That pain is usually denied, repressed, or disavowed and the armor which covers it can be very complex, involving interrelated affective, behavioral, and cognitive maneuvers. As Reich pointed out, the armoring may also be energetic, involving the way the body is held to prevent the experience of this overwhelming pain. This kind of pain requires the gradual dismantling of defenses and the working-through of the underlying emotions.

Unnecessary pain, by contrast, is best understood through those factors which maintain it, rather than those which elicit it. In Phil's case, for example, the unnecessary component of his pain was that maintained by the internalized introject of his punitive father and brother. An awareness of the nature of this pain was provided by the working-through of the necessary emotional pain. Yet, the emotional pain did not stop with that working-through. What maintained it had to be attacked directly by the cognitive interventions described above. Other forms of maintenance of unnecessary emotional pain include the secondary gain or payoff that it brings, the defense functions that it performs (as in an affect defense or racket feelings) or those kinds of payoffs, both internal and external, that accrue from playing games as outlined by Berne (1964). A careful analysis of such maneuvers, well-placed and empathic confrontations of them, and other therapeutic strategies to directly dismantle them, as in Phil's case, are most useful. Unnecessary emotional pain rarely, if ever, exists alone, without any underlying necessary-to-experience pain. Where humans have created such elaborate painful structures, there has been a reason—a reason which must be uncovered in characterological psychotherapy.

WHAT IS WORKING-THROUGH?

In this context of differentiating necessary from unnecessary emotional pain, it is probably also useful to answer the question often asked by my students, "What exactly is working-through?" Working-through is a process much more easily alluded to than defined, and any definition will fall short of describing the beauty, drama, simplicity, and complexity of that process. My bioenergetic colleagues have offered a simple rhyme to describe the process, which I have embellished slightly. In relation to dealing with the necessary emotional pain in the working-through process, they have offered this prescription: "Claim it, name it, aim it, tame it."

"Claim it" means to own the feeling—to acknowledge its existence, to experience it, to feel it, to focus upon it, to admit to it. This, we are often loath to do, not only because the feelings feel bad, but also because they often violate our standards for ourselves. They are not good feelings to have. Good people don't feel envious, rageful, competitive, petty, etc., etc., etc. Men don't cry. Women aren't selfish. Contemporary enlightened people don't get jealous. Liberated women don't feel helpless or liberated men possessive, etc., etc., etc. It takes a big person to admit how small he can be. For me, "claiming it" is the most essential part of the entire process and the one which people are most inclined to skip over or leave incomplete. This part not only feels bad, but is embarrassing.

The feelings to be claimed are often so deep that they threaten to overwhelm the organization of the self. This is, in part, why the process takes time and work. One should not claim more painful affect than one's ego structure can handle. Much of "working-through" is experiencing deeper and deeper levels of the necessary pain as the strength and organization of the self are enhanced through dealing with the painful feelings themselves, as well as through other ego-building therapeutic processes. Claiming the necessary painful feelings is the most crucial step in the entire working-through process, which typically needs to be returned to again and again. It is often the most resisted part of the process and the one that takes the most ego strength or self-organization. Often, if this first step is merely set in motion, the rest will follow with little additional intervention.

"Naming it" refers to the process of bringing some labels or cognitive understanding to what goes on in the first step of the working-through process. Typically, we wish to rush this step prematurely in an intellectual avoidance of the experience of the pain itself. In doing so, we cut short the most necessary part of the process and miss much of what is necessary to label either in depth or in content. Often, the best therapeutic strategy is to help clients to forestall naming it. Nevertheless, the naming part of the process is valuable; it reduces the disorganizing confusion necessarily elicited in the first step, brings and strengthens organization, allows communication with others who may facilitate the necessary process, and permits real sharing of this essentially human experience. In the process of "working-through" the naming will often become more and more refined, exact, pinpointed, or explanatory. In exploring jealousy, for example, narcissistic patients will frequently elicit deeper and deeper levels of the inadequacy which underlies the more simply labeled affect "jealousy." In this and other ways, this step of "naming it" builds a bridge to and complements the third step of "aiming it."

When you "aim it," you direct the feeling where it belongs. Because psychotherapy often deals with historical pain, to aim it means to associate the feeling with the original injury and the injury's original source. For narcissism, of course, this often means the original shame, humiliation, and using perpetrated on the patient by his or her caretakers. But it is important to note that the necessary feelings are not always historical. When we are used to suppressing our feelings, it becomes a natural, automatic process. We don't know, for example, that we're angry, or at whom, or about what. So, an important part of the psychotherapeutic process is to elicit current *necessary* emotional responses and to assist the client in the process of claiming, naming, aiming, and taming them.

Learning this working-through process is ego-building and essential in characterological psychotherapy. Working-through is often seen as the essential aspect of traditional analytic therapy which is conflict oriented rather than deficit oriented. With Kohut and others, however, I see it as a process which both builds structure and resolves conflict. Structure is built in learning the process and in steadily building greater tolerance for deeper levels of it. The process resolves conflict by bringing the conflicting feelings or demands to the surface, thereby demanding resolution. This demand for resolution again challenges the structure and thereby builds it.

As the necessary painful feelings are aimed at their rightful target, there is usually the demand for even deeper levels of feeling than originally experienced. When the aiming is historical, for example, the person may have to feel all of the pain associated with being repeatedly shamed or sexually used or persistently ignored. This may lead to a refined naming of the feelings or thoughts and a more exact and affectively genuine set of feelings toward those who perpetuated the injury. With this, there will usually be more authentic and often more primitive expression of the necessary painful affects. Often, when a session of such "working-through" is complete, a person feels cleaned out or unburdened of a load which he only dimly knew existed before the session began. You literally have to see it to believe it. I have had to repeatedly see the beneficial, releasing results of years of working-through before I could deeply understand what I am communicating here. It is an incredible experience; though it may be trying to see others through it, it is never boring. It is inspiring to see people rise to the courage it requires. It is unfortunate that it takes so long and hurts so much. I still welcome the possibility that it may be done more quickly or less painfully. But I have no problem being the merchant of this necessary misery because I see how the process works and the fulfilling life that people can have on the other side of it.

The necessary pain is tamed by going through the first three steps of the process. The taming is a natural outgrowth of what comes before. It may be useful to name the taming and have some philosophical label for its existence. But essentially, the desired result is a byproduct of the painful process. When it is not, one may then strongly suspect that some unnecessary pain is cluttering up the picture. In this case, an exploration and analysis of pain maintenance factors are in order. It is, of course, always difficult to know when a "working-through" is "complete" or when the pain is completely unnecessary. This discrimination often requires experience and the help of a trusting therapeutic alliance, and this judgment should always be held tentatively. Guidelines for this discrimination are probably possible, but for now this discussion will serve as food for thought as we move on to other issues.

MOBILIZATION IN THE BORDERLINE NARCISSIST

Though the underlying structure is similar, the surface manifestations of mobilizing the grandiose false self will be noticeably different in the borderline narcissist. Like everything else, the mobilization will be more gross, obvious, and unidimensional. Typically, the patient will withdraw from interpersonal contact in therapy and life and indulge in fantasies of grandiosity, superiority, and hostility. He will often manifest an impatience with the vulnerabilities or imperfections of others. In therapy, he will often denigrate the therapist, deny therapeutic benefit, and move toward premature, ungrounded termination. Knowing that empathic connection with the therapist will be the undoing of this grandiose self, he will resist this in every way possible, including missing sessions, coming late, avoiding eye contact or meaningful interaction.

In the case of John, presented in Chapter III, every mobilization to leave town, quit school, and terminate therapy was preceded by a nearly intolerable annihilation-abandonment crisis. During each crisis, John was extremely needy, desperate, lost, in panic, or depressed. In every case, his mobilization to leave everything terminated much of this dysphoria and malaise. On each occasion, he attempted to avoid further therapeutic contact both individually and in group. Yet, he had previously committed himself to a more orderly termination and I remained firm insisting that he stick to those commitments. In part because he was a man of principle, and in part because he sensed value and caring in the relationships he had formed, he repeatedly assented to further contact. Each time, either in individual or group work, he would break through the defensive posture, achieve human empathic connection, and ultimately revise his plan. I cannot overemphasize the importance of the group and John's extratherapy contact with its members in achieving this repeated outcome.

In cases where a group and its resources have not been available, there has been more pressure on the therapist and the patient's significant others. In the case of Edward, a 30-year-old student, the annihilation-abandonment crises always revolved around the one-sided perception that no one had ever cared. At these times of crisis, Edward would assail his parents and fiancée, with whom he lived, for their inability to care for or appreciate him. On two occasions, the crisis resulted in his striking out and significantly hurting his fiancée, and on one occasion he got into an unnecessary physical fight with another man. During one crisis, he became seriously suicidal and went so far as to place a loaded shotgun in his mouth.

As with John, the most obvious mobilization of Edward's grandiose self always came on the heels of these crises. At these times, he would, like the person with the narcissistic style, overextend his work commitments and see therapy as an unnecessary drain on his time. He would complain, both during the period of crisis and into the period of mobilization, that I gave him inadequate "advice" to deal with his problems. In spite of above average intelligence and a fair degree of psychological sophistication, he would maintain at these times that if someone would only tell him the right thing to do, he could solve his problems. A flight into grandiosity, overactivity, and disdain for everyone provided a very imperfect and fragile escape from the uncomfortable annihilation-abandonment crisis.

Edward was the son of a very rigid professional man who had himself been disappointed in his career. The father had high potential and a prestigious education but was a relative failure professionally and was a disappointment to both his wife and himself. This resulted in a multiple narcissistic injury to his son, the patient, who witnessed the father's failure, the mother's consequent rejection, and the father's resulting depression. As with many narcissistic males, Edward's mother inappropriately idealized him and, in classic fashion, replaced the father with the patient as her primary cathected male. The father resented his son, humiliated him, and was always booming with criticism and "advice" for him. Edward never received the kind of paternal modeling and support that he required.

In therapy, this is what he unconsciously wished for and needed from me. However, for reasons of history, he looked to me for "advice." When this was not forthcoming, and when the unconscious needs for idealization and mirroring were not realized, Edward became enraged. He had fantasies of destroying my office and killing me.

From this nightmare, he would periodically escape to the shelter of the grandiose false self. During these periods, I would tell him that his father had given him plenty of "advice" but that it had not been what he needed. I told him what he needed was the support of someone he could trust. I interpreted the distrust as a direct avoidance of feeling the deep need for a father he could love, look up to, and ask for help. I directly encouraged him to embrace the crisis and interpreted his acting-out and withdrawal from me as avoidance of it. It was only when he began to give in to this need that he could hear interpretations around his archaic needs for complete mirroring from his family and fiancée.

In both of these more borderline cases, it was necessary to reestablish the empathic human connection. With these patients, the techniques of Gestalt or bioenergetic therapy are at once too much and not enough. They are too much in that they can too persistently pull for affects that are already threatening to overwhelm the patient. If these techniques are mistakenly used in potentially dangerous situations, the client will usually effectively defend against them or completely withdraw from therapy, but one cannot count on that completely. Their use could potentially cause a decompensation. These techniques are too little in that they are so obviously artificial, potentially manipulative in the context of great distrust, and fly in the face of an emotional intensity which is already at fever pitch even as it is being denied.

What is required in these cases is that very hard-to-describe "touching" of the client where he most needs to be touched, yet not so deeply that he is frightened into greater distancing mobilization. The intervention is more difficult because you must connect with a person barely capable of connection. You must trigger the human need for support in a person whose human need is deeply threatening. You must elicit trust in a person who is deeply distrustful and similarly threatened by the collapse into the archaic transferences which occur when trust is realized. This is, obviously, a very delicate balance. It is natural for a therapist to be intimidated by this task. And it is wise for even an experienced therapist to avoid having more than a handful of borderline or borderline narcissistic clients at one time.

Though it is difficult to find this key with the borderline narcissistic patient, what I have found to be most encouraging is that these patients will often give you many chances. In spite of their distrust, disillusionment, and narcissistic rage, they will keep coming back to therapy—in part because they have nowhere else to go. I believe that if we understand the problem and work to understand the client, we can eventually come up with that key which will expose at least one opening in the pathological distrust. Even our persistent fumbling attempts to find the key will be duly noted by the client. After a certain number of attempts, she may let one key work just because you have passed the test by trying enough times.

Edmund White (1983, p. 234) has written "a wounded part needs a special welcome back into life." It is our job as therapists to understand our patients well enough to provide that special invitation. The words, the timing, the tone of voice, the facial expression may all need to be "special" in order to move through the labyrinth of defenses to that terrible hurt. Paradoxically, however, we must give up our need for specialness, brilliance, and cleverness to deliver this special message. The message must come out of our seeing the injured child in the defensive adult and speaking to it in such a way that he or she can know that we truly see. Our narcissistic needs to be special in doing this seriously impair our ability to do it. Though all our knowledge will be useful in finding the key, it is often found in that spontaneous moment when our informed humanity gently reaches out to that of another. Whatever techniques are used or eschewed in psychotherapy, these are the moments of deepest healing for our clients and deepest satisfaction for ourselves.

There is very little to be said about how to give this special invitation. A little more can be said about where to come from when giving it. To be grounded in your own humanity, accepting of your own limitations, and solid in yourself is a firm ground of being. From here, you can see with empathy and love the wounded child protected by the facade. If you speak repeatedly, soothingly, and patiently to it, it will probably hear you. It will not be forced or tricked or impressed by your knowledge or cleverness. It will respond to your authenticity, which may be bolstered by the strength of your knowledge. Neither your knowledge nor your realness are enough. Yet the combination of trustworthiness, empathy and knowledge concerning what the injured child really needs will heighten the probability of your having an impact. And, even if you do all this, you will probably still be continually frustrated by the injured child, who will not reveal himself until he is very, very sure.

THE EXISTENTIAL SHIFT

The objective of all this work with the narcissistic style or borderline narcissist is to stop the frantic pursuit of the self in activity and accomplishment and shift to that moment when one experiences the reality of one's existence in the present. That moment is the entry to the real self. A good therapist, seasoned by experience or blessed with intuition, seizes that moment to touch the patient at his core. Through recognition, empathy, or the sharing of the despair or simple beauty that emerges then, the therapist reinforces reality with human connection. By repeating this process again and again, the therapist helps the patient acquire a taste for and strengthen the natural propensity for attuned relationship. When that attunement is achieved in the moment, the false self has been demobilized and there is no further need to concern oneself with any strategies directed toward that objective. From that moment, the therapeutic relationship may most profitably be used to deepen the encounter. It is quite enough that the therapeutic interchange be pleasurably honest, real, and meaningful. It is not even important that the content of the interaction be all that meaningful, but it is important that the affective quality achieve meaningfulness.

As therapy progresses and as the client has internalized caring and respect for his real self, processes that actualize the reparenting of self with enhanced acceptance and nurturance can be most useful. A detailed description of some of these procedures will be offered in the next chapter, which is devoted to the enhancement of the real self.

Therapeutic sessions which involve the transition from the mobilized false self to accessing and expressing the real self are among the most profound. Indeed, they provide a model for what we hope the narcissistic client will eventually be able to do for himself. Though an extraordinary crisis of false self failure will often be a watershed point for the healing process, it will always be necessary for the patient to traverse this false self-real self course again and again throughout therapy and probably thereafter. Repeated experience of this shift is necessary and it will be very useful to assist the client in understanding what facilitates movement from one state to the other. For one client this may be the increased sense of reality which comes from the effects of body work in enhancing body awareness. For another, it may be a cognitive cue or reminder. Another may need to do certain things to ground himself and tame the mania or compulsive activity.

It is at those times when a transition has been accomplished that an inquiry concerning the *willingness* to give up the false self may be most productively undertaken. Particularly when the transition results in positive feelings, the client may be asked if he is *willing* to give up the compensation—to be ordinary. Never mind in such a discussion whether he is able. The simple statement of *willingness* is in itself therapeutic. The Socratic inquiry concerning how long a client thinks it will take him to give up the compromise and what he needs in order to relinquish it is also highly therapeutic, particularly at these poignant times.

In these discussions, I think it is especially important for the therapist to accept his own inability to get the client to change. The motivation for change must be the patient's. While the therapist may demonstrate his concern and caring by his commitment to such change, he cannot accomplish it and his awareness of his limitations can be very useful. It is very facilitative to philosophically accept the natural timetable of the patient's change and, with that acceptance, go about the exercise of one's therapeutic skills with "quiet competence" (Kohut, 1984). You give the client the message that you are there when and if he is ready to change and accept your help. You know that he will cling desperately to the grandiose illusion that he can do it himself. You know that he *needs* desperately and that he desperately *hates to need*. You can observe this epic struggle, quietly and competently takes sides in it, but for the most part leave the passion of the struggle to the client. You cannot do it for him. Your attempts to do so rob him of the necessary autonomy, which will motivate true change, and reinforce the archaic narcissistic transferences, which lead to temporary cure only through wholesale identification.

No part of the foregoing discussion should be misread to discourage a well-placed or impassioned confrontation. Nor do I wish to discourage the communication of caring to the patient which will encourage and sustain surrender to the real self. Rather, I seek only to emphasize the importance of the "guardianship of autonomy" (Greenacre, 1959) and the criticalness of avoiding the superficial improvement that comes from fostering an unresolved narcissistic transference. The healing of narcissism is an epic struggle, and that struggle must be owned by the patient. No amount of skill, caring, or passion on the part of the therapist can release the patient from the responsibility of that struggle. To attempt aiding such an escape is to be like that well-meaning but harmful parent who does not allow her child to experience and learn from the natural challenges and frustrations of life. Such actions only bolster the self-image of the parent or therapist, who may congratulate themselves on their compassion and effort but who fail to have the wisdom and courage to allow their charges to work out their own lives.

As with the parent, the therapist's task is to walk a fine line between too little indulgence and too much, too little challenge and not enough, etc. It is possible, even likely, that most therapists will err from time to time in walking that line. Occasional errors, particularly when quickly corrected, are not of great consequence; indeed, they probably assist the therapeutic process by requiring the narcissistic client to deal with human imperfection in his therapist—a parent substitute. As long as the therapist is informed and respectful of the kinds of principles outlined here, she will be able to offer enough confrontation, empathy, and support so that the client can trust her to be there when needed, yet not offer so much that she extends the false promise of doing the patient's work for him.

CHAPTER V

THE REAL SELF

Your self is now.

– Hugh Prather

IN THE BUDDING of the real self there is hope. But as the real self emerges, one is fragile, vulnerable, and full of feeling. The feelings may be very negative or too much when positive, but they are undeniably real. It is this realness that one learns to cultivate and cherish. In the birth of the real self, there is always a profound need for others—a need which one has long denied or avoided. The new bud of the real self cannot exist very long without the sustenance provided by a welcoming other. Our most essential therapeutic task with the narcissistic person is to provide that welcome.

His history doesn't matter, really. He is 40 years old and just beginning to find himself: "My drive to be a *universal genius* is destroyed. I'm throwing out many of the books I've collected, never read, and never will. I've finally admitted that it's a loss to give up that hope, and yet I feel really clean dumping all this stuff. I'm giving up collecting all that music, too. All that collecting was just my poor way of being that *universal genius* because if I couldn't know it all or do it all, I could at least have a copy of it—hold onto it. It was all just bogus.

"Last time I was in here bent backwards over the stool making those wailing sounds, I liked what you said about my mourning for myself. I've been mourning more since the last time. I feel awfully sad with the big waste of my life over the last five years. I feel like there's been an accident in which I've been injured. The compromises to keep up the front have been deadly. It's as if I've been living someone else's dream—the *universal genius* that my mom always wanted. I *can't* do that anymore, but then *who am I*? I feel anxious, empty, unsure. I'm scared. . . .

"There are those moments, and sometimes it lasts hours, though, that I feel alive again. I'm playing music again instead of listening to so much of it, and I'm lifting weights a little now, and running. These things make me feel good. My sense of smell is better. Out on the running trail, I smell the pine needles again like I haven't for years. And last Friday, when I was lifting weights, I slowed down and enjoyed it and didn't hurry from one exercise to the next trying to get it all done as fast as I could. Instead, I felt my body and joked with some of the guys in the gym and took a long rest in the Jacuzzi afterward. Sometimes, it's as if I'm coming back to life. And then there are those other times when I get so incredibly anxious. I don't know what to do with myself. I'm frightened I'm losing my grip. I can get very depressed and feel so lost and childish. It's awfully hard for me to be less than knowledgeable and competent. I feel like I've always had to put a face on myself, and now the face has been stripped off and I am really at a loss. It's like there's always been a thin crust over the void that is myself. And now I'm in that void, and sometimes I cry and make this sickening retching sound, which is just an expression of how sickened I am by where I am and what's happened to me.

"And still there are these good moments, these alive moments. And those two states of mind vacillate back and forth, though I am depressed or sickened by it all more than I feel good. I feel good mostly about the fact that something is changing, something is happening. There is movement. But most of the time it isn't much fun. When it is good, though, I get very hopeful."

This is the kind of thing you hear as a person begins to rediscover the real self. There is an upside and a downside. On the upside, there is a realness to the experience of life, a discovery of genuine likes and dislikes, moments of pleasure or freedom in self-discovery or self-expression, genuine liking or love for others, etc. Similarly, there are episodes of the discovery of real competence in valued activities, together with a genuine enjoyment in those activities. There are episodes or at least moments of enjoyment of the most simple pleasures. And, there are moments of discovering that the world and the self are not what one has always seen them to be. The introjected attributions of the parents or the script decisions of the young, uninformed child are no longer unconsciously driving one though they still are operating and influential. It's not the way one always thought it was; it doesn't have to be the way it's always been; one sees the potential of choice.

Therapeutic intervention is required to support and to sustain the profound change. This kind of self-expression and renewal leads to internal crises for three basic reasons. First, the self-expression automatically leads to the activation of the old introjects. In or out of awareness, the client begins to "tell" himself that he cannot be this way, that the world is not friendly to his self-expression and not worthy of his faith—that this self-expression is too much, too little, or dangerous. Second, the openness that this kind of genuine feeling and self-expression requires accesses the underlying structure at its point of developmental arrest. For the narcissist, the arrest in rapprochement is revisited and the person must begin to deal with the frustrated demands and overpowering affects of that developmental crisis.

Finally, the uncertainty of this new aliveness is experienced as threatening. The defensive structure has worked for many years. While painful, the defensive perspectives make the world understandable and predictable and prescribe one's dealings with it. So, in summary, the individuation and aliveness achieved through the expression of the emerging real self lead to the expression of negative introjects, the activation of the annihilation-abandonment crisis, and the threat of facing one's life without knowing what it's all about. The emergence of the real self leads to the experience of overpowering affects, which then lead to the reactivation of the defensive structures either in grandiose or symptomatic accommodation. Masterson (1985, p. 8) has noted this same pattern and labeled it the borderline triad; "*individuation* leads to *depression* which leads to *defense*."

It is important for both therapist and client to be aware of the great upside-downside affective polarity that exists with the expression of the real self, particularly in its initial expressions. The affects of the annihilation-abandonment crisis are powerful, infantile, and often more than one can stand. But, they are real. I believe they have been misnamed depressive in that they are truly expressive of the developmental reality which the client is experiencing. When they are indeed too much, they may lead to defensive depression, but they are not themselves depressive. When defensive depression changes to expressive despair, there is real hope for reclaiming the self. As understanding and tolerance for these archaic and unpleasant feelings are developed, there will be more upside experiences of the emerging real self.

The therapeutic tasks in relation to the real self can be put quite simply: (1) Assist the client to *welcome the unwelcome* feelings of the arrested real self through developing understanding and providing the necessary support. (2) Encourage, support, and participate with the client in the process of self-discovery and self-expression. (3) Help the client to understand and manage the truly double-edged sword of the emergence of the real self and manage the inevitable tendency toward defense in the face of this epic challenge.

To accomplish the first of these objectives, it is almost always necessary to repeatedly reassure the client through *reframing* the meaning of the downside of the real self. The crises of real feelings are different from the deadness of the defensive depressive state. There is more affect, more movement, and more hope in the genuine sadness, rage, or panic of the archaic, but real self. The narcissistic patient may need to be told this many times and assisted in making the discrimination, which becomes more difficult as these genuine feelings trigger the defensive symptomatology. You may need to repeatedly review with your patient these transition episodes and help her learn how they work affectively, behaviorally, and cognitively. For many, the distinction will have to do with expression versus suppression and social contact versus isolation. Where there is expression of affect, there is movement and change; where there is inhibition, there is frozen affect, physical contraction, and no change. The effects of expression are even more profound when it is accompanied by meaningful human contact. The narcissist's pride often forces her to withdraw when feeling vulnerable. To the extent that she can face others and express to them her real vulnerability, she can work through the archaic demands and affects, maturing herself through that process. Typically, withdrawal and suppression of affect are defensive. Expression, particularly with others, is working-through.

This is one of many situations in which the direct education of the client concerning human psychological processes as they apply in the present context can be tremendously therapeutic. A therapist's calm and experienced comprehension of such familiar patterns is in itself very soothing. The client is thereby encouraged to continue to feel and express these archaic longings, fears, and frustrations, up to but not beyond the point at which they become disorganizing.

Any therapeutic techniques or significant others that make expression more likely or fruitful are recommended. Thus, Gestalt or bioenergetic processes, which loosen defenses and pull for expression, may be undertaken outside of the usual therapeutic hour in most cases. When, for example, a client is anxious or panicky but is having a hard time understanding these feelings, the classic Gestalt technique of simply repeating, for sentence completion, the phrase "I am frightened because . . . " or "I am anxious because . . . " can be very enlightening. Similarly, if the anxiety creates an inhibition in breathing, the client might be encouraged to do the backbend, which typically employs the bioenergetic stool, using another available structure (the cushioned arm of a couch is usually appropriate for this). Alternatively, if a client suddenly accesses a lot of anger in his day-to-day life, he might be encouraged to do some hitting of pillows, some screaming in his car or in the shower, or to assume and then hold an aggressive position. Finally, if a client is feeling a good deal of grief or sadness but finds himself unable to release it, he might be encouraged to make sounds that express this feeling and thereby access its deeper levels and experience release.

Typically, the more purely narcissistic clients will be more resistant to these extratherapy exercises than most other character types. They may, however, be more willing to explore the resistance to doing them and even express that resistance verbally. It may, for example, be useful to ask the patient to directly verbalize his resistance to expression—to have him say, for example, "I'm feeling bad, but I'm not going to let anybody know it! I'm tough and I can handle this. There's no use in complaining, and I'm not gonna do it. My therapist is a wimp and wants to make me one too. He has no idea what he's talking about," etc., etc. This identification with and expression of the resistance at least moves the person off the conflictual isometrics of dual containment. The expression of such resistance actually lessens it in most cases and, in any event, gets the patient to begin to play the expressive game. The existence of primitive affect and resistance to it are highlighted by these procedures and thereby become more accessible to the client in therapy and beyond.

CASE EXAMPLE: LARRY

This kind of intrapsychic struggle between the emerging real self and the defensive false and symptomatic selves is often most clearly seen in the clients exhibiting the narcissistic style. Because they possess greater ego strength with firmer reality relatedness and less tendency to project than the borderline narcissist, they do not act out these conflicts externally. Rather, they experience the conflict internally—predisposing them to psychosomatic illness, depression, and inertia. Often these clients require therapeutic strategies which externalize the conflicts in order to bring them into the light of awareness and force expression.

Larry was a 38-year-old professional man, successful in his work but very isolated from important interpersonal relationships in spite of a very affable style. He was particularly isolated from important heterosexual relationships, for which he longed. The most significant element of his history involved his relationship with his mother who was, to his memory, very nurturing and supporting up until the time he hit adolescence. At that point, she became hysterical about his expressing any aggression or sexuality. She greatly restricted his adolescent expression of self and would go into hysterical fits, rolling on the floor and screaming, when there was any threat that she would not be obeyed in her restrictions. The father capitulated to this coercive control and Larry internalized his mother's fears concerning his expression of assertion and sexuality. Larry remembered that during adolescence, even when he left home with her reluctant approval, he felt that he was abandoning her and experienced guilt around these normal adolescent activities. As a result of this, and, I suspect, earlier training of a similar nature, he developed a highly polished false self, the purpose of which was to cover his sexuality and male assertiveness and to also cover the early embarrassment he felt at being a poor country boy. In summarizing the person he was discovering in psychotherapy, he said, "Success is how good I am at following the rules. Mimicry is my only living strategy. In any activity I need to know I'm right early on or I evaporate. If you would just tell me how to be me, I would be it. Wherever I am, I'm always looking about to see that everything is okay with everyone else. I'm always concerned that someone may need me to 'fill their coffee cup.'"

All of this, of course, led to an ever-increasing desire in Larry to express his real self. But his initial attempts to do this in active therapeutic technique led to aggressive and sexual feelings, and this repeatedly led to the following conclusion: "If I let go, I will be completely inconsiderate; if I let go, I will be horrible and awful and evil; my anger is scary, wrong and dangerous. I wish I could just find someone who could tell me what to do, so I could do it. I'm scared that these bad feelings are all there is to me. I feel it's all or nothing; I'm either totally constrained or totally out of control. That's what my mom taught me. There were no limits for her. Holding hands led to babies. Your feelings, your body, were an evil guide to what you should do. They were unreliable and dangerous. And I still believe all that."

But, of course, he didn't. The strategies and safety of psychotherapy allowed him to discover all of these internalized beliefs and all of the compromises to self-expression that were made in their service. These discoveries then brought the beliefs and compromises out into the light of adult consciousness for examination, feedback, and eventual accommodation. There was little need to challenge or confront these simplistic ideas, though reassuring support for Larry's rejecting them was offered on the few occasions when it seemed necessary or appropriate. A more borderline narcissistic client may well have projected these parental injunctions onto me, or alternatively, projected the polar opposite attitude, making me the embodiment of aggressive or licentious endorsement. The therapy would then involve the working-through of transference.

In Larry's case, and others where the narcissistic style is more prominent, it is often very useful to externalize this conflict by the use of Gestalt or role-playing methods. This was done with the Gestalt strategies mentioned in the last chapter. I had Larry role play his mother delivering these absolutistic moral commands and to play himself as a child in response to them. After this was fully developed, I then asked Larry to take the role of adult and address his mother concerning these issues. Among other things, I asked him to tell her how it really is and to tell her what she was doing to her child by the instructions she was giving. Larry did this well, but at a feeling level he began again to exhibit the guilt of abandoning his mother. This time, the guilt had more to do with moving on to a more mature, balanced view of life and morality, leaving his mother, and indeed his father, caught in their coercive-compliant patterns and life-destroying views. In this, and in a number of other episodes, we worked through his very common "survivor's guilt." As a child, Larry decided to sacrifice himself to save his mother from the grave discomfort she experienced and to garner her approval. Now, he had to face turning his back on his mother's ways of seeing the world and deal with both the internalized injunctions and the upset which his turning away engendered.

In this redecision process, as in all working-through to higher levels of accommodation and maturity, the simple presence, support, and understanding of the therapist are most critical. With many high-functioning people with narcissistic styles, it is often unnecessary to offer a great deal of explanation, interpretation, or reconstruction. The client knows, especially after the first few rounds in which these strategies can be used, the explanation, the interpretation, or the reconstruction. In each successive round, he most requires a safe and empathic hearing and witness as he works through these issues himself. With these kinds of clients, repetitive interpretations serve only to make the therapist feel useful, competent, and involved, thereby indulging his narcissistic needs and distancing him from the client. Much support can be given in silence, and this kind of silent support is most appropriate for this kind of client. Sometimes such clients do need, however, to hear very simplistic messages of reassurance or reprogramming from the therapist (e.g., "You are a good person, you deserve to live for yourself and be happy"). Often when I deliver these messages, I will say, "You know this, but it's my job to tell you . . . " in order to acknowledge the adult intelligence of the patient while speaking to his vulnerable child.

Larry had his shaky periods, which he saw as the insecurity of losing the "rule book" for how to be. Repetitive reassurance to trust one's innate wisdom and humanity is called for in response to this problem. Such reassurance is reparative of the original loss and encouraging in that it gives courage to the person for the risks of self-expression. In many ways, it takes more courage to find oneself at 40 than it does at 4 because at 40 you are quite a bit behind schedule and the habit strength of the alternative is formidable. Trance or altered state work can also be very useful with this particular problem. The metaphors of nature, with its apparently unconscious yet miraculous self-expression, are a natural for this objective.

But, we are prematurely getting to the upside here, though that is what inevitably happens. The downside and the upside of the real self go hand in hand and vacillate at times even moment to moment as the incredibly uncomfortable archaic feelings of the real self yield to true self-expression in spite of discomfort. In many ways, the therapeutic hour is a training ground in which the narcissistic client discovers that his self-expression is not only accepted, but openly welcomed. The real healing begins when such self-expression is generalized to the person's everyday environment and when those who care respond with the same kind of encouraging support that is initially seen as possible only in the therapeutic setting. Successful narcissistic individuals who have kept others at a distance with their perfect false selves are usually surprised by the overwhelming welcome they receive when they begin to share their vulnerabilities and insecurities with friends and family. This process of learning self-expression and generalizing it to one's real life can often be greatly facilitated by the use of small—or even large—group therapeutic experiences.

THE ANNIHILATION-ABANDONMENT CRISIS

The annihilation-abandonment crisis represents the most stressful part of the therapeutic process for the client and often for the therapist as well. With a borderline narcissist, there will be marginal control over these intense emotional states with a concomitant predisposition to blame others for the trauma. It is common for the borderline narcissist to viciously attack the therapist during these crises for her lack of caring, inability to help, insensitivity, etc. While it may be easy at an intellectual level to understand and disengage, it is simply not an easy task to be the target of the blasting rage which these individuals experience and act out. During these episodes, it is very likely that the therapist's own issues will be triggered, as these clients can injure, provoking anxiety and retaliatory rage. Typically, therapists are attacked for just those qualities in which they are invested and, indeed, for which they are being paid. Any doubts one has about one's competence and caring will be reinforced in this process, as will one's fears of any intense emotion. The propensity for countertransferential errors in therapeutic work is at its highest in the throes of an annihilation-abandonment crisis. To maintain the necessary balance of support and confrontation is not an easy task under these circumstances, particularly with the client who externalizes his own conflict and acts it out with the therapist. Almost anything you do may be responded to negatively.

One of the most common therapeutic errors in this period is to subtly or not-so-subtly try to prove to the client that you really do care for or are helping her. This intervention, which errs in the direction of regressive support, prevents the client from appropriately dealing with the necessary frustration in the process of rapprochement. In doing this, the therapist overextends and in that overextension sows the seeds of her own resentment and eventual retaliation toward the client, who cannot really ever be satisfied by the level of support that is currently possible.

The other most common countertransferential error in this situation is to act out one's anger at being placed in this uncomfortable position by excessive or nonempathic confrontation of the patient's destructive interpersonal patterns. The therapist can punish the patient in this situation with confrontations that are correct but countertherapeutic, deluding herself that such frustration is "good for" the patient. It is in dealing with this annihilation-abandonment crisis that one needs to be particularly in touch with one's feelings to maintain the necessary therapeutic neutrality.

Personally, I find it useful in these situations to remember to breathe and stay with myself and to err in the direction of saying too little rather than too much. If I do find myself hurt or threatened, I am inclined to share that with the client, albeit at a level of depth moderated by my sense of the client's ability to constructively respond to that kind of sharing. It is during these periods when I most liberally use my resources for collegial supervision and support. Because the client is so regressed during these episodes, we are inclined to believe that we must maintain the most self-control; in doing this, we are prone to deny our own emotional responses and then unconsciously act them out. Giving oneself permission to make mistakes is the requisite condition to recognize and then correct those mistakes. As I have stated earlier, the correction of such errors can be extraordinarily therapeutic for the narcissistically injured patient, and this effect is probably enhanced during these crisis episodes when both therapist and client are in a vulnerable, human position. Such corrections will also often either establish or deepen the therapeutic alliance. Finally, each such recognition and repair represent important movement in whatever narcissism exists in the therapist.

Though the client with the narcissistic style will be less problematic for the therapist as he goes through these crises, the therapeutic problem can be more difficult because it is more concealed. The individual has too much ego strength to act out his rage either on the therapist or others. Yet the rage is intense and will be released in less obvious ways. This type of patient will also experience a great deal of panic, despair, and loss and will also often unconsciously blame the therapist for getting him into this mess. The fact that he "knows better" in some ways makes the problem more difficult. Because of this, it is particularly important in treating the client with a narcissistic style to keep bringing him back to your relationship and to his feelings about you and the therapeutic process. It is often useful to actively encourage the client to express his resentments and disappointments as well as his disapproval of you personally. Among other strategies, I will often ask such a client to list all of his negative reactions and, using the Gestalt frustration principle, require him to do this beyond the point at which he feels he has exhausted all his negativity.

There are several therapeutic responses to this negativity listing. One is to join or support the client in his negative feelings. The therapeutic process does make life more difficult for the patient in that it dismantles a set of assumptions and strategies that have protected him for years from catastrophic feelings. After one has left that safe, if chronically uncomfortable, harbor and has no other even in sight, life can become very threatening and one can become very dysfunctional. The journey is sustained by the client's recognition of the pain engendered by the old assumptions and strategies. It is also sustained by faith in the therapeutic process, but mostly by faith in the therapist personally. That faith is sorely tested as one feels worse and despairs of ever feeling any better. The patient, of course, wants to believe and it usually takes a high degree of consciousness on the therapist's part to stay with herself, avoid the easily committed errors, and repair them when they do occur. An unrepaired error may well destroy the client's faith permanently.

The patient with the narcissistic style will generally retreat more quickly from the crisis in ways which are superficially effective. For this reason, it is necessary for the therapist to encourage and support the vulnerability and employ therapeutic techniques that access its expression. Once it appears, it is important to reinforce. The primary reinforcement is usually the profound intimacy and realness that can be experienced by both of you at these times. The therapist must be ready to offer that profound intimacy when the client is ready for it. This is one more crucial reason for the therapist to have handled or cleaned up her countertransferential reactions. In a very real sense, this kind of intimacy is a form of human love. It cannot be offered in the context of bitterness resulting from therapist injury, overextension, and withheld resentment.

I believe that it is the sharing of this profound human intimacy around the vulnerabilities and discoveries of the real self which provides the ultimate cure. While there is a kind of intimacy that occurs through the analysis of the symptomatic and the false selves, there is always a quality of newness about the intimacy that is possible around the discovery and acceptance of one's vulnerability, essential humanity, and emerging uniqueness. There is a higher level of human connectedness in it—a hopeful open-endedness. It's special. It is difficult to capture this kind of intimacy in writing because so much of what makes it profound is the context and the nonverbal communication. It exists in the final therapeutic scene in the film "Ordinary People" and in the final scene between the father and son in that same film. It can also be seen in "The Breakfast Club" as the adolescent strangers in that film discuss their common humanness. I have tried to capture it in the transcripts of therapy which make up the greater part of chapters six and seven of this volume.

THE REAL SELF AND AFFECT

The therapeutic orientation to the real self, particularly in the initial phase of its development, must primarily be at an affective level. Attention or intervention at the cognitive level takes the patient away from the critical awareness of her fundamental physical self and into language and constructs. Behavioral interventions, while ultimately useful, similarly take the client away from the overriding necessity for attention to current experience and emphasize prescriptions for correct behavior, which is always the narcissist's undoing. When you finally get the narcissist client to his feelings, by all means stay there. Do not analyze. Do not prescribe. Simply be there, with immediacy, to further this most essential experience of self-discovery and self-expression.

It is, I think, primarily in this arena that the successful therapeutic analyses are separated from those unsuccessful ones in which the patient more or less understands his dilemma, keeps trying to do those things that might bring him to a more real way of living, but continues, nevertheless, in his self-defeating style. For it is, after all, these threatening feelings which led to the construction of the defensive compromises in the first place. It is the avoidance of these feelings that maintains the character structure. If they are not fully expressed and worked through, there can be no real relinquishing of the defensive lifestyle. Because the expression of these affects so automatically leads to the defense, it is important to remain sensitively vigilant to its remobilization. When this occurs, you may, if you catch it soon enough, head it off. Alternatively, you may get the client to identify with the resistance or reengage in those maneuvers that will relax it. For all of these responses, I find the techniques of Gestalt therapy, focusing, bioenergetics, and other active therapies to be particularly useful, in addition to more ordinary verbal therapeutic methods. Intervention, as opposed to simple presence and immediacy, is most appropriate in response to the inevitable remobilization of defenses. When the real self flows, be there; when the unconscious defenses emerge, intervene.

The three major negative affects to be elicited in this process are terror, rage, and grief. In the classic cases of "narrow" narcissism, the primary fear is of the narcissistic reinjury—the fear of being shamed or humiliated for being too little, too much, etc. Where narcissistic adaptions overlay earlier characterological issues, the terror of being annihilated or the panic at being abandoned will also be elicited by self-expression. Additionally, there will be that inevitable panic associated with the experience of void in the self. Finally, the client will often experience fear of her own profound but prohibited feelings, including anger, sexuality, power, joy, or fear itself. While understanding such fears is an ultimate objective of the work, it is usually better initially to allow and encourage simple experience and raw expression of feeling than to call for its labeling, which can pull the client out of direct experience. As the client becomes more experienced at expression, the explicit and implicit calls for labeling will mobilize ego function and thereby enhance the self.

The grief, mourning, and sadness elicited in the therapeutic process are, of course, aimed at the original injuries but are often much more profoundly experienced in relation to the loss of life and self sustained over many years. It is necessary, to complete the therapeutic process, to experience the grief at the original injury but equally necessary to mourn the loss of a life shaped by that injury. Similarily, one must experience the rage at the original injurers, but one must also experience the rage at those internalized structures which have kept that injury and the consequent denial of self alive. Without initial rage at the perpetuating internalized patterns and beliefs, the requisite motivation to really change is lacking. History then becomes an excuse to justify the continuation of the patterns which deny the true self.

Any therapist attempting to alter characterological patterns must possess a great deal of tolerance for negative affect. Indeed, in the more borderline cases, she must be able to tolerate being the frequent target of these feelings. While there is the upside to this psychic garbage collecting, the working-through and completion of these downside affects are absolutely essential and, unfortunately for both therapist and patient, must be encountered first. Repeatedly, the client will need to experience and work through her despair about her particular injury, compromise, and consequent losses. The "good enough" therapist will have to be present, immediate, and congruent through that experience. To the extent that the therapist has not worked through his or her own despair, there will be a strong tendency to move the client away from this experience and to prematurely resolve it through interpretation, explanation, or "forgiveness." Herein lies much of the incompleteness of psychotherapeutic work. It is often most difficult for us to just do nothing but be with the client through those most difficult emotional crises, which he must traverse to regain his origins and himself because to do so requires us to access what we ourselves must still confront. The therapist's limits are most sorely tested in those cases in which there is some kind of similarity or interlocking fit in the issues of therapist and client.

It is in this area—the therapeutic response to the downside of the real self—in which the cliché "physician, heal thyself" is totally apropos. Such healing makes true therapeutic presence possible in these otherwise extremely difficult situations. And, real presence is all that is required. When we can't be really present and immediate in these situations, we cling to a therapeutic technique, stance, or theory and thereby block the working-through. All therapists are prone to do this and such an error can provide a marvelous therapeutic opportunity if it is recognized and corrected. When we are not present, we need only be human enough to admit it and to use the resources we have available to us to effect a return to that presence through recognition and repair of the therapeutic error. A therapist who can do this can complete the psychotherapeutic process. One who cannot will leave the job ultimately incomplete.

In forwarding the above propositions, I am not denying the value of understanding through interpretation or explanation or the ultimate role of forgiveness in the resolution of underlying characterological issues. On the contrary, both are essential. Rather, I wish to emphasize the fact that the typical client, particularly one with the narcissistic style, needs the least therapeutic assistance with understanding these genuine negative feelings once they arise. By that time, the client will have experienced a good deal of analysis with respect to his psychological defenses and will usually be able to interpret these feelings himself with very little assistance. A well-timed question, an appropriate Gestalt or bioenergetic exercise, or even a well-timed interpretation may well be useful. It is simply that therapist overactivity at this point is most likely and most detrimental to the process. When this kind of affect is flowing, it is most beneficial to let it flow. Analysis can always wait.

THE REAL SELF—UPSIDE

As the defensive functions of the false and symptomatic selves are accessed, analyzed, and diffused, and as the annihilation-abandonment crises are worked through, positive spontaneous expressions of the real self will emerge. Characterological psychotherapy is like an archaeological excavation. Layers of compromise, interpersonal games, and intrapsychic defenses must be cleared away to reveal an arrested, injured, angry, and frightened self. With the safety and acceptance of these feelings and deficits, a person can begin to rediscover who he or she really is.

There are a number of signs of this emergence of self. The first of these is often a return to a deeper sense of one's physical self—a return to physicality and response to the senses. Some, like the client introduced at the beginning of this chapter, regain the sense of smell, touch, or sight. The experience of the senses deepens, sometimes only momentarily, but that is noticed as a profound shift. Others report an enhanced sense of integration of the physical body, such that they feel more grounded, centered, or "in touch" with themselves. Many begin or return to physical exercise, which enhances this feeling of integration and physical self-awareness. This return to physicality is experienced with pleasure, as different or long-forgotten.

Concomitant with this, all individuals who rediscover themselves develop an enhanced awareness of their likes, dislikes, interests, curiosities, etc. This is often accompanied by amazement at the extent to which they have had no real interests or the extent to which their interests were determined by what others wanted them to be or what was judged appropriate. This enhanced awareness is usually accompanied by an enhanced sense of self-initiated behavior or decisions. The client may report more consistency in his or her behavior in a certain area, or begin to be less "field dependent," or she may report having stood up for herself in ways that she would not heretofore have done. One client reported, for example, after an intense period of self-expression, that his handwriting mysteriously became consistent rather than reflecting three or four different styles of penmanship. Another sign of this kind of self-actualization is enhanced responsibility for self-care. A person may spontaneously report that she is taking better care of her health, apartment, diet, or schedule.

Somewhere in the process of enhanced self-expression the person will take a personal stand opposing the longstanding sacrifice of self in pursuit of compensatory objectives. He may, for example, refuse to continue to sacrifice his health to a workaholic career that sustains an inflated self-image, or refuse to pursue activities that rescue others but that torture him, or stop denying his real needs in the pursuit of perfection. An enhanced real self always brings more genuine self-expression. So, the person becomes more assertive, more able to say no, and more congruent when she says yes. While such self-expression may well engender anxiety and other symptoms initially, the trend will be toward greater self-confidence and less anxiety in that expression.

Finally, the client will exhibit and report enhanced self-acceptance. She will be better able to see and appreciate her strengths and the rewards they bring. She will continue to value herself while recognizing deficits. In line with this, she will also be increasingly amenable to feedback, responding realistically to both praise and criticism. As she relinquishes the need to live up to perfection, she can realistically respond to input, either positive or negative, about her performance.

Welcome as are these changes, the therapist's role surrounding them must be *primarily* reactive. The narcissistic individual is so accomplished at falsely giving what another wants that one must be particularly careful with this character structure to avoid prescribing genuine or spontaneous behavior. Recall Larry, who said, "if you would just tell me how to be me, I would be it."

True spontaneity and genuineness, however, stimulate the fear of annihilation, abandonment, or rejection, even though the patient's adult ego may perceive the value of the new behavior and the folly of the fear. So, especially at first, the patient's new realness needs support, mirroring, and prizing. Masterson (1985) suggests a strategy of *communicative matching*, in which the therapist empathically shares the patient's new discoveries and, wherever possible, communicates some of his own experiences in the areas of interest opening to the client. The level of required communicative matching declines over time as the client internalizes the supportive functions and needs less "refueling" from the supportive therapist.

As with the downside of the real self, the upside primarily requires therapeutic responses that are empathically attuned, supportive of the reality, and genuine. Here, however, the support can be more active and self-disclosing. This is another area in which the techniques of the more active psychotherapies can be particularly useful. In one session, after Larry had stopped working and had begun to use his time to travel and pursue long-lost interests, he was sharing his process of self-discovery.

Larry: The way I have lived life—or have in the past—is "What's my assignment today? What's my obligation? What rule do I satisfy? What image do I please? What bad feeling do I avoid?" It came to me when I was wandering around the Northwest this week—I encountered a kind of fear, which was a fear of feeling something . . . you know like . . . oh, maybe that's the important part of this whole lifelong story of being frightened. That, among its elements are just that I am afraid of feeling something. I'm afraid of feeling aimless. I'm afraid of waking up in the morning and not having anything—I was gonna say, not knowing what to do, or who I am.

Therapist: Well, can you go underneath that feeling? What does it mean, that feeling?

Larry: Hmmmm? Umm. Somehow value gets in there. It's like I don't feel valuable. I don't feel like I'm achieving anything. I. . . . You see, the whole new idea that you've introduced here over these years is that unless I'm doing what I want to do, I'm going to be unhappy all my life. That's one version of it.

Therapist: That's right.

Larry: Unless I can get it, you know, I'll be pursuing false self things. And it's true. And, so . . . it challenges the whole structure that I've been living according to and makes all of this seem like an important thing for me to do. But the feeling I'm in, is—I don't find satisfaction yet. I don't find a whole opening up and my new identity coming down to me. It's like . . . I start out with these loneliness and emptiness feelings—often when I wake up in the morning—that relate to my not having a mission. And, I think that I must have . . . I don't know . . . I'm looking for the way to count my worth—achievements, work, collateral, admirations from staff, and friends and family. . . .

One thing that just came was that I . . . I don't want to go back to work. Am I just lazy? Is that all that's goin' on? Maybe I spend my whole time just spinning stuff in my head. 'Cause it's a way of staying busy, and the years go by. Then what?

Therapist: I would say that anybody who's had as much pain and fear around work as you have is going to have a period of not wanting to go back to work. And that's real expectable. It doesn't mean that it will always be that way.

Larry: Yeah, it may not—but I . . . feel fear about that, and all sorts of things about that. . . . You know, in the midst of these feelings a few days ago, I was by myself somewhere, up in Idaho. I think it was a Sunday. I started just doing some writing, and I thought, you know, I have friends, other people, you and others, whose primary motivation—not the exclusive experience of, but the primary motivation—for their work is the joy they feel, the pleasure they feel in it, not the kind of relationship I had in the late stages, at least, with my research team, but in writing they find something.

Therapist: Self-expression.

Larry: Yes, yes, okay, that. And so, here I was about to have another opportunity to either face it as a place where I was avoiding the punishment of not doing anything—and, if I did that, burying an opportunity to have something pleasurable. I mean, it might be, that if I approached it somewhat differently, I might actually find something I like. So I banged around about that for a while and decided that what I could sort of do for free, that was without judgment about it, was just calisthenics—in writing. One of the simplest of which is just descriptions. Just try to do a good description. So, I found myself in a little abandoned and sort of really half-refurbished-for-tourists coal mining town out southeast of Boise—and sitting in the car on Sunday morning, and there was a scene, there was a street. And, I thought, well, describe it. And somehow in the act of doing that, I was dealing with this issue about whether or to what extent I was living to avoid punishment and to what extent I was living for self-expression—it comes in and out all the time.

Therapist: At least there's some variation.

Larry: Yeah, there's some variation. And, I found myself, as I was describing various things, being able to get it. And, it would click a little bit, the phrase, then I'd blow it, then there'd be a little more and I had something, you know, I had something! And what I began to do is to get fairly rhapsodic about, you know. I went through, and I wrote for a while, and I just stopped. It didn't have any conclusion or anything, but—there were some things going on, there was four or five people trying to beat some life into an old blue Datsun that didn't want to live, and finally it gave up a couple of its cylinders—and all the people were crowding around. You know, it's the kind of car that only runs back and forth in a little town up in the woods where nobody's looking. And I went through several such scenes, and then I wound up over in Boise on Monday, to visit my father's grave. I had only been to that graveyard once as a child three or four years old and when we buried him. And it's a maze, and it's complicated, and I went right to the grave without any trouble. And then I sat there in the car for a while and—I continually feel like I am overwhelmed by the subjects that I think I might want to write about. Like there's too much emotion.

It's that thing about . . . I can't get it all set at once, you know? And yet I found an entirely different thing happening. And that was, if I set about trying to describe very small events, just to be very unflowery, and as clear as I could, about capturing that area of the graveyard and what was going on and what I'd been through arranging for the tombstone, all this other stuff comes out, all this stuff about Dad—you know, what was he like? What was it like for him to be there in the depression and the war? What was Boise like? Hotter than hell in summer, freezing in the winter—and it was a delight to discover it, just a delight. I didn't have troubles getting started. I didn't—there's something in me.

Therapist: Right, right. That's it. You don't believe that a lot of the time.

Larry: Too true. I went down to an old fort nearby, and I went down the road. I had tried to do one more thing, in the piece of writing, and I got way off too far into it; it was lousy, and it quickly came to me why. It was just wonderfully useful. I had lost track of the simple fact that just staying grounded and just being descriptive, and I had gone way off in—in adjectives, you know? Descriptive writing is adjectives, so now it's "and," pairs of adjectives where there was only one before, and complete with one.

Very commonplace. Loss of staying focused on what it is that makes for good description, which isn't lots of adjectives; it's just the right words, and those are mostly just the right feelings. And what I had done was I had—"Okay, boy you're on a roll here, you can just write."

So—off the road and started writing. And I gave myself no time to sit there and "get it" about that place. I just didn't. And foom, it shows right up, in crap. It's just not good. And I went, and I looked at some of the other stuff and it was—you could see the good parts in it—and I went down the road saying to myself—having a conversation with you, something like, "Well, gosh, somewhere there's real substance in me."

Therapist: It occurs to me that there could be a way for you to remind yourself of that because that's what you forget, and that's all you need to remember. It's that simple. Although it's just that difficult because you have a whole childhood of training not to believe it. Being told that that wasn't true, that you have to live up to something, or prove something, or make up for something.

Larry: Yeah. These little things are really sweet and making my life feel a lot better. I almost stubbed my toe this afternoon. Bette's house is out in the country, and I run from there. I was tired of carrying my keys around, laid them down, and went out the door and closed it and locked it behind me without a key. And that was quarter to two. I was going to take a long run, 11 miles, and then—everything's locked in the house so I can't get into town, the car is fully locked up so—and the house is weatherized and tight as a drum. Bette had locked all the window latches. So after ten minutes or so I realized I really was stymied, couldn't find an opening. There was nobody in the main house, so what to do? Call you, call the landlord—nobody's going to be home. So finally I said to myself, "Cool down, you'll think of something." And, so I did. I would have never done that before.

This enlivening reflection provided the opportunity for some communicative matching around the creative process, particularly writing, and the shared experience of the inspiration of trust in oneself in creating. Artistic production as the result of proving oneself to others versus self-expression, the quality of the experience of creation in each of these states, and the quality of the products of each provided an opportunity for profound human sharing. This also provided the opportunity for some mild indirect confrontation of the residual idealization which Larry displayed in characterizing my motivational structure. By this point in the therapeutic process, such confrontation of idealization was appropriate and significantly contributed to the profound intimacy of this and other sessions.

In addition, these peak experiences around writing and later photography provided an ideal opportunity for the use of those active therapeutic strategies that assist the client in reaccessing these desired states. Not only do such strategies facilitate conscious memory and accessing, but the hypnotic use of such methods can also cumulatively affect more unconscious, spontaneous living in this creative, playful reality. Thus, I jumped at this naturally occurring opportunity to utilize and "install" this desired state. Because Larry was a relatively sophisticated trance subject as a result of earlier work, I quickly reestablished a trance and re-elicited all of the visual, kinesthetic, and auditory cues of the small town street scene which had been so transportive. After this state was reaccessed, I suggested that Larry establish his own idiosyncratically meaningful cue which could be used to re-elicit this full experience. Once this was accomplished, I then simply future paced the use of this cue and its associated state in other foreseeable situations in which it might be useful. Finally, all through this hypnotic "rap," I indirectly suggested that this kind of trust in self and life could occur naturally and spontaneously without any deliberate effort to access it. Concomitantly, I attempted to inoculate Larry against the almost inevitable fear that this kind of trustful letting go would elicit by reframing the fear as wonderment and awe in one's participation in a universe of infinite complexity, beauty, and balance.

Like almost all good trance inductions and utilizations, this one was spontaneous and unique, guided only by some very general principles or messages that I wished to deliver. Such trust in one's own unconscious provides a very useful model of surrender to faith in the process which we had been discussing, as well as enabling a deeper trance in Larry. Trance work of this kind can significantly further the desired processes of internalization, which must be accomplished to enhance appropriate ego function and strengthen a healthful real self. Presently, I will discuss even more direct procedures, both in and out of trance, which can facilitate the required internalizations. The process described above is a straightforward application of *resource accessing*, formulated by the neurolinguistic programmers (e.g., Cameron-Bandler, 1985).

The development of new interests or of new approaches to old ones provides an opportunity to assist the client in discovering and developing pleasurable and effective strategies. Larry was writing an article and, in two subsequent days, experienced both profound success and profound failure. In exploring both experiences in detail, we discovered Larry's high-performance strategy for writing. We found, for example, that Larry knew he was ready to start writing when he felt he had enough to begin to list what he had to say. Particularly important in this step was permission to not have to organize the material. From his unsuccessful experience, he found that this compulsory requirement to organize things initially created a block to movement. So, it was important to give himself permission to brainstorm and to forestall organization.

The third discovery was that Larry needed to give himself permission to define the activity as play rather than work and to again give himself permission to "play with it." To Larry, this meant permission not to make everything sequential, not to use every point in his original outline in his eventual product, to write and then throw out segments which did not work, etc.

Larry's fourth discovery in this dialogue about writing was that he needed to reinforce himself for the quality of his work, his approach to it, his judgment about it, etc. Particularly important in this was his acknowledgment of the validity of his own unique way of writing. It was important for him to credit all the activity in the writing process rather than counting only the pages of the eventual product. Reading, brooding, discussing, listing, and incubating were all necessary elements in the process. Remembering this and acknowledging himself for the effort in each area were important.

Fifth, Larry realized that it was important for him to notice when writing felt good, when he saw it working—particularly when he saw a piecemeal, unorganized, and imperfect approach working. Allowing himself to experience pleasure in the process even more than pleasure in the product seemed to be essential in differentiating the successful from the unsuccessful experience.

Finally, as I knew from my own experience, it was important to establish when he had done enough—a signal to stop. In reaccessing the successful experience, he realized that the primary signal was that he was tired. He had told himself, "I have done enough for now," and he remembered experiencing faith that he could continue at a later time. He recognized the temptation, as have I, to squeeze every last ounce of energy from himself when he was "on a roll." This tendency imposes a scarcity consciousness on the desired state and thereby serves as a self-fulfilling prophecy. If the real self knows he will be driven to exhaustion if he allows himself such productive periods, he will understandably protect himself. If, on the other hand, he knows he can enjoy this kind of self-expression and exit it when appropriate, he will be much more willing to embrace it again.

The simple elicitation of this effective strategy in comparison with the ineffective strategy, together with the opportunities for communicative matching which it provided, was in itself very therapeutic. The final step of this work on strategies, modeled after the work of Bandler and Grinder (e.g., 1979, 1982; and Dilts et al., 1980), was to "install" the effective strategy. To do this, I induced a light trance in Larry and then proceeded to simply run him through the strategy in the appropriate contexts. In doing this, I was careful to specify and elaborate on each point we had established as part of the effective strategy. In this procedure, I used written notes to ensure that I covered every aspect of the effective strategy in sequence.

This intervention of eliciting and then recreating effective strategies can be particularly appropriate when a client comes to therapy during unusually healthy periods. In Larry's case, for example, there was one session, close to the end of his therapeutic work, when he realized that he had been very reliably choosing himself over his "duty" or "balance sheet." Narcissistic individuals typically sacrifice themselves to their *abstractions* of self: business people to their balance sheets, students to their grade point average, academics to their vitas, professionals to their case loads, etc. When Larry began to notice that he was very reliably changing in his predisposition to do this, we explored *how* he did that. Larry was amazed to discover that there were about a dozen ways of thinking and behaving that maintained this healthy choice. After accessing these strategies, I employed once again the simple procedure of helping Larry to recreate these helpful attitudes and behaviors in the appropriate contexts.

These sessions with Larry serve to illustrate an active kind of supportive therapy which I believe to be consistent with developmental psychoanalytic theory (object relations, ego psychology, and self psychology) and the kinds of supportive therapies which derive from it. While these active strategies derive from cognitive and behavioral approaches that have heretofore usually been seen as antithetical to most psychoanalytic thought, we see here that a very significant rapprochement is possible between the "new psychoanalysis" and the cognitive-behavioral tradition. When these more active strategies are contextualized within a developmental-characterological view of the psychotherapeutic process, they become much more than band-aid coping strategies, which they may otherwise represent. At the same time, they complement and add powerful alternative strategies for the supportive therapist, whose strategies may be quite limited if he or she is restricted to those techniques employed in the traditional analytic literature.

As long as the objectives of ego-building and "guardianship of autonomy" are respected and the risks of excessive intervention are appreciated, these more active strategies can be used in the service of individuation and self-enhancement. As long as these techniques are used to further the growth of the client, rather than prove the usefulness of the therapist, they can be of service. The risks of wholesale identification with the idealized, powerful therapist will be realized only if the therapist is unaware of these risks and/or practicing therapy in the service of his narcissistic needs. But if this is the case, the damage will be done anyway and the selection of particular procedures will be largely irrelevant to that unfortunate outcome.

Larry also provided the impetus for using several of the exercises derived from Gestalt therapy that serve to enhance the immediacy, spontaneity, and genuineness of communication. In both individual and group therapy contexts, Larry persistently struggled with his tendency to perform socially, giving others what he thought they wanted rather than giving of himself. In the group, he was caringly given the feedback that he was experienced as phony, paternal, arrogant, and controlled (see Chapter VII for transcripts of this work). He very much wanted to be more himself, but his pleasing behavior was often automatic. He needed a good deal of assistance in even discriminating his controlled from his spontaneous self. As a result, I was drawn to use exercises that pull for a kind of interpersonal altered state. One of these, the "What Are You Experiencing?" exercise, requires the client to simply report on his direct, ongoing experience whenever asked to do so in an interaction which may productively last for a good deal of time. This exercise is accomplished in a dyad in which one person (the therapist in this case) simply asks the other on a variable schedule to answer the question, "What are you experiencing?" After the first couple of trials, the question may be abbreviated to, "Now?"

In Larry's case, particularly at first, I would periodically stop the process and debrief, eliciting information about his process, giving feedback, etc. Over time, Larry became more and more expert at simply letting go, trusting himself, and verbalizing almost automatically without his usual screen, which filtered for acceptability, appropriateness, etc. I also employed an adaptation of this exercise, which more closely approximates the desired interpersonal interaction. In this application, Larry and I alternated in our spontaneous sharing of our immediate experience. This process, like the one before it, is most effective when it continues for 10 to 15 minutes or longer, as this extended time can break down the usual barriers to free-flowing contact and, in this way, create a profound altered state. I have used this process with hundreds of people in workshop contexts and seen the profound altered state effects that can be achieved when it is used sequentially and over a substantial length of time. Larry began to refer to this effect as communicating in "real time"; he cherished this state and began to trust himself more and more to elicit and be safe within it.

In addition, I engaged Larry in simulated situations in which he would share with a specific other all those feelings that he was withholding. In this exercise, I played the role of the significant other and heard whatever he had been withholding. Consistent with his history, Larry was particularly prone to withhold both positive and negative feelings from any woman with whom he was involved. He tended to project onto women his mother's propensity to become hysterically coercive when displeased and so he inappropriately feared sharing anything negative. Similarly, he also projected his mother's possessiveness and would therefore withhold positive statements for fear that this would be taken as a "proposal of marriage" and lead to possessiveness which he was loathe to actively resist. The simulations acted out in therapy led to freer sharing in his relationships with women, which usually led to his discovery that these contemporary female figures were able to handle negative input and appreciate positive statements without moving in to own him. Where this was not the case, and his projections were in some way justified, he then had the opportunity to stand up for himself, changing his historical predispositions. At one point in this process, he said, "Confronting the disappointments of others in me are now really opportunities for me to stay with myself. I'm beginning to see that others' reactions to me do not necessarily mean I'm wrong. I am not continually playing for good reviews."

Larry worked very hard at his humanization, his release from the negative introjects and scripts of the past, and his development of new interests; more importantly, he risked a new approach in pursuing these goals. In addition to writing and photography, Larry renewed his commitment to running and took a class in tai chi. If this seems excessive, it's important to note that Larry had quit his research job and had stopped working for a time, devoting himself to this kind of personal self-discovery.

One symptom of Larry's social anxiety was the excessive sweating that he experienced both in social situations generally and particularly in the tai chi class where he was, perhaps for the first time, just one more nonexcelling member of a group. Indeed, he was slower at it than most others in the class. As the changes outlined here were accomplished, the excessive sweating was diminished and then disappeared as he began to welcome the experience of just being one of the group. Toward the end of his therapy he remarked, "I'm feeling more on the ship of humans: more like one of us."

PROMOTING TRANSFORMATIVE INTERNALIZATIONS

Kohut has enlightened us concerning the furtherance of internalization through optimal frustration. It is necessary, however, to highlight the fact that internalization can occur through simple modeling. This mechanism probably accounts for a good deal of the internalization processes that occur throughout life. Blanck and Blanck (1974), for example, have highlighted the particular value the therapist has in communicating to the client that he in fact has a "right to be soothed." In addition to self-consciously employing the modeling mechanism, even more direct procedures may be used to promote and enhance the naturally occurring internalization of beliefs, behaviors, and beneficial orientations to oneself.

In *Characterological Transformation* (pp. 202–206), I presented transcripts of three hypnotic utilization procedures which were designed to install self-soothing abilities. In one of these, I ask the client to remember a time when he was soothing to another. After building a full representation of this experience, I then call for a shift in the characters of the visualization such that the client becomes both soother and the one soothed. This is a particularly viable therapeutic strategy for most individuals exhibiting the narcissistic style because they are typically great nurturers of others while simultaneously neglecting their own deprived child. This is only one of several strategies, hypnotic and otherwise, which can be self-consciously used to facilitate and more firmly install the desired internalizations.

The simplest level at which this internalization can be furthered is probably the most universal among supportive psychotherapists. One simply plays the role of child advocate to the neglected real self and encourages self-love, self-soothing, and self-indulgence. A theoretical appreciation for the developmental role which this activity plays can very much enhance its effectiveness as well as eliminating its overuse, which can be regressive. Beyond this, one may employ even more direct strategies, like the hypnotic one alluded to above, which can serve to install internalized qualities, behaviors, or attitudes. One can, for example, review the client's current and previous life for promising objects of internalization and directly or indirectly suggest their incorporation. With the use of hypnotic technique, you can deliberately construct a composite internalization figure or edit the qualities of an external object for internalization. Alternatively, through the use of hypnotic metaphors, one can indirectly suggest both the process and content of desired internalizations.

Although all of these strategies can be most useful, I believe the therapeutic context which consistently and unflaggingly supports the real self will contribute the most in this process, which must take time for its full integration. I don't believe, in other words, that a simple trance, by itself, can produce the kind of profound change that is required. I do believe, however, that trance and other directive work can certainly further these effects. It is most important that the therapist know she represents a potential object for internalization, like it or not, and that she direct her behavior accordingly.

Additionally, I believe it is important to keep one's eye out for any other internalization objects or effective models which the client may incorporate in developing a more mature and nurturing self. This kind of "parent transplant" is much of the work of psychotherapy and of the continuing work that an individual must do on his own in the construction and utilization of a community which loves, supports, and challenges him. Further, a knowledge of the continuing need for self-sustaining others (*selfobjects* in Kohut's language) attunes both the therapist and the client to these continuing human needs.

Further, the need for and maturation of the forms of *selfobject* transference—merger, twinship, mirroring, and idealization—can further orient the therapist and eventually instruct the client to gather about him and construct within him the kinds of figures that sustain a healthy real self. *The construction and maintenance of such a self-sustaining community are probably the most essential factors in guaranteeing the continuation of the therapeutic gains in the real self.* A therapist's consultive and ego-supportive functions in this regard are appropriate and valuable. It is important to communicate to the client that he not only deserves to be sustained by such a supportive community but also deserves to avoid those individuals and circumstances which will call up and reinforce his compensatory self. Such avoidance is particularly warranted in the first few years of the infancy of the real self developed in characterological therapy. Typically, the narcissistic client needs a good deal of support to justify this kind of self-love. He is so used to self-sacrifice and painful challenges that these sensible forms of support and protection seem somehow wrong and immoral. He may need to be repeatedly told that he deserves to be with others who love and help him and to shun those who use and abuse him.

Very gifted narcissistic individuals can be remarkably retarded when it comes to realizing their legitimate need for a benevolent environment. I remember one very poignant session with John (introduced in Chapter II), in which he was lamenting his imperfections and saying, "I don't believe I have the right to be forgiven." I responded, "I just want to tell you, John, that you do have the right to be forgiven." He said, "When you say things like that, I know that you don't know me." I said, "No, John, you are the one who doesn't know who you are when it comes to this." At this, after almost an entire session of hostile resistance, with accusations about my failure to understand him, he said, "You're right," and began to cry (see chapter VI, pp. 191, when John deals with this very issue in group therapy).

Before closing this section devoted to strategies for enhancing the real self, I wish to highlight one other set of interventions, deriving primarily from the consciousness movement, which can serve this self-enhancing function. They are meditation and affirmations. Meditation, of almost any form, serves a self-organizing and self-soothing function. Most of the research on meditation has been done on the transcendental meditation method and the results of that research are truly impressive. Those results suggest that this form of meditation, at least, diminishes anxiety and depression while influencing a sense of well-being, enhancing a feeling of independence, and improving general personal functioning in a myriad of ways (e.g., Orme-Johnson & Farrow, 1977). There is certainly reason to believe that meditative practices that focus on the real experience of the body, such as the "I am" meditation introduced earlier and others of a similar nature, would slowly serve to enhance the experience of one's real self. In addition, there is reason to believe that meditating on affirmations, which confirm values or attitudes to be internalized, could also have a curative effect. While it is often difficult to get people to routinely engage in either of these activities, I believe the evidence is sufficiently positive to continually advocate their use in spite of often low rates of compliance. Personally, I can attest to the soothing and cumulative curative effect of an affirmation which I might recommend to anyone sharing the narcissistic style. It is, "I deserve just to be."

CASE EXAMPLE: CHUCK, THE TRIP HOME

Chuck represents a person functioning at the high end of the narcissistic style continuum. I saw him for only six months and in this time we accomplished a great deal, as much by my simply normalizing, encouraging, and supporting the already healthy aspects of his personality as by anything else. Chuck was referred to me in the context of dealing with a separation and divorce, around which he was experiencing some rather normal levels of grief, doubt, loneliness, and guilt. A normally high-functioning person, he was unusually concerned about these very natural emotional responses to this crisis and felt that there might be something seriously "wrong" with him. My therapy with him was brief and analytic in nature, having a great deal of similarity with the brief psychoanalytic psychotherapy of Davanloo (1980) and Malan (1979). I could take the gloves off with Chuck and not be concerned too much about injuring him through confrontation. Indeed, he needed and respected psychotherapy which was much more active, confrontational, and concomitantly present- and past-oriented than what he had received in two prior counseling experiences. At the same time, of course, Chuck's intrinsic health offered plenty of opportunity for supportive interventions when they were called for, and his level of functioning afforded a high level of therapeutic rapport and alliance.

Chuck came from a midwestern, monied, upper-class, "country club" family. There was, in short, a sort of "dynasty" aspect to this family, with the concomitant demand for distinction, achievement, and polished social facility. Chuck's father and older brother were both fairly rigid, hardworking, achievement-oriented people who provided a formidable challenge for Chuck to live up to. These more immediate family figures were contemporary representatives of a family pattern requiring achievement, distinction, and social grace. Though Chuck exhibited some solidity in the experience of a real self, he also exhibited some widespread insecurity with regard to living up to all this. The narcissistic injury in his case seemed very much to have to do with the obligation to live up to these standards and his inevitable failures or near-failures to do so. The humiliating or shaming experiences that he recovered during therapy primarily had to do with experiences with his older brother and father. Both of these figures had, however, often been nurturing and supportive of this youngest male in the family and one grandfather also provided a very positive role model. The history did not uncover any difficulties around the mother, who was remembered as a very nurturing person, but one who provided little stimulation or interest for Chuck once he had reached middle adolescence. Being the youngest of three children, Chuck appeared to have received more permission than his older siblings for some deviations from the more rigid patterns in this familial dynasty. He had broken the mold before in various youthful adventures and his divorce was a current breaking of that mold. So, while there was a history consistent with the development of some narcissistic issues, and while Chuck was preoccupied with meeting challenges, being good enough, proving himself in relation to the other males in his family, etc., there was also a strong strain of alliance and connection with his own real self.

Other narcissistic issues came out in relation to the psychotherapy process. In sessions, for example, he frequently alluded to his fear that the process would lead to the uncovering of some terrible quality or complex of which he had heretofore been totally unaware. Particularly during the early stages of therapy, he presented himself in a very controlled, hale-fellow-well-met mode, displaying his well-polished and quite successful social façade. His initial treatment was one of those in which I relied on the use of free association as a method to dismantle the oversocialized façade and get down to business. This simple maneuver was most successful in his case and dramatically eliminated a good deal of the defensive façade.

Other narcissistic qualities were also demonstrated in his relationships with women. He demonstrated to some extent that common split often seen with narcissistic individuals of both sexes: women whom he found safe, loving, and soft were women he found somewhat boring and insufficiently challenging. Those women, however, who were very physically attractive, somewhat hard, independent, and not so easily impressed by him were women who presented a challenge, even a badge of worth or accomplishment. Frequently, of course, these women would reject or otherwise hurt him, fail to provide him with the intimacy that he truly wanted, or, once dated, be found to be "hollow beauties or aggressive bitches." He could get hooked with these women by the challenge of initially not being good enough and eventually proving himself.

This same challenge had hooked him in business. Being a bright and powerful person, he repeatedly proved he was good enough but, of course, each victory was hollow and short-lived and resulted in his moving on to the next challenge. In both career and personal relationships, failure frightened him, and a significant portion of his life had been spent in counterphobic pursuits to prove that he was good enough—handsome enough, bright enough, responsible enough, caring enough . . . you name it. But, as stated earlier, there was a significant degree of health backed by a history which was in many ways nurturing and supportive. While Chuck may very well need therapy beyond the brief course that I have described here, there was significant progress in his case within a short period of time.

In the therapeutic process, Chuck was led to self-discovery with remarkable speed. By way of illustration, I think my most successful intervention in his case was to make a direct challenge when he was discussing the possibility of our being friends. At that point, I shared with him my reluctance about becoming his friend if this in fact were an option—that is, if we had met outside of the therapeutic context. I told him that I wasn't sure whether I'd want to work as hard as I would have to work to break through his social façade to get to know him. I said something to the effect, "You're just too perfect, Chuck. Your clothes are perfect, your hair style is perfect, your conversation is perfect, your recreations are perfect, your social graces are perfect—it's just all too perfect. And that's a little intimidating and even makes me a little envious. On the other hand, I just know all that's not you, really. And I know I'd have to work pretty hard to get to the real you. I think if we had a friendship, you'd offer to give me more than I could or would give you and I'm afraid the relationship would put me just a little bit one down, while at the same time not really giving me *you*. And, while I find you to be an attractive, bright, interesting guy, I'm not sure I'd want to confront all that."

Well, this made Chuck sit up and take notice. It jarred the smoothness. But it didn't hurt him much. Indeed, Chuck was grateful for that intervention and used it as a springboard to get in touch with a number of his friends and to directly check out the status of these relationships. In this session, Chuck said that he felt something like what I was describing was probably operating in some of his friendships. It seemed that his so-called friends were avoiding him a bit and he had to initiate to them far more than they initiated to him. The checking-out process with friends that followed this session led to some very useful intimate conversations and helped Chuck sort out the people with whom he could be real from those with whom he could not. Further, it marked a watershed point in the therapeutic course, reducing Chuck's façade-like behavior in the therapeutic sessions. In the final session of psychotherapy, in which we were reviewing its development, Chuck spontaneously remarked on this as one of the more powerful and influential interventions.

Chuck's issues with women, competitiveness, and proving himself through career successes were dealt with much as they were summarized here—through insight, appropriate confrontations, therapeutic processes, etc. An analysis of a dream provided valuable insight for Chuck into his pattern of projecting his own weaknesses and vulnerabilities on women and then taking care of them rather than himself. This is a common pattern among narcissistic style individuals of both sexes, where control is maintained in relationships by denying and projecting vulnerability on the other and then becoming the other's caretaker. This session, and others which reinforced it, assisted Chuck in coming in greater contact with and owning his own vulnerabilities, fears, and human emotions.

The final piece to be summarized in this case involves Chuck's overdetermined efforts to "save" his brother, who in many respects resembled his father. In one session, Chuck recognized that the rigidity, overwork, and consequent unhappiness produced by this pattern had effectively killed his father. He saw the same pattern recurring in his older brother and spent a good deal of time thinking of ways to rescue his beloved brother from that fate. Almost every try was frustrated and disappointing. I offered the "undoing" interpretation of this pattern and helped Chuck see how his current attempts to save his brother were, in effect, attempts to undo what had happened with his father and to get the kind of continuing and supportive fathering that his own father was unable to sustain. As we shall see in the following transcript, when he understood this, his attitude and behavior toward his brother changed and he was then able to see his brother clearly, to accept from him what he could get, and to let go of his overdetermined attempts to save him.

Because of his high level of functioning and his response to a relatively short-term intervention, many therapists who adopt an analytic perspective would be inclined to see this patient as oedipal or rigid (à la Lowen, 1958). While I was very attuned to current and historical material that would be consistent with this interpretation, I didn't find much. Though some of his relationship patterns were consistent with this interpretation, the entire picture was far more consistent with the view that Chuck was an example of a high-functioning person with a narcissistic style. While I will acknowledge that extended analytic psychotherapy may very well have revealed more oedipal material in his case, the material I do have does not lend itself all that well to this interpretation. Rather, I think this case, among many others, argues persuasively for a theoretical construction of patients that takes into account the prevalence of character style. In this construction, these individuals may exhibit a good deal of ego strength and self-formation but also display features of psychopathology which are best understood as the traces of characterological, often pre-oedipal, issues.

In the last month of therapy, Chuck took a trip home. His report on this and other aspects of the two-week period since he had seen me demonstrates what can be accomplished and what will be seen and heard as the narcissistic patient humanizes and begins to live for himself rather than for the internalized standards which separate him from his own life process.

Chuck: The whole vacation focus was 10 days of doing what I haven't done in years and that was just family and old friends. Every time I've gone back to Ann Arbor it's been a lot of business and very little family. Once I even kept a cab waiting while I stopped at three places—two grandmothers and my mother while the cab waited outside—just to say hello since I was in town. But this trip was relaxed and I just kind of let things happen. There was plenty of time for that. The main thing was to catch up on my brother. We had a telephone conversation about what our thoughts were about each other. We got in the car to go have some fun bicycling out in the country and it was a beautiful day (chuckling) and I thought Jesus, I kind of hate to ruin a beautiful day by talking. And, I said, "Let's talk a little bit in the car here. Do you want to start or do you want me to start?"

And he goes, "Wha . . . what, about what?" And I said "Well, you know, I think we got, you know—we talked a little bit on the phone and I think we ought . . . "

And he goes, "Well, you know—let's chat for a minute. I think you pretty well heard my side on the telephone that day."

And I said, "Look, guy, we said there was a need to chat about some of this stuff, so even if you don't talk back I just want to tell you a couple of things. Just for the record. Simply, you know, simply, you mean a lot to me, you always have, I love you a lot, and my relationship with you is real important, but I do feel that as I'm kind of pursuing some other interests in life—as I'm really electing not to be so involved in business, whether it's for myself or with other people, or with you, you know I'm a little afraid that that's going to cause a problem between us—that you're not going to be as open to being as close if I don't do business and things like that with you. And I want you to know it's—you know, the business. It's not just *you*. In part it is, I'm suspicious about some of the business deals you get into and some of your motivations and I'm a little concerned about those things, but if I really wanted to be in business, I think we could work those out—some of those concerns. But I just don't want to be in business. You know, I've done my share in my own life for that and I really want to pursue some other things. There's only so much time in a day, and that's what I want to do for me and, and. . . . Really I hope that we can continue to be really close and, you know, like we're taking a bicycle trip today, and I hope you don't think that I'm a ne'er-do-well because I don't want to be in business, but if you do, fuck you. You know."

And that was . . . it was real nice. And he just said, "Look, you know, . . . it's not for me to tell you how to live your life, really," he said, "and I wouldn't want you telling me how to live mine, and we can be brothers and kind of share some concerns about what we see is going on, within reason, but that's what makes life sort of interesting. You know, if you were like me it wouldn't be any fun." I think he was pitching me more than he was . . . I don't know . . .

Therapist: Pitching you?

Chuck: Pitching, . . . he was selling, I think, and saying the right thing. I don't know if he really meant it. . . . Part of that he did mean, but I feel he probably has some suspicions about what I'm doing that he didn't come up with and I also think that . . . that, while they're concerned, he—and his wife in particular—would rather have their stereotype of how I am and just leave it at that. I think they're comfortable with that. I don't need to beat 'em over the head with it. You know, the whole time I was there, in regard to her in particular—it was mostly just kind of superficial sort of: "How are things going?" None of it was: "Oh, so you took this new course. How was it?" None of it was really, "What's going on?" or, you know, "We're really interested." You know, so I thought, well screw it. That's . . . you know, so what? What can I do about it?

Therapist: And you didn't really get caught up in sort of needing them to understand or trying to make them understand?

Chuck: No, I just thought the hell with it.

Therapist: Good, great! Great!

Chuck: And, typically I just tried to be in their universe when I was there. They'd say, "Well, let's have dinner" and I thought, "Well, no, . . . I really need to take some time to see some of my other friends," and I spent a lot more of my time doing that and being with people I am interested in keeping in touch with and who are interested in me in a little different fashion—

Therapist: Uhm-hmmm.

Chuck: a little bit more intimate kind of fashion. And that was really time well spent. Even though it was just touching base in some respects, it was still in-depth touching base. And, you know, one was a former history professor so we got to kick around some of the ideas about my going back to school and we had a few beers with some of his friends that, you know, teach at Michigan State, and you know. . . . just stuff like that. That was kind of nice. And an old friend of mine named Nancy, who's just a friend—a woman who's been through lots of experiences with me—very intimate but never lovers; she's just a fun person to be with. And I wanted to take my niece and nephew on a major day . . . y'know, since I was in town. We did things I never would have done on my own; I never would have gone on the water slides and the merry-go-round and all of that. God, it was wonderful. It was so much fun. Y'know, it was 80 degrees and she's six and a half and he's four and y'know . . . you know, I've never done anything like that and . . . it was a ball, I loved it.

Therapist: It sounds wonderful.

Chuck: Yeah, you know, Nancy was a big help with all that and Christ, we did everything there is to do and all the cotton candy and ice cream. It was a great exposure for me.

Therapist: That's the real life that you wanted, you know, as opposed to achievement of the real estate business or full professor of history, or whatever, you know. It's like all those things are nice, but this is . . . but this is real life.

Chuck: Yeah, and that's what I felt when I was doing it, you know. She bumped into some friends of hers and we spent some time with them, and . . . you know . . . it was just . . . and that's all I could think about when I looked around. I thought, Jesus, here are all these people who haven't sold any real estate—who haven't come close to selling as many buildings—and they've got their finger on the button better than I do about what's real and what's fun and what's valuable and . . . you know, they were out there with their kids and and . . .

Therapist: You know, you could have both.

Chuck: So there was that, and there was that contrast. There was this great day, the three of us—the four of us. We all got really burned out and tired. It really exhausted all of us. And then we tried to fit too much into one day. My brother arranged a big family birthday party for my mother at a fancy country club. I mean the change was unbelievable in terms of the rigidness of that compared to the . . . you know, the fun of spending the day with those kids versus an evening at the country club. The kids were dressed up and my brother was sort of in charge and he's director of the club, and was very . . . conscientious about his kids who were cutting up and a little tired and—very apologetic and also got a little stern and—you know, tried to show his authority . . . you know, it was just bullshit.

Therapist: The contrast was rigid versus . . .

Chuck: Well, the contrast was amazing. He'd never taken them on a day like that. Now, he's done some fun things with them, but you know, he just doesn't skew as much toward that. I think a little bit, but not as much. And, you know, it was just . . . it was just the artificial roles of the country club compared to the other world and just the tightness . . .

Then, I picked up my grandmother and we took a long drive in the country and we had a great picnic and it was a beautiful day, and just, you know, along the river in Michigan we just sat down and did that for ourselves and had, you know, really long talks about her youth and her parents and her grandparents and her relationship with my grandfather. And it was just wonderful. We didn't stop talking for the whole time, and she just loved just being with me and I loved just being with her and . . .

Therapist: That's great.

Chuck: And, and, so, on the way home . . . I just kind of talked about the various sides of who I am and how much of the side that I like probably the best kind of came from their side, which is true.

Therapist: It's nice to hear all of that.

Chuck: The focus on family and the things that are—as far as the simple pleasures, and why I'm in Oregon, and things like that—are very much my grandmother and grandfather. And we talked about that and we talked about the fact that she ain't gonna live forever and that, you know, we're not gonna probably get a chance to take a lot more trips like this and you know, how glad we both just took the time to do it. And we talked about what it might be like to be 82 and not sure you're going to live for that much longer. And, we didn't get into that subject real deep, but I . . . you know, I just kind of said, "You know, we talk on the phone a lot and I hope that during those conversations we talk about lots of things that are not just topical. I hope that if there's fears or things like that, or things you want to talk to me about, you will feel free to do it." Because I remember before my grandfather died, her husband, that one of the things that was so nice was that I had a chance . . . to really know more of who he was. He grew up here, and I didn't really understand all of who he was until I was here and just looked out the window and could see what was here and why he was who he was and what have you. And he and I had a real nice conversation, talking about how much we'd meant to each other. And he died a week later. And, you know, I've always been happy about that conversation. We did a little bit of that kind of talk in the car. It was really sort of emotional. You know, we didn't cry a lot . . . it was real nice.

Therapist: A very touching time.

Chuck: It was real nice, and it was . . . yeah, yeah, it was a nice time we had. And, ahh. And, in Ann Arbor, it was great to be with my nieces. This one niece is 14 and I've seen her more than I have the 11-year-old, but God, you know, every time I would call on the telephone it was always—we didn't have much to talk about . . .

Therapist: Phone things with kids are hard.

Chuck: And, just to be there for a couple days—I mean, God, their mother just couldn't go on enough about it. She said, "It's just so great. They're having so much fun getting to know you." You know, we went out and . . . it was a little different with them. Their father is out of the home—divorced and not really into kids that much. He likes to be a good father, but he's not really into it. And so we went on a river trip together, which was really a very pretty river for back there. I was surprised how pretty the country is. That was one of the things we did other than just poking around and having lunch together and things of that nature. We went . . . I took them on a shopping trip. I said, "Now I've got 15 years of guilt to get over with, so I need to . . . do a little penance." I was just kidding about that, but I said, "Really, your grandfather whom you have never known was a man of many personalities and one of the sides which I liked was he was very generous, and you know, had a real flair for certain moments in life and being a little overindulgent—not as a rule, not all the time. But there are certain ways he spoiled me and he spoiled your mother, and they're sort of nice moments that I remember not for his buying affection and things like that, but just something I thought was fun. Part of the money I have was from him and part of it is what I've earned, and let's just go out and have some fun. Let's just go out and buy some stuff and go shopping."

Therapist: Wow.

Chuck: Yeah, I said, "I'm kidding about this retribution for my guilt for not knowing you for 13 years, because I don't really feel that terrible about that (laugh). I feel sort of sad that you grew up so fast, but I wasn't really into uncle-ing. You were born 13 years too soon, as far as I'm concerned. But, let's just go out and have some fun along that line. I never get a chance to do something like this. I just . . . I would enjoy doing it . . . so let's just have fun at it." So we went to a fancy store and bought some necklaces and we went to the department store and bought some stuff and just had a great time. I just sat there and enjoyed it, you know. And they were very shy and said, "Oh no, we can't spend any more"—and I'd talk 'em into spending more and . . . said when we went into the store, "Now, don't embarrass Uncle Chuck . . . I know some of the people in here, (whisper) . . . you have to spend this much money, otherwise I'm gonna start dancing to the music in the store." And just kiddin' with 'em. And they really had a . . .

Therapist: They're so easily embarrassed at that age.

Chuck: Yeah, yeah. And it was just—JEEEsus, was it cute. It was a great time. And so they were getting ready to go to camp, so didn't spend all the money that I had figured on spending, so I gave them a gift certificate for the remainder and said, "When you get back and you get ready to go to school, you know, you can come in here without me and . . . "

Therapist: That's so marvelous. I had an aunt who was like that, and I think she was really responsible for a lot of the ability to let go and have fun that I have today. One time someone asked me, "Do you have any brothers or sisters?" and I said, "No, but I have an aunt."

Chuck: (laughter) That's great! It was a fun thing.

Therapist: It can make a big contribution . . . even now, at 11 and 14.

Chuck: Yeah. And I had a good time also, saying it was . . . yeah. It was fun for me to bring my Dad into it because that's a skill that I really learned from him. . . . I mean, he takes a bum rap for . . . well, let's say "generosity" . . . just the fun of it. He takes . . . not a bum rap; you know, he gets what he deserves in certain areas. You know, it's not all positive. But there are certain areas in which he really had something . . . the sense of play and generosity. You know, taking his kids to Chicago to look at schools . . . or just having fun together, you know, going to New York and shopping and going to shows. And just, you know, sharing that other side of life with us when we were growing up. And I kind of liked giving him a little credit for that, you know. It was appropriate, you know. It was just neat to be with them and they enjoyed it and I enjoyed it. It was just great fun.

Therapist: It sounds wonderful. It's such a good thing for you to be a model of some looseness and play and generosity.

Chuck: I said . . . 15 years from now we may do this again, or this is just to get you indoctrinated so that five or six years from now, if we go to New York, we can have another big one. Don't expect this every time I come to town. But, I'm trying . . . I'm trying to see them in August when they come to Lake Tahoe, if I can be there. I said, "I want to show you the other side," which is, you know, we're going to go camping for two nights, so anyway . . .

Therapist: Marvelous.

Chuck: So, anyway, and I had as much fun as they did. And I got my head straight about some other things just, you know, as I've grown up. . . . I've known my relatives in Ann Arbor. Some of them are, you know, very wealthy and have big plantation-type homes, and all these big parties and it was kind of fun to be on the deck for one of these huge parties like I remember when I was a kid and think, you know . . . I don't know, I just have a little different view of who they are and what their values are and, you know, they're always funny and nice but it's a very manipulative, powerful type of thing. I recall sitting around the dinner table with my nieces there being the way they are, and this drunken 80-year-old, very much in control of this plantation, says, "I notice you're not eating any of your dinner. But, of course, you don't have to here." Really embarrassing these two kids in front of everybody. And I just . . . didn't like it, you know . . . just that kind of stuff.

Therapist: Yeah. Sure.

Chuck: And, anyway. So, I sort of had my eyes opened to some of these, some of these ways. I did some reconnaissance on my own. I got on my bicycle and rode all around, just saw all my old haunts in Ann Arbor. I went to my high school and poked my head in the window and looked, you know, all around.

Therapist: Great.

Chuck: You know, I could sit here and say, gee, I had a great childhood, and all this, but I'm so glad I'm not in that world that I grew up in.

Therapist: Because . . .

Chuck: Well, because it is very rigid in terms of what your possibilities are or what your possibilities aren't. I had to think to myself when I was in Ann Arbor, would I want to be a professor at Michigan or Michigan State?

Therapist: Umm-hmmm.

Chuck: Given my understanding of the politics, you know, of the communities and of the people that run them and, you know, what their particular value systems are. I wouldn't want to be involved in that. You know, I wouldn't WANT to teach history in Ann Arbor, particularly.

Therapist: Mmhmm.

Chuck: You know, it's . . . it's interesting to me how the possibilities for a life that I perceive for myself here sits much different than anything back there. It's . . . just the possibility to explore the . . . really who you are as opposed to what you're supposed to be is much greater here. It might be different if I had a lot of family here, but . . . and I'm sure there are certain undertones of all that politics here that exist back there.

Therapist: There is that.

Chuck: There's some of that everywhere. . . . But, I'm just, you know, very pleased with my decision to be here.

Therapist: Umm.

Chuck: Boy, it's just that . . . as far as figuring out things like that. That doesn't have to be Eugene. I think it could be Portland or Seattle. But, just the difference in mentality here. You know, I cruise up and down the streets in Ann Arbor . . . just that flat land, the telephone poles, and these old buildings, and just sort of really old values that just . . . just made my skin crawl, really. Just . . . I just thought, God . . .

Therapist: Yeah. That reminds me of Garrison Keilor? Do you know him?

Chuck: Yeah, um-hmmm, um-hmmm.

Therapist: He really puts me in touch with my origins, which are somewhat more Scandinavian, real midwestern.

Chuck: Ummm-hmmmm. In what ways?

Therapist: Well, in every way. The accent and the work ethic, and not saying too much and not really disclosing what's really going on with you and keeping your life kind of a secret. He has this great list of the 95 theses that a man wanted to nail to the door of the Lutheran church all about what they did to him to make him restrained and restricted and not have fun. I identify.

Chuck: Uh-huh, Really! Well, it's like the comment at the office . . . you know the senior old guy who I respect, was talking about somebody and he said, "Well, you know, of course, he's a perfect demigod—every time he opens his mouth, he shows how stupid he is." Well, you know, that's the kind of talk that just makes you . . . anybody who ever heard that . . . never want to talk or say anything that might be even questionable . . . you know, and . . . it's very tight. Very tight back there. One of the things that was nice is I ran into someone back there. . . . . It turns out that there's . . . a law firm that's doing some work for some of the deals we're working on. . . . This guy I went to school with when I was 15, when I was really a run-around, letter-jacket, track star, you know. . . . He didn't study a book, never opened a book. And you know, God, I ran into him and I just thought, this is hard! He's somebody. He was a real bright little kid, you know, just. . . . I said JEEEsus it's hard to face somebody who I knew in that era. We just talked for a minute and it was kind of fun, the sort of little rapport that developed . . . and, you know, then the conversation . . . well, "Are you married?" and I kind of say, "Well it's sort of difficult right now." I think he picked up on it. . . . He was glad to hear that I felt comfortable saying that and he kind of went on to say, "Well, you know, I went through an awful one myself and, you know, everybody said we should get divorced. We ended up not getting divorced and it's worked out well. I don't know what your situation is, but it is hard. . . . " It was just kind of nice that . . . that was the kind of a conversation we never would have had 18 years ago. And it was after so many years, even in the corporate setting, not really knowing each other well, it's nice to kind of just get over some of the gobbledygook into something a little more personal. And that was fun. And, I think that . . . you know, I think that's a function of being open to that happening and I think that people read that.

Therapist: Ummm-hmmmm. I think that happens because you're projecting it's okay to talk about those things,

Chuck: Umm-hmmmm. It's a conversation you wouldn't have had with my brother, you know.

Therapist: Right.

Chuck: And, so you know, all these little . . . in lots of ways, things are improving. You know, this woman . . .

Therapist: This is a success story.

Chuck: (rather embarrassed chuckle) Yeah. There's a woman that came over once that I didn't really want to go out with again. She has been calling me up . . . and I've kind of been hoping that we wouldn't connect on the telephone. And this kind of went back to what we talked about earlier. It's hard to let somebody down, especially maybe if it's a woman or whatever. And I just . . . I just said, "You know, this. . . . " Let me just tell you what happened. A couple weeks ago, or a couple months ago, I went out with a woman and I liked her and I wanted to take her out again, you know. And I called her up and she said, "Listen, I think you're a nice person . . . but I really, for a variety of reasons, I'm not really interested in going out with you." And, I kind of hung up the phone and I thought, you know, I didn't like hearing the message, but I loved the fact that I didn't have to call her and have excuses and go six or seven phone calls before you just kind of eroded into just not calling back . . . you've just exhausted yourself.

Therapist: 'Cause that's kind of what you wanted to with the woman now? You wanted to just let it erode away.

Chuck: Well, that's typically the way I'd do it. It's easier for me to behave that way. And I kind of thought, well, what would I rather get, a straight message like that or erosion? So this woman who I don't want to see . . . I said, "Listen, let me just tell you how somebody hit me over the head two months ago, and I wasn't wild about the message, but I sure liked the style (laughter). You know, basically, I enjoyed the evening we had, and I like, you know, many things about you, and the fact that, you know, you're a runner and you're kind of trying to integrate a bunch of stuff in your life and have a balance, but you know . . . I don't know if it's me, or whatever it is, but the way I'm conditioned or programmed, but from a male-female thing, you know, whatever it is I'm looking for just didn't seem to be there. And, I . . . you know . . . so I . . . I just want to level with you about that, in terms of you and I gettin' together, and . . . (smiling).

Therapist: Great.

Chuck: I hung up, and I kind of went whew (great exhale), I don't know if I want to be in this arena or not . . . but then I thought, well, fuck, it's life, you know.

Therapist: Being single has its hard moments.

Chuck: It's life you know. So, anyway, she called back and I said, "You know, I'm glad you called back . . . because I don't mind, you know, talking about this a little bit more." And, she goes, "I just want to talk about that just for a second more." And I said, "That's fine." And she said, "The more I thought about it, I really was happy that you told me. I didn't like it at first and I just kind of hung up, and I probably wasn't as thoughtful for how hard that was for you to do and, you know, I . . . you know, and I just kind of hung up and what have you. But the more I think about it, I really do prefer that method."

Therapist: Yeah, it's a much more caring thing to do.

Chuck: Yeah. And she said, "You know, I really did enjoy that evening, and this may be a really hard question and you don't have to answer it: But, can you give me an idea of just what . . . what . . . what hit you that . . . you know . . . ?" And I said, "Well, boy that's a tough one. I'd be happy to, but shit. You know, take it for what it's worth. I mean, you know, I think we're all on some kind of a quest trying to work things out, and God . . . I don't . . . you know, who knows, you know, what kind of little things I've got. But I'll just tell you . . . just give you a hit, just to think about . . . and I think from a conditional standpoint, there's a certain, you know . . . I think there's a certain softness that I'm sort of looking for in a woman, or whatever, that I didn't pick up on from you. And, you know, I think you're really . . . I sense maybe a little bit of anger and harshness in the way you're trying to be in the male world, and maybe you have to do that to be successful in what it is that's important to you. I don't know. I don't know what that's all about, but I picked up on . . . you know, for me . . . you know, I . . . I'm just feeling I'd like a little more softness in a companion and, you know, amongst perhaps a checklist of certain (chuckles) attributes, if I could have a wish list. But, ummmm, you know. But, you know, maybe there's some neuroses I have that maybe I, you know, I don't want to have somebody competing with me. Maybe it's all kinds of things that, you know, you wouldn't want to even be a part of my world, for whatever the reasons are. I say, 'Who knows?' but that's just kind of what my hit was, for what it's worth." So, anyway, I said, "I'm really glad we're doing this." I said, "This gives me a lot of hope for the way people can behave." I said, "I just . . . " then we started talking about running more, and she wanted to give me the names of some people that . . . and all of a sudden, I think a real communication evolved to the point where we may have dinner again a couple of months from now.

Therapist: Right. Once you're that honest with someone, it's such a peak experience in a way, that it leads to more. Not necessarily marriage, but a relationship.

Chuck: Yeah, but sure . . . and I said, "You're a nice person and you know, you're a good runner and I'm really interested in that, and I want to keep open the possibility that, you know, if you're going out for a run and . . . you know, and you wanna take me along, I'd enjoy doing that. I'd prefer for that sort of a thing to exist as opposed to the male-female thing."

And, uhhh, and then the other day I got my . . . you know, I got my first exams back in this re-entry to grad school. They weren't perfect, but out of two essays, I got an A on one, and he said, you know, "really a great command of the subject and control of the way you wrote the essay" and the other was a B, it was very disorderly. (Laughs) But, but . . . you know, it was . . . but I thought, shit, you know, there's progress! And, I'm feeling like I'm getting some of those skills back because the one essay was really good. I knew it when I was writing it, I knew it when I was finished. And, I'm getting a sense of how to continue to do that. And, at the same time, I opened the dividend check for my company for the quarter, you know, and it was no small sum, but the thing that turned me on more than anything was the goddam A. I mean, I just . . . it's so CLEAR to me, you know, that I'm on the right track. I mean . . . I'm just . . . I'm not convinced that it's the right thoroughfare. The right thing may be an offshoot of that where I am . . . you know, who knows what it is? But, I think I'm on the right scent in making these priorities in my life.

Therapist: Trying them is the only way you're going to discover . . . and as you said, there are a lot of offshoots.

Chuck: Yeah, but clearly, you know, putting the business as secondary—even if it . . . doesn't work. If it goes bankrupt tomorrow, I'm feeling so good about what else is going on in my life, and all the other possibilities, and you know my nieces and nephews and kids and relationships . . . it is not just . . . I'm not holding everything you know, in that business anymore. You know, it's real slow now in business—frighteningly slow. But, what's money. Yeah, so what? I am concerned, I do want the structure to go well. I want the people to do a good job. . . . I want that to exist. 'Cause that would throw me into a crisis now. I could sell the business, but I'd prefer to deal with that down the road. I certainly would prefer to sell a little bit down the road if I sell it at all. So, anyway, that's a little about what's going on, and it's been really pretty positive.

Therapist: No shit. It's wonderful.

Chuck: Yeah.

Therapist: I don't know when I've heard a more positive report—it's positive on every angle, in your communications, your self-concept, your lack of need to win the family over, your ability to sort of fit in and be real with who's able to be real with you and sort of just understand and let go and rest and notice that your brother is being a little, um, a little—

Chuck: A little phony, selling, yeah.

Therapist: Without really trying to nail him on it or be offended by it. The communication with that woman. Great.

Chuck: Yeah, it's been—I think things are starting to piece together. You know, I think they're just piecing together a little bit so I keep it on a roll, you know, but then going back and seeing those kids, it really kind of opened my eyes, and that was, you know, the country club in Ann Arbor with my sister and I'm just sitting there by the pool watching all the little kids, you know, dive in the pool and swim across, and then they were doing the back stroke and kind of criss-crossing and bumping at each other. Yeah, I mean, I don't know, you know, either the kids are getting cuter or they're . . . or I'm getting older, I don't know what it is, but I'm just really, all of a sudden I'm just open about it. I'm much more open to that and thinking it would be really fun.

Therapist: Being a parent, you mean?

Chuck: Well, kids or to be a part of something that involves kids. Whether it's—you know, even doing something with the Parks and Rec. in town, just something that, you know—

Therapist: Or even the Big Brother or Big Sister program might be interesting.

Chuck: Exactly. Exactly. So I'm just, I don't know, I'm sort of enjoying it and I'm sort of thinking this family thing's sort of important to me. The things I keep homing in on are of importance to me—I like this business of family as a possibility. It's not right now, and there's, you know, not the right person to do that with, but I have a hunch that that'll roll along in due time, and it may take a few years or whatever, but I sort of think that is a real possibility.

Therapist: It is.

That's my boy!! Of course, the seeds of this transformation were ready and just waiting to be nurtured into this full flowering. Still, this transcript documents many of the changes that take place as a narcissistic client discovers, nurtures, and expresses his true self and it documents what short-term work can do with appropriate clients. In this transcript, the development, the contrasts, and the very realistic positive hopes for the future are so sharply drawn by the trip home and by this most humane dialogue with the woman he no longer wanted to date. This is what the narcissistic transformation looks and sounds like. It is a reentry into the incredible joys of ordinary life.

CHAPTER VI

THE INTEGRATION OF GROUP AND INDIVIDUAL THERAPY: *THE NARCISSISTIC CHARACTER DISORDER*

I find my way because you find yours.

— Hugh Prather

IT IS 5:30 Tuesday night and time for the group to begin. I look forward to this particular gathering because it has been among the most profound learning experiences of my career. I am the therapist to these six people, all men, each of whom has been or currently is in individual therapy with me. Most in the group are not unlike myself, on the threshold of middle age, successful in work, but somewhat to severely isolated. We all share the experience of pursuing achievement and assisting others in compensation for insufficient self-regard. The popular male curse of the narcissistic style is well-represented here. Larry is here, and so is John, the youngest member of the group, introduced originally in Chapter III, page 96. John is in the throes of one of his crises and is considering dropping out of the group. In the taped segment which follows, he masterfully outlines the central issues of narcissism but does so with such honesty and poignancy that every man in the group sees himself in John—in the beauty of his real self-expression and in the tragedy of his sacrifice of self.

THE INDIVIDUAL IN GROUP: PART I

John: I've been feeling a need to get to work, to achieve a lot more than I have been recently. (very very softly) Last term I ended up not getting the grade point average I wanted. The feelings that come up in this therapy just get in the way of wanting to achieve. When I feel, I usually don't want to achieve that much. But you know, I feel weird if I don't want to achieve. I feel that I'm not a good person—being a good person to me means to go out there and try to be the best at whatever you do. I haven't been putting in that effort, and I get very angry with myself for not doing that. I don't feel strong enough to be able to achieve and feel at the same time.

Therapist: Strong enough?

John: I don't have as much capacity as I would like to both feel and achieve at the same time. And I guess I feel I've disappointed myself with that. I'm seeing some of the vulnerabilities that I have, and I don't like them, and I don't like being told that I have them, and I want to prove to everybody that I don't have them. I don't feel like I achieve anything here in this group. I don't give enough to be here; I don't have as much knowledge; I don't have as much to share and because of that I don't feel good about it. It's like I can't achieve here; I can't do anything. It's annoying. And I put a lot of time into this, a lot of time. I feel myself wishing that I was as developed emotionally as some of you. I'm angry at you for being where you are compared with where I am. I feel strange, I feel sad—I feel like a jerk, is what I feel like, for not being better than I am. The only way that I can judge myself is by picking up on other people's reactions. If they don't react positively, then I think there's something wrong with me. And I get real depressed. I've been sort of playing a game with myself these past few days of going out and achieving things, setting myself up in a position of going to job interviews, giving a lot of positive responses. But I also notice how I act when I give those positive responses. I pretend that I'm great, I pretend that I know it all and that nothing bothers me; I'm real strong. People seem to eat that up. They respond positively, "You are great." And though I don't believe that's true . . . I like the response, I like the attention. I want a lot of people to respond positively. But I'm just fooling them. I got all those positive responses and then I just felt real lonely. But I was getting confused tonight when I came in here. I was listening to Bill; I liked what Bill has said—because it seemed *real*, it seemed *real honest* and it was—*real*. It's hard for me to express it any other way besides just saying real.

I can listen to that kind of thing all night long; it's great to get rid of all these pent-up feelings. But I don't feel strong enough to do both. I have seen you around town, Bill, and you're different, you're much more focused on a goal. Now I'm thinking to myself, I wish I could be that way, to be able to feel when I want to, and then seemingly block it off. Let nobody know how I feel until I want to express myself. But I don't seem to be able to do that. I carry my feelings on my face a great deal, and in my voice. And I don't like being reminded that I can't do both, that I'm not strong enough to be both at this time, or maybe ever. I don't like being reminded of that, and that's what therapy seems to do for me, to be reminded of how weak I am.

Jeff: What do you want?

John: If I could feel, but yet control it, I would, but I can't keep it under control.

Larry: Strength is—to you is—not showing it so much. At least that's the message I'm getting.

Jeff: At least for me, emotions and control are somehow at odds—pure feeling is something that—to me that's when the control is at a real low level. So you don't try to control it when you're really honestly feeling, you know. There's a lot of area between them. I almost see control at the opposite end of the spectrum from feeling.

Bill: Are you saying that it's just really hard for you to pull it back together and get out there and sort of do what you gotta do? You come in here and come apart, go back out there and start to compartmentalize all this stuff that you do here so you can just be Joe Robot out there.

John: It's impossible for me to do that.

Jeff: I've been in situations . . . sometimes what's been going on in my life has been so powerful that I can hardly bear to face anyone or anything. . . . Fortunately that's really only happened about two times in 12 years, but sometimes it happens.

Bill: I guess the way I think about it is that the more that you let go here, the less you have on your sleeve out there. Does that make sense to anybody?

John: Yeah, but it doesn't work that way for me. I start feeling and I can't stop it.

Therapist: Part of the dues that you're paying for the work you're doing is that you're carrying an emotional rawness around with you. Can you accept that? It's part of the deal.

John: I understand that. You see, the thing is that, I think I understand pretty much what I'm doing and feeling and why I'm here, and I pretty much understand the process. Not totally, but I understand why I get in these moods, but that doesn't take me out of them. The understanding really doesn't change a lot for me. I had a final in physics Wednesday morning, after group last Tuesday. You weren't here, Larry, but that was—it was a pretty emotional time for me. And I flunked it. Well, actually, I got a D, but that's bad enough. I ended up getting a C in the course. That's not like me. I've gotten straight A's, and now I'm really pissed off. I was totally pissed off. You know, I was saying, this fucking therapy's screwing me over. I can't even think anymore in class. So when somebody tells me, sure, take the time, you have the time to feel, go ahead—I don't have the time. I don't have it. I don't have the opportunity to fuck up for a day and come back, because it's on my transcript.

Bill: What's your grade point average?

John: I don't know, it's a 3.7, something like that. I mean, it took it down from a 3.9.

Therapist: I think you can't do what you're doing without having some of that happen—from what I know about how it works, you can't do what you're doing without having some of those days. It's just too bad it was finals day.

John: I know that too, and that's—that's what I'm wrestling with.

Therapist: Before we go on with this, I was just wondering if it would be possible to take it over since the test measured your upset, not your knowledge.

John: No, it's not . . . I don't want to do that. I don't believe in that. That's not what I'm here to do. I understand the thought behind it, I appreciate it, but I'm not going to do that—I took the exam like everybody else. Everybody else had their problems and I fucked it up. I don't get special treatment just because I'm trying to do something.

Jeff: If I understand correctly, you know the stuff . . .

John: No, it's my conscience and my conscience says not to do that. Maybe in the future I'll feel differently about it, but no. No, it's my responsibility to go through life and take responsibility for it.

Therapist: It feels so much like an ordeal—

Bill: ordeal by fire. And this is an opportunity to ask somebody to briefly turn the heat down.

John: I don't like the idea in this case. I think I'll think about it in the future but not in this case. My GPA is a 3.7, with, almost 100 units. Before, my GPA was a 2.7. Combine the two, my overall GPA is like a 3.1. And every time I don't get an A, it doesn't go up, it just hovers around that. And there's so many people out there that get better GPAs—God, I'm going into my spiel about why I want to do well, and it's kind of boring, but it's like I get real intense on it, because I'm not—I am not allowing myself to be forgiven for what I did before, as a motivation to do better in the future.

Martin: I understand flagellating yourself forward, and I think everybody else here sees that process. We're all experts.

Bill: One of the things that I would just like to offer back to you is that—you had said, a bit ago, that you had a fairly good understanding of how this process works and what its characteristics are. I have a great appreciation for how much time you spend in your head working on these issues and how much energy you devote to them, and I'm wondering if you also understand that in this choice between achievement and feelings, you really don't have a choice, in the sense of turning off your feelings, of turning away from them, of condemning those processes that bring them up and rub your face in them. If your objective is to get over what's hurting you, and learn how to have a good satisfying life with women and other people, you don't have a choice. I know you know what I'm saying. . . . I am just saying that a transcript is a piss-ant small piece of life.

John: I know that, too, but I—see, no one really pushed me in my life. My parents were afraid to say anything to me because of how they fucked up my older brothers, and I got it into my mind when I was about 18 years old that I didn't push myself hard enough.

Jeff: Now here was a guy that really could accomplish things if he was pushed.

John: I didn't know that, but I wanted to find out, and—so every time if I don't do well now, I have to kick myself a whole lot to get going, because I don't feel anybody else, well, helping, you know, pushing. And I do it too much, I think, I overdo it, but—

Therapist: Do you think there's any ending . . . if you won the Nobel Prize, would that do it? . . .

John: No, but what it would do, it would feel real good for a while, and it would give me something to fall back on, to say that I deserve the respect I want. It's more respect, because I deserve respect.

Therapist: My experience is that when you get into that, nothing is ever enough. Once you set that path, you'll never rest.

John: I'll always want to achieve more, I know that.

Therapist: It's worse than that—

Jeff: You always feel the need to achieve more in order to prove this thing, and it doesn't work.

Larry: And because the feelings aren't being served, you will continue to feel bad about the long years and hard hours that go into winning those Ph.D.s. Yet you'll be . . .

John: I believe both of you, I'm not arguing with you.

Therapist: It's because they've done it—we've all done it so much.

John: But it's like, I feel like I have the right to do it too.

(group laughter)

Jeff: I'll bet you every one of us here knows that you'll achieve a lot.

Larry: Yeah.

Bill: Part of the deal is that it is satisfying. You know, I mean, part of it is nice, making it. The other part of it is the dark shit that's—this doesn't prove nothing.

John: I think it does prove something.

Bill: It doesn't prove what I neurotically wish it would. It does prove some other stuff. It proves some good stuff, but it doesn't disprove the dark stuff.

Therapist: Part of the dark stuff, John, is that you are so hard on yourself, so incredibly hard on yourself. What I know is that accomplishment won't ever stop you from doing that, from being so *hard*.

John: No, but it will give me. . . . See, this is how I'm thinking right now—is that if I do accomplish a lot, and, let's say, if I make a lot of money, then I can say, well, why don't you leave this weekend to do whatever—you know, go see the top guru in psychiatry for a weekend. And, I've earned the money to do that, and I'm doing it for me. In other words, it's like—I earned it for myself. No one's giving it to me; I give it to myself. Whereas now, my parents give me something, I don't feel real good about it, I feel hollow. I don't feel a lot of motivation—it's not for me, so much, I almost feel like I'm getting this therapy for them. You know?

Bill: You ever feel like you're doing it for us?

John: No, I don't feel like I'm giving enough to you, like I said before, that I don't know enough to see past what you're saying, because my feeling is we all pretty much say the same thing, but I want to—I have this thing, for me—I have this quest for greatness. You know, I feel I should be able to just say in one sentence what would encapsulate the entire thing for all of you, but have it not be so profound that you wouldn't understand it, but it'd just hit the spot for everybody.

Bill: Sure, we all want to do that.

Jeff: Right.

Therapist: Perfect, cure us all in one sentence, one perfect sentence.

John: And it's really weird, but, it's like I say to myself, push hard enough, do it hard enough, and maybe when you're 50 years old you'll have it, be able to get closer to it. But then I say, well, if I keep on at this pace, I'm never going to get there.

Therapist: If you don't come up with that one perfect sentence, what would you think of yourself?

John: I wouldn't feel bad for me alone, but if I had to see the rest of you people, I would feel guilty that I hadn't done it—that I wasn't good enough.

Bill: Then I want to tell you that, even now, you have been very helpful to me. You've been very helpful to me. And I'm saying that because it's a very true and very simple fact. You've got a trap set up for yourself, where if you don't achieve this elegance of Confucius, you're shit, and guilty. You don't have to do that. And this may not affect you the way I would wish that it could affect you, but you can help in the way that the rest of us can help each other. I believe that your intention is to help, and I need that help, so I appreciate that. You don't have to say anything special . . . I don't need that from you. You help me most by your intention and your honesty and by the mirror you give me of *me*. I see me in how hard you are on yourself, how little kindness you give yourself. One way of practicing kindness to yourself is to recognize how you do help me. Practice kindness with yourself.

John: It just sounds so much like counting your blessings before you go to sleep, and I never bought that.

Therapist: Could you start?

Jeff: You need to program yourself to feel good about yourself, and you can, with what, among other things, you achieve for the rest of us.

Therapist: As you've said many times, John—love yourself.

John: The only time that I really love myself is when I feel loved by others.

Therapist: Right. And that's what I would like to do. I'd like to tell you all the good things I think about you, and put it in a sentence. If there's any way that I could make you feel the love I feel for you right now, I'd like to do it, but I also know there may not be any way to do that.

John: Yeah, it wouldn't work, it wouldn't work for me, because I have to prove it to myself. I have to prove that I'm worthy.

Bill: That's the tragic thing.

John: I'm listening to what everybody's saying, but what I'm really telling you is, it doesn't matter what you say.

Martin: What doesn't matter?

John: That you're telling me that achievements really aren't the Holy Grail.

Bill: How did you feel when I said what I said to you—that you had helped me?

John: You said it to me before, so I understood it.

Bill: How'd you feel?

John: Well, I felt the same way about what you said as I did about what Steve [therapist] said, because I think you were saying the same thing. It just doesn't matter—I have to prove it to myself.

Bill: So were you unmoved or unaffected? It had no impact?

John: It made me feel good, but it wasn't enough.

Bill: Wait a second. What felt good about it? What feels good about it when I tell you that you've been helpful?

John: Well, it makes me feel that there are nice people in the world and I think you're one of them. That's what it makes me feel.

Bill: Uh-huh. And what's that say about our relationship?

John: I really don't think it says a whole lot about our relationship.

Bill: But it says something, doesn't it?

John: That you're able to express the fact that you're a nice person.

Bill: What does that say about how I feel toward you?

John: I don't think it says a whole lot.

Bill: I agree with you; it doesn't say a whole lot, but you know that it says something and you keep moving away from it.

John: Well, because, see, the truth—if I said the truth how I felt it wouldn't be very nice.

Martin: We can take it.

John: Well, it's like, my feelings are it doesn't matter, because it *isn't enough*. What you're saying to me is just—I feel like I'm just being stroked, and I feel—I feel like you don't know what you're talking about in my case.

Bill: I wasn't talking about your case, I was talking about my case. . . . you are helpful to me . . .

John: See, that's how I think.

Bill: What I'm getting at is that I see a very fast short-circuiting away from anything positive, so that it's never enough, it's never enough, it's never enough. It's like the intensity of the experience has to be incredibly strong for it to mean anything. But I think you are feeling something. You feel good about yourself when you feel loved by other people. My experience with you in this group is that there have been times when you have felt loved by people in this group, so that you could be open and kind with yourself.

John: That's true, I do. And I enjoy it a great deal. But I have to go home, and I'm not going to get stroked anymore. I don't like having to feel the stroke, and then not be stroked anymore.

Therapist: Does it help you for me to say that I think you're getting better at letting yourself be stroked?

John: I can let it all in, but it hurts more if I do, after I leave here. Usually, when I leave here on Tuesday, I feel terrible. I kind of unravel, and I don't feel good about the world, and I feel like what the fuck am I doing? I feel terribly weak, and I usually end up going out and doing something self-destructive—drinking or . . .

Therapist: What would help you . . .

John: Well—see, it's kind of a fix, that if I was to be helped after group, then the next day I'd want it, and the next day. I want it every day in my life; I want it all the time. And . . . that's what I want and I can't get it.

Jeff: Oh, but you can.

In prior sessions, both group and individual, John had discovered the very intense feeling that only the unconditional love and support of one woman would ever provide the "enough" that he needed. This is a most common dysfunctional feeling in anyone having serious difficulties in the nurturing-holding periods of the first 18 months of life. As a result of this formidable deficit, it is often very difficult, as in John's case, to be affected or to internalize any caring which does not emanate from this one, perfect source. Working-through this need is perhaps the central issue in the characterological therapy of one with schizoid or oral issues, which John clearly manifests here. Both Bill and I were trying to help with this problem by offering John the caring feedback illustrated above. Even though these overtures were obviously deflected and labeled as "not enough," they still had a therapeutic effect. Once again, they highlight the "nothing is ever enough" stance which John acknowledges when he says, "See, that's how I think."

John, like so many others in his position, lets in more than he is willing to admit. Fully acknowledging the input would be emotionally overwhelming, and while it typically leads to tears of relief and ecstasy as it had in the prior group meeting, it leads to a level of openness which is still disorganizing and therefore disruptive to his day-to-day functioning. This was illustrated by the fact that the emotional incidences of the last group meeting resulted in poor performance on the physics final. This same theme—letting in positive input which is less than perfect, unconditional, or from a feminine source—will be returned to later in this group dialogue.

Martin: You'll never achieve enough to impress me, John. I don't care what you do, I won't be interested in it.

John: That's the greatest thing in the world that you can say to me, Martin, because I'll never let you get away now. I'll keep in touch with you forever to prove to you that I can. (group laughter) It's like, that's the greatest carrot you can give me, for anyone to say that to me. It's like I'll prove it to you.

Martin: You'll never impress me with achievement.

John: Hey, I hear you, but you're just feeding the fires.

Martin: The things that you've really got are the ones that you are trying to keep hidden. The things that you're sharing with me are the things that are going to be important . . . are the things that are really you. If you succeed in achieving, what you are telling me is that you will be better at hiding your feelings, who you really are, what you really have to give.

John: I feel this—isn't fair. You shouldn't say that to me. That doesn't feel fair. Because it makes me want to be more like how you're saying, but that isn't fair, because if I want to be that way, no one's going to hire me. I'm not going to make a million bucks.

Martin: I would rather have you poor and happy than have you rich and hate yourself. If you could be poor and like yourself, sure . . . I'll wish for your poverty. I don't think it's either-or, but if it had to be, I know how I'd vote.

John: I'm still hung up on the fact that I think success means, . . . well, money, and I want it now. I don't want to wait. I know therapy, for me, is a time to let myself unravel. But I want to tighten up and make it now. I don't want to wait. I'm in a hurry. I'm very impatient . . . what I really want is to *blow people away* [aggressively].

Jeff: Impress them?

John: No, I want to *run 'em over*, you know, beat 'em bad. I think I know how to do it, but I can't feel while I'm doing it, because then I wouldn't do it. But somehow, when I do achieve that way, I feel a sense of power, a sense of strength that is just the opposite of how I feel now.

Therapist: How long does it last?

John: Until the next achievement—how long depends on the achievement, the recognition that I receive.

Therapist: The bigger it is, the longer it lasts?

John: It doesn't usually last more than a week, sometimes a month. And in the meantime I'm working on the next achievement. So I can take a vacation of a week, but I feel in touch with jobs moving all the time, documenting things, hurry up so I can get back to life.

Therapist: I think Martin told you that it's not your continually bringing in additional achievements that would move him closer. He doesn't give a shit about that. He wants *you* in your life.

John: Well, that's why Martin's special to me. Because of that, I don't have to be up. I can call him when I'm down. You know, it's like it's almost more appreciated when I call him when I'm down.

Jeff: That may be true for the rest of us, too, and you really don't know it. It's true John.

John: But there are some people in the world that I'm angry at. They tell me that I'm not good enough.

Therapist: And they want the million bucks.

John: Yeah, they want the million bucks, and their terms of success is to achieve monetarily, to become the boss, to own the world.

Therapist: And you're going to show them.

John: Yes.
Therapist: You're going to sacrifice yourself if you have to.
John: Well, I want my cake and eat it too, but I'll sacrifice first. Seems more important. Sacrifice is a religion for me. It's what a good person does.
Therapist: That nicely expresses that disease, it was nicely put.
John: Gee, thanks. Well, my paranoia is based on the fact that I don't believe people love me. And . . .
Jeff: Love yourself.
John: Well, the reason I don't love myself is because I don't think I'm worthy to be loved because others don't love me, and I had to learn that from someplace. I don't believe that I was born with that.
Therapist: If you did believe that you were loved, then what would you . . . ?
John: God, I don't know, I don't know what it would be like. I really don't. The only thing I know is that when I feel strong is when I achieve. Feelings are so. . . . But achieving—that's more powerful than any drug. It's greater than anything.
Therapist: What about feeling loved?
John: Well, I don't believe it exists.
Therapist: Well, what happened last week—remember that time when you felt seen and understood . . . and you cried some and you felt you didn't have to fight anymore, or prove anything? In that instant you had it.
John: I try to forget those moments pretty quickly.
Therapist: Remember it now.
John: Umm. I remember it, but I don't like to talk about it because that's the way I really feel and because if I really was to be honest with myself, I'd feel that way, and wouldn't do anything. I wouldn't—nothing would really matter.
Bill: Do you realize what you would have to give up?
John: To do what?
Bill: If you kept experiences like you had last week, which threaten your whole model of your life, you'd have to give up this model of your life.
John: Yep. And I'd have to give up my reasoning of how to achieve.
Bill: Yeah. And you've got this 1962 road map of the world—and then you had this experience that you have to throw away, you have to delete it, because it doesn't fit the map. So something's got to go. Either the authentic, real experience has to go, or the old road map of life has to go.
John: Yeah, I know.
Bill: You continually choose to delete authentic experiences in service of the old map.

John: I believe you believe that.

Bill: I know I'm right.

John: I don't know that you are. I'm beginning to doubt what the right way to go is, because I feel good when I achieve, and I feel like shit when I just feel. And isn't the whole point of life to feel good? I mean, ultimately.

Therapist: As you describe those achievement experiences, there has always been a somewhat hollow feeling about them. They don't really do it.

John: Yeah, like my athletic success in the east or my academic success at Washington. They were just a start and I gave them up.

Therapist: And, you have always given them up, because they don't fill the bill; they don't do it.

John: I guess. But I have the choice that I have to make now and it would call for a total commitment, one way or the other. And I guess I still need to have less doubt that you guys are right about this. Let me share with you, though, the way I feel about people in this group, is that I almost feel like you don't have a right to tell me what's going to happen to me, because you've all already worked your butt off and achieved something. But I haven't yet and you're telling me I shouldn't, because it's not the way to go.

Jeff: We're not telling you you shouldn't achieve, we're telling you, don't expect that it's going to give you what you really want.

Martin: Just don't sell your soul for achievement.

Therapist: No, achievement is fine, fine, but it's just frosting on the cake. I get to live in this wonderful house, I get to drive a nice car, I get to buy new records and books when I like. It's fun, I like it. It doesn't make me feel loved, it doesn't make me love myself, it doesn't make me happy. It's just frosting or it is better than nothing.

Bill: It's money. I get to live in a really nice house, too. I go on a nice vacation. If I want to get something, it's more likely that I can buy it, so there's a lot of things that can happen with having money. I get to make a lot of money doing something I like. You know? And there's really nice stuff connected with achieving, because in a lot of ways it can get a person in phase with something that they really want in a very high-level, successful way, and it's great. But, it's not core stuff.

Martin: (sarcastically) Go on and be even better at achieving until it's all you've got and then get back to me.

John: What?

Jeff: All Martin does is achieve.

Martin: I don't have a fancy car, I don't even live in the house I own; I sleep there. I work all the time. I don't enjoy anything. I wouldn't wish that on you. (tears up)

Jeff: Yeah. If you take Martin's route, you take the whole package.

John: Well, I feel jealous of you, Martin. I was talking to you on the phone the other day, telling you about a job that I was thinking about taking, and you were telling me that you worked in a warehouse while you were in a graduate school, worked your way up to foreman after being just a person who unloaded boxcars, and they wanted you to be the manager of the whole fucking warehouse after you graduated. And I was feeling god damn jealous. And I was thinking, I'm going to do that same thing, you know? And, it just flashed in front of me, it was like, I've got something to shoot for.

Jeff: Oh god, now if you don't get invited to be manager of the whole warehouse, then you will have failed. He's just presented you with a new standard. And if you do everything, if you do all that stuff, and then right at the end, when the guy's just about to ask you if you want to be manager of the warehouse, he says, "Well, we're going to hire Joe Smith," you're a failure!

John: But I want that. I want respect.

Jeff: You're trying to prove something, and it doesn't work. Look at Martin.

John: I respect Martin a lot. I know he's struggling. But, see, I respect him, I can see myself being in his position when I'm that age, having people respect me, and somehow that feels good to me.

Therapist: It would be better than nothing.

John: Yeah, I think it'd be great.

Jeff: Listen, you're not getting what he's telling you. (Martin crying quietly) If you take Martin, you get the whole package, and that's a whole lot of emptiness and pain.

John: Believe me, I know what he's saying. I don't think you're listening to me. What's more important to me than feeling the love is getting the respect, achieving. I understand what you're saying.

Jeff: And I'm saying you're wrong.

John: That's the part I don't believe. I don't know it yet.

Bill: John, that's what I said about 10 minutes ago. And I don't want to get patronizing, but I think you need to get there.

John: I know.

Bill: And my wish for you is that you have that disillusionment as soon as possible. I want you to become disillusioned. I want your heart to break as you recognize, here I have made a million dollars, I own every railroad in the United States, and it doesn't work.

Martin: (crying) I've done it. Look at what it got me. No one loves me for what I've done. No one cares about me for that. I want out.

John: I just keep on thinking that no one will know how happy I am if I don't achieve.

Martin: If you are happy, it doesn't matter who knows.

Martin's input in this interchange went far beyond what may be apparent in this transcript. In many ways, John and Martin were twins in their psychological makeup, and Martin had lived out the kind of self-sacrifice and achievement to which John aspired. Martin's empathic understanding of John had been demonstrated within the group countless times before, and his authority with John was further enhanced by his tears. Martin had just come through a period, both inside and outside the group context, of working through severe early child abuse. As this was completed, he was finally able to begin letting go of a successful but very self-denying career. I believe that Martin's hearing his own internal dialogue given so clearly here by John significantly contributed to his final letting-go of these patterns. Martin's heart had been broken and John's struggle provided him with a still necessary reminder of that, enabling him to be more fully released. If he couldn't save John, he could at least save himself. And Martin's saving himself became an example for John, more important than anything he ever could have said.

Later in the session, John was struggling with the decision of trusting the course that the entire group was advocating for him versus staying with the old road map that Bill had described to him earlier. We pick up the dialogue here:

John: If I go your way, I'll have to trust something that I never believed in and achieve for a different reason. I don't think achieving's wrong.

Therapist: Is there some way we can help you in connection with what you just said?

John: You can tell me where a great woman exists who will tell me that it's okay to feel that way, and will not be some scatterbrain who goes back and forth, someone who will say I went through this shit, I know it's real.

Larry: Does she have to be single and available to you, or just someone to talk to?

John: I don't know.

Larry: I can deliver one.

John: It'd take me a while, because I'd want to examine this person very carefully. Yeah. It's very hard for me to believe that there are women like that out there. This really gets to a good point, because if there are women out there like that, it would take away some of my incentive to achieve, if you know what I mean. Martin, are you with me?

Martin: Damn right.

John: Because my mother was very achievement-oriented, you know—and I would like to believe there is something different. I don't. But what wouldn't be fair is that this person would almost have to be perfect.

Therpist: But then you have to struggle with that. And—that's a lot of what you're struggling with, is *perfect.*

John: I can accept imperfection in a man. I can't in women.

Therapist: Well, then you won't ever be happy with a woman.

Bill: I'm not so sure. Because that sounds like some of my stuff—I mean, this is my great wish and working theory—as the relationship becomes more and more real, I become more real, she becomes more real, then all the perfection stuff begins to dissolve. You know what I mean, and then she doesn't have to be perfect and you don't have to be perfect.

Therapist: That's my theory, too.

John: I don't want to be Hank Reardon, I'll tell you that much.

Therapist: Well then, Albert Einstein, Arnold Schwarzenegger—take your pick.

John: No, no. There's a specific reason. You know who Hank Reardon is?

Larry: Oh, yes!

John: I didn't say it for nothing. I don't want to be Hank Reardon. All he wants to do is produce. He doesn't even want a woman. His woman is production. I don't want to be Hank Reardon.

Therapist: Now there's a start! (group laughter)

Here John has acknowledged again that what he really wants is the love and understanding of a woman, though both the woman and the love she gives must be perfect. He is again confronted on this and given hope by a group member, Bill, who alludes to the process by which his perfectionism in relationships is dissolving. In saying he doesn't want to be Hank Reardon, John lets down, joins the group, and acknowledges that they have had an impact on him. Later, Martin shares the extreme difficulties he's having with a work situation that could conservatively be described as "crazy" and gets a good deal of support from the group for his efforts to detach himself from it. As the group ends, John says, "As I came in here tonight, I was thinking of leaving. Now I feel you guys are too wonderful to leave."

INDIVIDUAL THERAPY: PART I

A good deal of the next individual session was devoted to continued uncovering and working-through of feelings associated with John's mother and women in general. The first part of the session, however, was devoted to working-through the resistance and distrust that John had about revealing those feelings to me. He said he was afraid that I might humiliate him with the knowledge or that in some way I would use it against him. He said that he felt this way around most men and, additionally, had the sense that he would lose them once he revealed these vulnerabilities concerning women. As he explored this, he discovered that the loss of other men would result from his unwillingness to see them again once they were aware of his great vulnerability.

I asked John to explore his own judgments of himself concerning his feelings about women. In response to this, he said, "I'm overly hurt. I'm difficult to deal with. If I were seeing me, I'd say, 'Here is a person who has an overabundance of pain with women.' I wouldn't know what to do with me. I'd want to send me away." Obviously, John was projecting his own judgments of himself onto others and I gave this interpretation. I reassured him that many men have an overabundance of hurt and pain where women are concerned and that I had helped a number of men with that problem.

At this point, John confessed that he had continually used his issues with his former girl friend to test out if I was a safe enough person to trust with these vulnerable issues. He felt that I withdrew from him as soon as he mentioned her name and took that as a sign that I could not be trusted with this level of information and feeling. I explored with him what I knew to be my reactions to his discussion of his former girl friend. I recalled that on many occasions he would analyze her and her motivations and that I would frequently try to bring him back to his own feelings and motivations, seeing such analysis of her as a real waste of his therapeutic time. On several occasions, we had talked about John's seeking out his former girl friend and I recalled on those occasions feeling apprehensive for the hurt I knew he would experience in doing this. Finally, John's paranoia about the relationship between myself and his former girl friend might have caused a change in my behavior as I struggled with how to respond to him when he brought this up. In each of these cases, there may have been a change in my behavior, but I was able to assure him that I was not afraid to deal with this issue, nor did I feel withdrawn from it. As we explored this, he also indicated that he felt the same kind of a change in the other men in the group when he discussed his former girl friend, which, of course, he often did.

After this admission to and working-through of resistance and distrust involving both interpretation and my careful presentation of the reality as I saw it, we could move on to exploring his vulnerable feelings with women. On this occasion, he was more willing to explore his feelings about his mother, but was still reluctant to discuss his feelings about his former girl friend or other women who might be in his life.

This is one of many examples of the dual use of interpretation and therapist self-exploration and disclosure which I find is therapeutic where there is therapist-client conflict. The patient needs a real object in the therapist who has human motives, reactions, propensities to err, etc. The communication of the therapist's process models intimacy, enhances client trust, and often opens the client to transference interpretations, which are then less likely to be experienced as put-downs from a superior source.

As John discussed the feelings of being treated like a doll by his mother, and as he related some bizarre stories concerning how she treated him as a child, he confessed again that it was so very difficult for him to feel and talk about these things simultaneously. In response to this, I encouraged him to simply feel and assured him that that is what I wanted and that I would like to simply be with him while he did this. In response to this, John said, "I don't believe you at all when you say that. No way. You're being nice to me—I mean out-and-out blatant lying. I don't even ask the question why you are lying, I just know you are lying. To me, to be allowed to feel means to be accepted. To me that's an impossibility that I wish I had. And that to me is extremely sad." John went on to tell me how he was criticized for all of his feelings as a child; in particular, his childlike happiness was ridiculed by both his parents and his older brothers.

John kept saying in this session that he wouldn't believe it if I were simply there for him and I kept asking him how it would be for him if he did believe it. In response to this question, he finally confessed that he would then experience even more pain for all the times that he wanted this kind of contact and support but failed to receive it. I offered him the interpretation that it was this that was stopping him from dealing with these issues. Just as in the group context, he was caught between feeling dissatisfied with the support which was never enough on the one hand and feeling even worse after he had received the support for which he longed only to have to return home alone.

In response to this defense interpretation, John began to get more deeply into his feelings, but just as he did, he began to criticize his fellow students, who could not feel as deeply, and judged me as a college professor who wanted him to go too fast, etc. Again, I made the defense interpretation that he used the criticism and judgment of others to move away from his own experience of painful feelings. John accepted that interpretation and said, "It's really me who doesn't think that it's okay to feel." At this point in the session, he began to cry and to discuss his desperate need for love. He said, "I would be with any woman who comes along who would give me compassion. I opened up to Brit (his former girl friend), and she left me. She betrayed me. She said, 'Believe me, I'm here for you' just like you say that to me. I believed her and then she left." At this point, John felt a good deal of the anger toward Brit and then toward his mother.

John then discussed the guilt he felt for being so angry with his mother and I actively gave permission for and normalized this anger. I told him, "You have a normal dislike for a mother who was bad to you. You are normal in that reaction. You deserve to be angry and you deserve to get what you want." In discussing his guilt, John said, "I don't deserve to have what I like, so I'm not allowed to have it. I wasn't good. I didn't live up to expectations."

John spent the remainder of the session discussing his beloved uncle, who was the one person in his family whom he really respected and by whom he felt really loved. I simply listened to a good deal of this, although I took every opportunity to suggest in various ways the internalization of this strong and benevolent figure. I suggested to John that if his uncle were around and could talk to him, he would tell him, "You have a right to be angry with someone who has hurt you. You have a right to be happy with someone who loves you, who's beautiful to you, and who has compassion for you." I also suggested to John that as he could use the strength that his uncle would want to give him, he could begin to see himself as trustworthy and deserving and therefore to experience others as trustworthy too.

At this point in the session, John cried quite heavily and said that he felt that he'd let down his uncle, who could look down on him and see how imperfect he was. John said, "I felt from the time I let him down that I couldn't call on him. I miss so much not being loved. That pain has gotten in my way so much of my life. The pain of not being loved is so great that I couldn't control it or my life." Again I reassured John of his deserving love, deserving the support of his uncle, and indirectly again suggested the internalization of this positive figure. I then gave a rap on emotional control. Since I think is of some general utility, I reproduce it for you here.

John: I still don't really understand what it means to have control over your life.

Therapist: What it means to me, John, is that you work through enough of this early pain and you change the decision, "I'll never deserve to get what I want" to "this is what happened and I'll never reclaim it, but there is life and love and success—what I want—out there, and I'm going to get it."

John: I'm not sure what it means anymore, and I don't have . . . pictures of a life I control.

Therapist: See, it's these feelings that cause you to have so little control, and it's the attempt to control the feelings which gives you even less control. The thing that needs to happen—the thing that is happening—is that you're getting those feelings out and learning that they're there, and that you *don't* have control over them, you *can't* control them. But you can release them and by releasing them, tame them or reduce them so that they don't control you. And when they don't. . . . The less they control you, the more control you have to live your life in a rational way. (pause) And some of those feelings, you know, may persist for quite a while; but, if you're not trying to control them, if you can just . . . if you can let them just pass through you, they just pass through and leave you in control of your life.

John: I believe you.

THE INDIVIDUAL IN GROUP: PART II

At the next group session, John continued on the themes developed in the individual session.

John: The feelings that I want to deal with, which are the ones I talked about last time in individual session, where you asked me to feel and think about my anger towards—my mother. I let her off the hook because she was so weak. But what I began feeling was just very very sad, that my mother never really loved me, that she was always leaving me, and, I was there—to give her love, because she needed love. And I'm beginning to see why I panic so much when I fall in love with another woman. And why that woman becomes my mother. And so I'm beginning to feel the pain associated with my mother. I really had it blocked out well for a long time. And I guess that's because there was a lot of pain there, you know, and I was just thinking about that. I was trying to wrap up a whole bunch of things about what we've been working on. And actually, it's very emotional for me. I get kind of confused in this situation because for me to talk would mean not to feel. For me to feel would mean, you know.

Therapist: Well, maybe you need to take a few moments of silence and work into it.

John: Yes, I'll work into it. (pause) God, I'm losing my train of thought.

Therapist: Let me suggest you just breathe a little and feel and then, be silent for a little longer, and then start talking.

John: Yeah.

Therapist: Shift gears.

(pause)

John: All right, now I remember what I was going to say. Um. This therapeutic process, for me, has seemed to have drawn me out in the open, what you, Larry, were talking about tonight. Um, it's really brought me out in the open. So now, I get terribly frightened about people seeing me, you know, about me being who I really am into what I think is growing up, out of it, to become who I can be. But the process of allowing myself to grow up through it is very frightening to me, because I think it would be very lonely for me, and I don't want to experience that loneliness again.

Therapist: It doesn't have to be lonely.

John: Yeah. And so, I am now noticing I am becoming in touch with my feelings more. Remember last week, when I said to you again, "You don't know me," and you said to me, "I think I really do know you. I don't think you know yourself"?

Therapist: Yes, that was about your being worthy of being forgiven, of deserving to get what you wanted.

John: I'm not sure exactly what it was about, but I looked at that all from different angles. And, there's a lot of truth in that, because I've been trying to hide from who I am. Been trying to deny it, deny my pain because if I don't feel pain, then I'm fine. But if I feel this pain there's something wrong and I have to work. And my pain is very expressive on my face, I can see it. Others can see it when I feel it, and I didn't understand that. I didn't know what was going on, I just thought, this guy (the therapist) is making me crazy, you know. Having all these weird physical reactions. But I looked at it, and this past week things came together a bit. And I saw every time that I started feeling this way

I was feeling a great deal of pain, and there was something inside me that was just extremely hurt. And it was all coming to the surface. And I noticed this because when I get tired it comes out faster, and more readily. When I'm strong, I can subdue it. But, I guess what I wanted to do here tonight was to cry—it was to cry when I first came here, to get this out. But I don't think I'm in that frame of mind right now.

Therapist: Let it be what it is, right now—you're great.

John: It's taking the machine out of me. I thought it was neat because I finally was able to see that what's happening is I'm coming to the surface.

Therapist: Yes, you're right. And there's a diamond underneath that hurt, just like with Bill. And some of what you show us, John, is just beautiful.

John: Right, but—all that's not that important to me somehow. It's not important to me that I'm beautiful underneath there, as it is important to me, as I'm finding out *what* is underneath there. And what this is telling me is that I can have control over my life. I don't have to be ruled by my moodiness, because if this comes out, and I know who I am, then I can operate with that.

Therapist: Right.

Martin: Right.

Jeff: It's great.

Larry: Right, Jesus.

John: And so, that was making me feel good. I was feeling the pain, but actually it was a cure kind of pain, it wasn't this muddled kind of stuff. I knew what to do with it, I could see more clearly. I still have a lot of confusion about certain things. Like I think I want to work more because I want people to want me. I want them to hire me, to want me. Actually, when I get there, I don't really want to work, you know, at that kind of job. I just want them to want me. And so there's this one gal that keeps on calling me, offering me these different jobs, and I keep on turning them down. I have a valid excuse, and I say, I have a class at this time, but I just—it's great. I just want her to call me, you know.

Therapist: You want to be wanted.

John: Right, but it's kind of a sick wanting, that was the point; it's not a good kind of wanting. It brings me in touch with why I want it so much.

Therapist: But, by getting that kind, maybe you'll get a clearer picture.

John: I do, yeah.

Therapist: Yeah. And it puts you in touch with why you wanted it and that's real painful. And that is what you have to get through to feel better.

And you are going through it and you are getting better. And I know it's hard, and I admire you for doing it.

John: Yeah. And that just brings to light the fact that I don't want to do it, most of the time. I'm very scared.

Therapist: Of course. Who wouldn't be?

John: I went out climbing on these miniature rocks earlier—whatever you want to call them,

Bill: Cliffettes.

John: Cliffettes—with Bill on Sunday. And I was thinking, when I first got there, these guys are crazy, you know, I walked up to the top of this rock and I wouldn't even go near the edge. I was terribly afraid.

Bill: I thought that was real wise.

John: And then when I climbed it once—I mean, it took me a whole long time, but I kept looking back down, and I was growing less and less afraid, you know, it was like—I can do it. And I was thinking, why was I so afraid? It brings me in touch with my family when I was young. Because I'm not good enough, you know, I'm not—there's a thousand reasons why I'm not good enough. I was not good enough, you know? And I was supposed to be competing with my brothers who were eight and seven years older than I was. And I was never good enough. I couldn't give Mom enough love. I was never good enough. And so I became afraid of doing things that I possibly could do because I was afraid of being told that I wasn't good enough. And so, when I was climbing this cliff, or whatever you want to call it, I'd sprint up a little bit, then stop. And it was like something inside me was telling me I wasn't good enough, but then—I'd make little spurts all the way up, I wouldn't just keep on going, and I was thinking to myself if I can make spurts, why the fuck can't I just keep on going straight up?

Therapist: You will.

Bill: He did.

Therapist: He did? All right!

Bill: Wonderful little metaphor there.

John: You know. The climbing that day wore me out, emotionally more than physically. And I didn't believe Bill would be there on the safety rope, to catch me, you know. There's just this fear in my mind of that.

Bill: I was there.

John: No, I know you were there, but it took me a while to believe that. Just being put in that kind of situation forced things to come out more.

Therapist: Yeah. It's a great metaphor for your whole life. Doing what you're afraid of, feeling your feelings, trusting someone to be on the rope.

John: Yeah, and you know, I really don't know what to do with the feelings now. I just know that I have them, and that, for me, is a step. And I'm pleased with that step.

Jeff: Yeah.

Larry: Me too, buddy, me too.

John: I am, but it's got me to wondering, why wasn't I the good person? And that makes me want to cry out, "Why wasn't I? What did I do to become a bad person?"

Therapist: Nothing.

John: And, so it didn't make sense to me to go out and work as much as you work, Martin, to prove that I was good, because why wasn't I good to begin with? And it was like, I was telling them that they were right, and I never believed it, but I couldn't figure out why they told me that I was bad. And so I would just sit there for, you know, years, trying to think my way through it. Well, why was I bad?

Therapist: Right, John. Just feel that question, "Why was I bad? What did I do?" Don't try to answer it in your head, feel the question. Breathe and feel it. . . .

(several minutes later)

Martin: It must have been four or five years ago for me when finally I just—I can't think of the words—I just hit this ultimate anguish. I think the question that came to my mind was just, "Why didn't they love me?" . . . I was just stuck with that thought for about six hours. You know, at that moment I cried. You know, I'd never cried in my adult life before that. So that's what that was all about, you know. I mean, it just took years to get to a point where that could happen. And then I felt really crazy.

Therapist: Just like you were crazy when you went through the child abuse stuff. You were on the edge; it was hell; it was like going through hell. We were all in on it but you've been much much better ever since. It is hell. You have to go through it and you get better on the other side. I've seen it again and again. And you guys (John and Martin) have been tremendous. The reason it's so hard, Martin, is your hell is pretty deep, and it takes time, but I swear to God, you have gotten better for it.

Martin: I've come through some bad times, but I can see it all now. I understand and I've relaxed. For the first time in my life, I'm waking up relaxed a lot of the time. Now I really want you to stick with it.

John: So do I, but I have fear—every time—every single time that I come into this group or come to see you, Steve, I try to read how you're feeling so that I'm allowed to feel. And the bad thing about it is I'm perceptive enough to see if you're having a good or a bad day. If you're having a bad day, it's like, no way am I coming out. I'll just talk to you for the rest of the session, but I usually start getting into a conflict with you at those times. Because I think I'm mad at you.

Therapist: For not having a good day, for not being totally there for you?

John: Yeah. It's almost like. Well, I can't explain it. It's just—you know, I wish I didn't do it, I wish I could just see past that, and, um, that's where my distrust comes from, that's where my—whatever you want to call it, my skepticism is that I look at people very carefully to see how they're feeling. And if I see something's going on inside them I get scared of them, so I'm not going to do anything, I'm not going to, you know, come out.

Therapist: You also know this, John, but it's part of my job to say it. It's that all or nothing thinking again; I'll be there for you completely and that'll be too much, or I won't be there for you at all and that'll be terrible. That's just arrested child thinking like Larry's thinking was earlier. And it's that child thinking that has to grow up, and that takes some time. It takes repetition of this over and over and over again.

John: Well, what I'm afraid of at those times is that, uh, if I come out, and you aren't there—if I feel you're not there, supporting me at those times, I'll die, because I'm not strong enough to support myself at those times.

Therapist: That also though, John, is a feeling which isn't necessarily true.

John: Uh-huh. It sure feels true.

Therapist: Fear feels true, I know it does. It feels true, but it's not necessarily true. You are stronger than you feel. And you will not die. You are an adult, not a child. I mean, that's how it feels for a child, and in a sense it's true; if the parent isn't there to take care of a child, he will die. And so your feelings are stopped at that point, so you still feel, if I'm not there you'll die. It feels that way, but that's not how it is because you're not a baby.

INDIVIDUAL THERAPY: PART II

The next two individual sessions needed to be rescheduled due to my travel requirements and, due to the tightness of John's schedule, were reduced from one-and-one-half-hour sessions to one-hour sessions early in the morning. He was quite late for the first session due to oversleeping, and both of these sessions were relatively superficial compared with what you've been reading about as well as most sessions in his overall psychotherapy. The highlight of the very next session involved a discussion of John's underlying, often preconscious, belief that his former girl friend was the only one who could fill the bill for him. I interpreted this notion, and John readily accepted the interpretation, as another childlike idea. When one is a child and attached to one's mother, she is the only one for the child. When the attachment is reproduced in adult love, and particularly where there is an early arrest, this same absolutistic, childlike thinking tends to be reproduced.

In this same session, however, John also dealt with his fears of being overwhelmed by all the feelings that were coming out in psychotherapy. He discussed the option of quitting therapy in this session because, once again, when he deeply felt himself, all he could feel was the all-encompassing need for love. He said, "When I want that love, I want it from you. And yet I realize you are a stranger. I'm entirely open then, and can be hurt, and I became very frightened of being hurt." He continued to nurture the fantasy of quitting therapy until he could become successful, whereupon he would reenter it and face the feelings that disrupted his ability to perform. While supporting the reality of the disruptive effects of psychotherapy, I continued to encourage him to continue participation both in group and individual work. Later that day, John called to cancel his participation in the group session that evening.

In the next therapy session, John was even more guarded and the session more superficial. He indicated that he planned to drop out of the group therapy program for an indefinite period, due once again to the disruptive effects of that kind of contact. He had some other superficial excuses, which I gently confronted. The positive side of this otherwise unfortunate decision was in his statement, "I have to make my own decision on this." I indicated that I supported that element of his process very, very much. I told him that I needed to make my stand clear on the issue, but that I recognized it was his decision and that I was glad that he saw it that way. Later in the day, he called to indicate he wanted to cancel future individual sessions as well. The next day he called again to ask for reassurance. He was afraid that I would retaliate against him for his decision to drop therapy, that I did not understand his reasons, etc. I gave him the reassurance that he asked for, told him I was glad he was making his own decision, and welcomed him to return to both individual and group work. I announced the decision of his terminating group work that evening and understand that he subsequently had outside contact with several of the group members, who essentially gave him the same message that I had given. That is, they recommended his return to the group, welcomed him, but assured him that the decision was his and that their relationship with him would not suffer as a result of whatever decision he made.

After missing two weeks of group sessions and one individual session, John called me to reschedule an individual session. In his first session after this final round trip, John said that he felt good about returning to individual work because he decided he needed it for himself. Prior to this time, he said, he had engaged in therapy as a duty. It was something he should do, perhaps even something he should do for his parents to be the perfect son they needed. From this time on, he related to the therapeutic process as something that he chose rather than something that was imposed upon him out of duty.

This first session was, however, still somewhat more superficial than many others. He was a bit wary of being humiliated in his return to individual therapy, but particularly so concerned relative to the group. I reassured him that he would be welcomed back and likened his departure and return to such a potential departure and return on the part of Martin, whom he respected very much. I suggested that he would very much welcome Martin back, had he made a similar decision, and probably not think less of him but be relieved at his return. I suggested to John that the other members of the group would feel this way about him. He left this session considering the possibility of coming back to group, but again reserved that decision for himself. He did return to the group that very evening and was enthusiastically welcomed back. He talked some about his decision to return, but was still a bit wary in this first session. He was encouraged by the group members' supporting him for making his own decision.

After these initial sessions in both individual and group, the change in John was truly dramatic. He evidenced a new calm and, for him, remarkable nondefensiveness in most subsequent therapy sessions. According to him, this was very much due to the fact that *he* had made the decision to return to therapy and no longer thought of it as an obligation but regarded it as a choice to do something that was good for him. In addition, as he talked, it became clear that his sense of humiliation over the kinds of extreme emotional reactions to which he was prone had dramatically dissipated. He no longer experienced it as a narcissistic injury to feel emotions which he acknowledged to be excessive or immature in the company of myself or the men in the group.

You have seen the degree to which John can be self-disclosing and admit very honestly and openly to dysphoric feelings and irrational ideas. But, subsequent to his final return to therapy, this capacity was much greater and much less defensive. He began to chuckle at himself as he would confess to various quirks in his personality. For example, during the second individual session after returning to therapy, he confessed with a chuckle how he was discovering that it was necessary for him to be Number 1 in any group situation. He'd become very angry at a person in a work group who had assumed that Number 1 position and had begun to attack this person for his arrogance, perfectionism, etc. He then saw that he was doing this, decided to change his behavior, and had a long, self-disclosing, and very productive session with this person with whom he originally had experienced such extreme rivalry.

During this same session he confessed how it was necessary for him to get all A-plusses in his school work without working. He said every situation that was less than this was an indictment of his okayness. He said he remembered many times having the reaction, "How dare you tell me I need to study more" whenever he would get anything less than an A-plus. Further, he confessed that in the past he had worked to build his grade point average to perfection or build his body to a satisfactory level and then would irrationally conclude that, having done this, he could stop studying or working on his body. All of this confessional was presented in a very uncharacteristically humorous mode, with a remarkable degree of detachment from these undesirable qualities to which he was admitting.

Similarly, he acknowledged during this session that he had been fighting to prevent intimacy much of his life, recently with me and the members of the group. He said, "I decided to no longer fight intimacy." He cried during this session at the losses of so many people over so many years due to his projection of disapproval, his rivalry, his perfectionism for himself and others, and so on.

In this session I, of course, gave John a great deal of support for what he was doing. In response to his bringing up his anxiety and embarrassment at social situations in which some intimacy was exchanged, I suggested that he would probably now be experiencing deeper and deeper levels of such intimacy, joy, and love. I likened this work to desensitization, in which higher and higher doses of such positive experiences would be coming his way and he would be developing an increased tolerance for them. At this point, John spontaneously recalled that before the age of eight, he was a very social boy who was relaxed with other people. I suggested that he access that state of mind whenever he went into a social situation and foreshadowed our use of more direct procedures (resource accessing) for this purpose. I correctly anticipated that, with this profound shift in attitude, he would be much more amenable to those active therapeutic techniques which had heretofore been too much for him.

While there is much more work for this young man to do, his work with me has been one of the most reinforcing in that he developed from a more or less borderline narcissistic character to a person manifesting more and more the narcissistic style. Contemporary with that shift, he became more and more able to be aware of his transference reactions as such and to be amenable to more active therapeutic procedures. Much of the early work involved the analysis and working-through of the negative transference, whereas work after the shift could involve other kinds of processes and procedures. Not long after the "breakthrough" reported here, John, not surprisingly, reverted to a defensive, closed stance in group, followed by a very painful individual session in which deeper levels of archaic needs and affects were experienced. Yet, he never returned to the pattern of leaving therapy while working with me and his transference reactions continued to be acknowledged as such, remarkably easing the therapeutic task.

COMMENTARY

Both Martin and John had to repeatedly access and work through what is the essential narcissistic issue presented by both of them at the end of the last group transcript: "Why was I so bad? Why didn't they love me?" As I said then, this is not so much a question to be answered as it is a feeling to be experienced, a feeling of disbelief, of grief, of loss. The answer to the question will ultimately be helpful. To come to an understanding of one's parents' or caretakers' human inability to really love will be healing. But, prior to that must be the working-through of the affective experience represented by the question. The ultimate affective resolution of this issue is: "I am not bad. I am good." Martin and John are both still working on this issue but both of them have made considerable headway on it, Martin after five years of therapy and John after only a year and a half. Once the narcissistic person knows he is good, he no longer has to prove it. He is enough, and he is free to simply declare that.

John's case, like that of his "twin" Martin, provides an excellent demonstration of the success that can be realized in the "hard work miracle" of working-through nearly intolerable levels of psychic pain. In this process, John became aware of these feelings, aware of their original sources in his family, and finally got that their experience was curative. He learned, albeit the hard way, to trust his feelings, to trust the therapeutic process, and to trust others (someone would be "on the rope" for him at last). With him, as with Martin, the therapeutic process was touch and go, and there was repeatedly the possibility that we would lose him. In both these cases, the negative affects were so overwhelming that they repeatedly tested the limits of the patients' ego resources. This was remedied, but only in part, by a consistent effort, in group and individual therapy, to offer supportive and ego-building interventions. While we made it in both cases, I was uncomfortably on the edge of my seat on a number of occasions and continue to be open to the possibility that this work can be less of a roller-coaster ride. At this point, however, it seems to me that work with narcissists who have borderline features is going to be a bit hairy given the state of our art. This may always be so.

In spite of the discomfort encountered during certain parts of the ride, however, the eventual results are incredibly rewarding. To see individuals like John and Martin really join the human community and feel its warmth and be nurtured by it is well worth the price of admission. We lose some of these guys, not only from therapy but from life itself. But we gain some too. And they are precious.

CHAPTER VII

THE INTEGRATION OF GROUP AND INDIVIDUAL THERAPY: *THE NARCISSISTIC STYLE*

A transformed individual is one who can tell the truth. A transformed environment is one in which the truth can be told.

—Werner Erhard

In the last chapter, we followed the development of self in a young man who initially exhibited a narcissistic character disorder through a seminal period in his therapy. By the end of this work, his attitudes, behaviors, and affective containment abilities were becoming more characteristic of the narcissistic style. In this chapter, we will further explore the interaction of group and individual treatment in the final stages of work with Larry, a professional man in his late thirties who exemplified the narcissistic style from the outset. Larry was first introduced in Chapter V, when some of his earlier work was reported.

The group and individual material to be presented occurred roughly over the same time span as that just reviewed for John. Both these men were in the same group and, in the two-month period covered by these transcripts, their stories unfolded in a parallel fashion. In the very same group meeting that began Chapter VI, in which John so poignantly outlined his difficulties to be worked through in the next several sessions, Larry was enjoying an exhilarating period of self-discovery. He tried to be helpful to John in that group session, but other than that was relatively inactive. As the session came to an end, however, Bill broke into the closure process and confessed that he'd been holding something back about Larry, which he felt obliged to say. He then said that, of all the members of the group, he knew Larry the least. He accused Larry of hiding out in the group and said he really had little sense of Larry as a person.

As this dialogue developed, I asked the men in the group to give Larry some feedback relative to this issue. George* told Larry that he, too, knew him less well than other members of the group and questioned why he, Larry, was there. Martin said he felt he knew Larry pretty well, recognized times when Larry was putting up his front, but felt that while that hampered Larry a bit, it wasn't a major difficulty. Jeff, however, confronted Larry with the fact that he felt Larry had been patronizing to John that evening and that Larry's smooth façade often made it difficult to really understand who he was. This was a difficult confrontation for Jeff to deliver and he confessed that he had withheld his feedback on some previous occasions. John also acknowledged that he had experienced Larry as somewhat overpolished at times, but did not find this to be a particular problem. He acknowledged that Larry had worked on this problem before and that he knew why Larry was in the group.

Though this kind of feedback had been given to Larry on prior occasions and this issue had been the primary focus of his work in the group, he took all the feedback particularly hard this time. He became overwhelmed, cried, and felt very hopeless. His reaction went well beyond what would have been expected given his history in the group and the nature of the feedback which had been given before and which was given very caringly on this occasion. Bill and Jeff both had to stretch themselves considerably to deliver these messages and seemed to be clearly doing so with Larry's best interests at heart. His relatively catastrophic response signaled an overdetermined reaction. Together with giving him some reassurance at that time, I asked that he look at what else he might be reacting to.

It was clear at the time that part of Larry's distress had to do with the fact that he felt he was being particularly genuine during this group session. Indeed, he was experiencing unusual expansiveness prior to this confrontation and was shocked that the group would see him as phony when he himself felt so real. In the reassurance I gave

*George was absent for many of these sessions due to vacations and was relatively inactive when present during this period.

Larry, I recalled a former group meeting in which Bill had told the group about a poignant experience he had had with his two nephews. At that time, the group had been similarly disaffected by the somewhat affected way in which Bill reported this incident. At that time, I had given reassurance to Bill by telling him that, in his individual session, he had reported the same incident to me in a way that was far more genuine, current, and real.

I offered the interpretation that Larry's behavior on this occasion was like that of Bill on the earlier occasion. Both men had the propensity to take feelings which were originally genuine and "coat" them for others so that they appeared phony. I recalled for them that they'd both caught each other in the act of doing this on prior occasions and, because of their similarity in character, were more exquisitely attuned to this in each other. Finally, I recommended to Larry that he look inside himself to determine, in the final analysis, whether he was being genuine or not at this and other times. I emphasized that the feedback could be useful to him in any number of ways but that ultimately he was the one who had to decide on the validity of the feedback and on the nature of his response to it.

INDIVIDUAL THERAPY: PART I

Nearly one week later, Larry came in for his individual session and began by working on discovering the factors underlying the powerful overreaction he had experienced in the group.

Larry: I've spent most of the week thinking about what happened at the last group session. And I want to save most of this for the group, but the part that I thought I would like you to help me with is this. You suggested, you said, "Larry, why don't you think about why you're reacting so strongly?" The suggestion was, I think, that my reaction to what they were saying was pretty strong, and you said, "Why don't you think about why that is?"

Therapist: Right.

Larry: And so, that's kind of what I'd like to start with. I agree. I think that that's useful, if I can get to that.

Therapist: Sure (pause).

Larry: Okay. I felt like the bottom fell out, and, well, I felt like I let the bottom fall out, in a certain kind of way. But what happened to me was that when Bill made his little opening, I sort of sat there and experienced it, and this thing came in, and I found myself feeling just awful.

Feeling like, oh boy, this is terribly embarrassing; I don't want to get into it. And then I found myself just sort of saying, "No, it's okay." Just opening to the feelings, saying to myself, "I know you don't like them, I know you wish you weren't crying. I know you wish a whole bunch of stuff, but just go do it. So I did. And with almost no hesitation at the threshold, I just sort of went right into my feelings. I felt pretty good about that, that I had let them pull me into it and that I didn't spend much time fighting it. I went with it thoroughly and quickly. And—so what is in those feelings is what I want to try to get to. One thing is that there was a sort of horror to it. Bill did his thing, said his piece, and George, and Jeff jumped on my back for what he perceived to be my patting people on the head. And—it just seemed completely wrong to me. It wasn't how I perceived myself; it wasn't how I felt I was being and so part of what hit me was this horrible realization that if they were right, then in fact I was going to lose them. And that's what it was like when my partner in the lab, Karen, said, "The team wishes you could come be with us." And I knew then, "I'm out. It's over." I knew. It was just the moment at which Karen expressed to me where the rest of the group was, vis-à-vis me.

Therapist: You were out.

Larry: That clearly got it to me—it's over. And that was sort of a special moment, because even though the room was spinning around me and I felt I was, you know, in a real bad spot, that realization came to me with a kind of cool breeze.

Therapist: And it felt good?

Larry: A little bit, like it came out without a trembling, without me feeling so terrified by it. I was just with it, just feeling it.

Therapist: Right. I know.

Larry: And although my having to leave the lab was many miles down the road, and in fact five months later, it was true. And it was the critical juncture, and I understood it as such. So now I'm back to what Bill said. Bill said a thing which I interpreted to be basically, Larry, you know yourself so poorly, so little, that you have no clue. It is not that you are lying to yourself about what is inside of you.

Therapist: You're just totally out of touch.

Larry: Right, I'm completely out of touch.

Therapist: I got that.

Larry: Okay. And I think he's wrong.

Therapist: I think that's wrong, too. See, what my experience was, was that you were being genuine and that other people would see you as phony, when you said it.

Larry: And you said that to me. Or something like that.

Therapist: I thought they might perceive it as phony, because the words were so good, it was so—veneered, in a way—but that doesn't mean it wasn't real, it was just, almost a too-good-to-be-true kind of thing.

Larry: So, what hit me there was that, Bill—I have no choice, except to stay with what I think is the me in me. And if it is true that the way I behave doesn't play well here, because it turns people off, then, as enormously difficult as it is for me, I'm going to have to stay with me and lose you.

Therapist: Right. Wonderful. I agree with your choice. I support your choice. (pause) But the dilemma—the need to make a choice—this thing about losing them is your projection. Just because they're turned off, just because they think you were patronizing doesn't mean you're going to lose them. The reason Jeff told you that is because he loves you in a way, and when he said, "I love Larry," he cried. Now *he's* not going anywhere. That's the child decision in you, it's magical thinking—if I displease my mother I will lose her. That's how children think. You may need very much to go to this, "If it's me or you, it's going to be me." That's great. And I think you may have to get to that point to really stay with you. But to your adult, I want to say that's a bogus choice, that's not the real choice now.

(pause)

Larry: (sadly) I did lose the team.

Therapist: Yes, you did lose the team. But that was complex. That wasn't just out of your own self-expression; that was for a whole set of different reasons.

Larry: Right.

Therapist: That was the people in Washington, the business that you're in, maybe some deficits in your management strategies, many other things—that was different. It wasn't because they saw *you*.

Larry: Oh yes, that's right. It wasn't. Ah, yes. (very long pause) You know, to my significant pain, you described me, in the Tuesday meeting—what I heard of it was, Larry has a very embryonic self. And I was hurt by how embryonic—I felt like what you were saying was, you know, we've got the eight-cell zygote stage here, birth is nine months off, and personhood is a lifetime away. And my struggle in trying to understand what happened Tuesday is, among other things, to try to sort out what came from the group that is for me, and what's their stuff being worked out on my time. And so it's quite true that I am just struggling to get a *me* out. I think there's more me here than my little resaying of your speech would indicate.

Therapist: You're aware I didn't say that you were embryonic—I hope.

Larry: No, I'm not aware of that.

Therapist: You're not?

Larry: No.

Therapist: Well, whatever I said then—that certainly isn't my view of you. I think that you're just beginning to discover yourself, yes. I also think there's a lot of self that's developed there that you don't even know, in a sense. It's like, you have a lot of abilities and sensitivities and other things that you've developed in the false self that can be rather easily transferred to the real self when the motivations have changed.

Larry: That's just how I feel. I—in a serious way, Stephen, I know that I still don't get it. You know? I don't get it.

Therapist: Don't get it—what?

Larry: Well, whatever the important thing is for me to get. And I have had the feeling that it is as if I know something but I don't know that I know it, you know? It is as if I have it, but I don't see it.

Therapist: Right, right. You're in the process of discovering what a wonderful person you are. And in that there will be some development of the self, but there's a lot of developed self that you don't even know you've got. You don't know how loving you can be, for example. You're a wonderful man who doesn't know it yet because so much of your attention has been placed on pleasing and avoiding displeasing. I would ask you again to look at this: I think you're reacting to what I said was overdetermined, that is, that you exaggerated what I said.

Larry: Yes, I think so too.

Therapist: It created more of an injury in you than was justified by what I said. That was, that was true all around. You are more injured than the input would have justified, the goal in there is to find out what else it was you were reacting to, what deep injury and humiliation did this hit? And we might focus on that one right now.

Larry: Yes, I would like to. If feels like an *always* condition with me. I say that just because it must have been pretty early or pretty frequent or something. It was in place, clearly by the end of grade school, and before, I think. Part of where I spun off into was . . . (pause) when I got a fairly clear notion about what wasn't true about what Bill and Jeff said to me—oh, oh, no, here's what happened, here's the thing that happened. I . . . after the group broke up, Bill stood up and said, um, and I probably will repeat this in the group, but he said, "Anybody want to go down for hamburgers?" And I was standing about an arm's length away from him, and to the side of his face I said, "yeah, me," and then I noticed that he didn't hear me, and so he said it again, and after he was done I turned to him and said, "yeah, I'll go," and he still didn't hear me. There was no response. So I walked up the stairs into your kitchen, and when I was up there and couldn't see him he said it again, and I yelled loudly from the kitchen, "yeah, I'll go," and then as

I was going out the door he turned to me and said, "Are you going to go?" So, I'm livid. At this moment I'm livid.

Therapist: About that.

Larry: Yes. And where I went with that was, oh, in fact, those fuckers lied to me when I asked them if there was anything wrong with me several sessions ago, a few months ago. They either don't know, or they won't tell me, and they really don't like me, and there really is something loathsome or unpleasant or distasteful about me, and it is that feeling, Stephen, that I'm telling you is very old.

Therapist: Right. (pause) Okay, now. Does any memory of this familiar feeling, particularly a childhood memory just pop up for you without you trying to remember it? Just go inside and don't try, just think back to where you grew up and just have something pop up, don't try. Just let it happen—it'll come later if it doesn't come now.

Larry: I get sort of a feeling in my lower bowel like it has something to do with toilet training or something—I don't remember any event. It's got—my mother is around it, and . . . (pause).

Therapist: OK. Just what kind of mother was your mother with regard to shit? Would she be real disgusted or would she be sort of like a farmer's wife, who feels—it's just shit, you know, it's everywhere.

Larry: Well, surprisingly in all of this, more like the farmer's wife. She grew up in agricultural environments, and I, in later years, saw her deal with children and just smile and go ahead with it without any particular problem.

Therapist: I see, okay. How about your older brother?* How old would he have been then? How old would he have been when you were two and three.

Larry: And four. It's a missing dimension, isn't it? Matthew is a missing dimension. He was 11 1/2 when I was born.

Therapist: So he would have been . . .

Larry: Thirteen to 15. Matthew and I had a strange childhood. The rap was, we were really close. The physical reality was, he had very little to do with me, until I went away to boarding school and he was going to graduate school. Prior to that, when he would come home, we had a standard interaction, which was that we went out in the backyard and we took sticks and fought.

Therapist: And this was in, what, college?

Larry: When he would be in high school, and then undergraduate school, and I was just in grade school. We went through several years of this

*This represents an intuitive, I realize, somewhat disjointed, leap.

traditional event, which was that we'd go out in the backyard and take sticks or something, and flail away at each other, in a way that never resulted in any injury.

Therapist: But it was fighting.

Larry: Furious fighting.

Therapist: And this was when you were in grade school and he was in high school or college.

Larry: Both. I mean, the period was long enough to cover that transition. And I can remember burning rage about things of mine that he destroyed. A little model airplane that he came down the stairs, having crushed, and was going to throw away, and the impotency and rage and the complete helplessness I felt about being unable to change that. Also, in dealing with this question, he told me in tears several times, as I was going through college and trying to grow up and so forth—when he got married he sort of turned to me and became a supportive parent, and a lot of the guilt that he had had to do with abusing me. He used me, once, to determine whether the current was working on an electric motor he had rebuilt.

Therapist: In other words that would shock you?

Larry: Oh yeah, it would be quite a shock. But I have no memory of the event. And he, I'll bet, five or six times when I was, like, late in high school and just going into college, he would tell this story, and I would be forgiving him for free, without any recollection of it.

Therapist: Six times that he went into the story about the electric motor?

Larry: Uh-huh.

Therapist: Are there other times when he'd do this—like when he broke the airplane, was it an accident or did he deliberately do it.

Larry: No. He deliberately did it. But it was like, what came through was that it was so trivial an event that it wasn't even that he was angry at me, it was just, anything of mine was too trivial to be concerned with. And that's trivial. *That's* how Bill made me feel up there. He completely *trivialized* me and my desire to go out with him.

Therapist: Tell him that, tell him that.

Larry: Oh, you bet, you bet. I'm going to—I'm going to give Bill a good dose tonight. I have always felt about Bill: I think he'd make a nice brother. . . . I think. . . . I packed a bunch of stuff and laid it on his shoulders there.

Therapist: Well yeah. A lot of projection goes on both ways with the two of you, because you are so similar. The phoniness, the pleasing people, and the doing it right. All that stuff. Are there any other memories about your brother humiliating you or making you feel trivial?

Larry: He made me feel stupid. In an effort I . . . I don't know how to characterize his motive. Matthew was a brain. And, um, in junior high school, seventh grade or something like that, some folks were rebuilding a Ford. And Matthew did the whole job on the engine. He rebuilt both the upper and lower ends—he did the whole damn thing himself! And so, um, with the credential and others, he went off to college, and came back and made lots and lots of time investments in me in trying to explain things. He'd get up on the blackboard and he'd explain and explain and explain, and one of the first experiences I have of having identified a feeling, as opposed to just being in it, was identifying, early on, somehow, after several years of it, that—maybe I was a junior in high school or something—that those sessions made me feel terribly bad, because I didn't get it. I couldn't get it.

Therapist: Which may have been his teaching, your learning, or the difficulties in the relationship which blocked that from happening. But you took it all on yourself.

Larry: That's right. I'm stupid. Or at least I'm stupid in the areas of math and hard science.

Therapist: Which since you've disproved. (pause) Well, isn't what you do now science?

Larry: A little bit, but my stuff is mostly nonmathematical.

Therapist: Fine, at least you haven't made a career of being a mathematician in reaction to that experience. There are lives like that.

Larry: Yes, you bet.

Therapist: This is a new piece for me—there is a great deal of sensitivity to humiliation in you, and it never quite made sense that that hooked up entirely with your mother. Some of the other stuff—pleasing people, being afraid to offend and tell the truth to them and all that stuff, that fits with your mother. But this great fear of humiliation, this "Can I be on your team?" never quite made so much sense before. What you've just recovered has the emotional juice in it to explain these overreactions. Don't you think?

Larry: Oh yeah. Part of what has made it so hard to find, what has preserved it so long has been that Matthew, by turning around and investing heavily in me, continued to enshrine himself in my eyes, and just made it extremely difficult to get at this stuff. I do remember a time—and I guess these must have been issues, but I don't connect to it—back about 1971, when I was leaving Seattle and just going through a couple of years of therapy there, when Matthew and I went out and invested in a boffing set—you remember boffing? Yes, they're yay long, big padded things like that.

Therapist: And you hit each other with them.

Larry: Yes. And I do remember we explicitly went after getting out anger that we had at each other and talking through this while we did it, but somehow Matthew has always been so—since I was in high school, Matthew brought me reality. He saved me from the sexual weirdness of my mother, and my father's acquiescence in it. I remember him and Mary, Matthew's wife, just sitting me down and saying, "Larry, look, women like it when men come on to them, do you get that?"

Therapist: Which mother said was wrong.

Larry: Right. "And you can have a drink of wine without becoming an alcoholic, and . . .

Therapist: Right, so in many ways he was a good brother, and that made it harder for you to see where he wasn't, where he humiliated you, hurt you.

Larry: Yeah (long pause) Humiliation is such a charged thing for me. Somehow it was central for my mother, too, and it must be that whatever I got out of that from my interaction with my brother was with mother, um, sort of strengthened like waves of the same frequency strengthen each other. It was so rich in emotional payoff, for her. I can't get the feeling anymore, but it's like the way people enjoy soap operas. It's like, you enjoy hurting, you enjoy being the person downtrodden, it's just so full of emotional power.

In exploring these reactions, then, Larry got that his behavior in group was genuine and real, that his choice, "I have to decide for me or them" was misrepresenting the current reality and that his emotional response to the feedback was overdetermined. In this brief excerpt, he recovered one more source of that overdetermined response to humiliation (i.e., his brother) while alluding to the other (the training from his mother). Finally, he decided to stand up for himself in the group, and particularly to Bill, who had initiated the issue. This kind of practice in sensing himself and then standing up for himself would become the central focus of his work in the next few weeks, both in therapy and life.

THE INDIVIDUAL IN GROUP: PART I

In the next group session, Larry continued this process with Bill. Jeff was not present for this session.

Larry: But I think most of the feelings that I've got going about last Tuesday have to do with you, Bill, and so what I would like is for you to be willing to go with me here for a while. Um, some of this isn't going to be very pleasant.

Bill: Oh no.

(brief laughter)

Therapist: Bill's the one who wanted us to stop being nice to each other.

Larry: Yeah, but that's Bill's agenda, it's not mine, and . . .

Therapist: Yeah, but he's up to it. He's capable of handling this.

Larry: Okay. Let me say a few of the things about it. Umm. (pause) These are . . . I've come to discover, issues that have propelled my life for a very long time, and so this is a real special opportunity for me to get a chance to work it out with you, but I'm not going to be very pleasant in a while, and I'm not going to be behaving very grateful.

Bill: Just go ahead.

Larry: All right. If you want to call a break or a halt or something like that, I'm rational enough to respond. (pause) The . . . the thing . . . some of the things you've said were, "Larry, you haven't been present, you've been hiding out. I know you least of all here." Along with not recognizing myself in how Bill characterized me, I didn't recognize myself in that, and here's how it went: I felt like, wait a minute, I talked at least twice as much as George. Not only that, you and I have a relationship, or a starting one, outside of this group.

Bill: A starting one. Yeah.

Larry: Where do you get off? Where do you get off telling me that I haven't been talking, that I haven't been here, that I haven't been present, or that I haven't been saying what's been going on. I *have*. I've been playing my one note, which is, how do I get to be me. And—it just isn't right. I haven't failed to reveal myself here. Yeah, I hide. Yeah, your criticism touches a true thing, but it was off somehow. It smells bad to me now and it did then. (pause) Here's part of it. That question, "How come you're here?"

Bill: Yeah, why are you here?

Larry: Well, that implies that I haven't been saying why I'm here, and I have been, so the question is why aren't the others hearing it, why aren't you hearing it? Why aren't the people in the group hearing me? Is it that I say it so softly or indirectly that the message doesn't come across? Is it that I haven't said enough? Or is it something else? Another aspect to it, and that is, I don't have to tell anybody here why I'm here. I get to be here. I don't have to pay any admission price in the form of saying, well, here's my reason for being here. And yet that's what the group was giving me. It was, "We don't know why you're here." Well, fuck that.

Bill: I think that's a distortion. I don't think you have to earn your way in here. And I think you're accepted here, and yet, what's going on is the mystery, and why you're here is the mystery, what your purpose is. Maybe it's most helpful—maybe you will be the most helpful to me as a mirror to me. The feeling I have with you is one of a kind of a fog—a fog somehow hiding something that I could really get hold of. I find myself tuning out when you talk. And I don't know what that is, that may be more me than you. The thing about the reporting that Steve brought up, something that I did at that session months ago, really works for me when I try to think of what's going on with you. It's almost like, real things before they get from here (the gut) or here (the heart) to here (the mouth), have been changed. And I just—I just kind of—I just disappear when . . .

Larry: Yeah, yeah, I hear you.

Bill: When you do that, I'm gone.

Therapist: Right, and it is a hard one to confront, isn't it, Bill, because it's hard to figure out what's going on?

Bill: Well, it is hard, because it's like you always say, you always present exactly the right sentiment. And it almost never feels right, and it never quite feels—I don't want to say never (pause). It doesn't feel right often enough, so that it feels like a problem to me. There's something a little unreal, a little synthetic about what you present to me. So when you put your hand on John's leg and say "I'm with you, John," I feel like, oh, that's such bullshit. And that's real scary—that's real scary for me because the fact of the matter is that I need people, and you're here, and I might need you, and I don't know if you're really with me, and so that's frightening for me.

Larry: Right.

Bill: So. That's what happens. We've said it 3000 times about how tuned in you and I are to other people, but by the time it finally gets said—I think I said it last week, it feels like it's been laminated. The times when I really feel like I'm with people in this group is when I or they are raw.

Larry: Okay, I can get that. But, what I felt going on last Tuesday was not an accurate perception of me. It was behavior shaping. Jeff said after I had broken down and cried and so forth, "Now there's the real Larry, now that feels real to me." Now inside here (points to heart), distinct from some other times in the past, you know, there was no difference in my authenticity. And what I saw going on was you being therapist, you being Junior Woodchuck leader, you being the assistant, you relating to me in therapist mode, and being Jeff's ventriloquist.

Bill: I said it first.

Larry: Yeah. You wanted him to say certain lines to me so that I would interpret his statements to me in a particular way. I'm supposed to understand . . .

Bill: Say that again.

Larry: Okay. You wanted him to say certain things, certain sentences, and you even said after he did, explicitly, hey, I wanted you to say those things. My feeling is, if you want to say something, say it through your own mouth. If you've got something to tell me, tell it to me, that what I'm saying.

Bill: Mm-hmm. I'll tell you why I was doing that. For one thing, I wasn't . . . I don't think . . . I may have been, but I don't think I was, doing the Junior Therapist trip. Because what I felt like was, we were about ready to stop, weren't we?

Therapist: Yes.

Bill: And I thought I might lose it, and I didn't want to—I didn't want to have it drift away without saying it, to lose the thought.

Larry: Well, I kind of don't know what to do with it, it still—it still doesn't feel right to me.

Therapist: Let me clarify this. You have the feeling that Bill was setting up Jeff to give the same message to you harder.

Larry: No, it was just the message. What I thought was going on was that Jeff essentially misfired that time on what is, in general, an accurate characterization of me. And I think Bill was handing him lines, that he was supposed to say, which he did, so that I was supposed to believe his version of reality—that Jeff was only doing this out of love for me. No, I think not. I think Jeff's working his laundry on my time, that's what I think!

Bill: Well, we're all doing that. You know, one of the things that I'm thinking is, here we're kind of working on something like this, and, uh, it's almost like we're talking about the novel that you didn't write, you know? Some stuff was going on for you last week that felt real right on, that touched something. Why are we talking about what wasn't going on? You said something that I or Jeff said touched something real and true. And it's as if we're talking real intellectually about other stuff.

Therapist: Not entirely. No, I think that Larry is giving you some feedback—some negative feedback, which he perceives may or may not be true. That's hot. And it is, he sees you orchestrating an interaction like that, and doesn't like it—he's sort of accusing you back, I think, of being phony in your own way. And that phoniness is in being the therapist and orchestrating things. And that may or may not be true, but that's what he's saying to you.

Bill: I guess I don't feel that was bad. I don't think it was bad at all, because, for one thing, I had something to say, and I didn't know if anybody else was going to say anything about it or whatever, but I needed to say something to you, and I think it was five minutes before the quitting time when I said it. I had no expectation of anything happening; it was my issue. Steve invited other people: "Well, why don't you check it out, see where other people are at." We checked it out with other people, and then this thing started happening with Jeff. I got the feeling that what was going on with Jeff was kind of hot, and my own feeling was that I felt more comfortable stepping back from what was going on with me personally, and just letting him go. I don't think that's feeding him lines. Maybe I was.

Therapist: Well, I think you were, but I think—I agree with you, they were good lines, and they were accurate. I do believe that Jeff is working some of his own stuff out on you, Larry. I also believe that it took a great deal of courage for him to lambaste you in the way that he did.

Larry: I see that.

Therapist: It was out of love, *and* there was projection going on there, just as there was with Bill, it's all true. John?

John: I just want to make an observation of what I saw going on. Apart from the words that were being said, is that I saw you, Bill, explaining why you did what you did and defending yourself, and I saw you, Larry, as not really expressing your true feelings to Bill. I mean, you opened up by saying, "I'm going to get mad at you." You never even got mad at him.

Larry: Well, we're not done yet.

John: I know, but you really don't seem to be getting down to it.

Larry: Maybe it's hard for me, it'll take a while.

Bill: I don't like it when people get angry with me. Phew!

Therapist: Well, let's get on with it.

Larry: All right. So. Hey, I'm feeling like you don't hear me when I am talking. I do talk, and I do say what's going on with me here. I have said why I'm here. I have said what the issues are for me. A thing happened after the group broke up that I think says some things for me. You were sitting here, Bill. I was sitting there right next to you. You got up and said, "Anybody going to go down and have hamburgers?" I'm standing right here. I say, "Yeah, I'm in, I'll go." No response. You say it again. "Anybody want to go out and have hamburgers?" I say, "Yeah, I'll go with you." No response. Nothing. It's like I'm not there. So I go up to the kitchen and from up there I hear you offer the same thing again. In a loud voice I say, "Yes." Now I'm leaving to go out the door, and you turn to me and say "Are you going?"

Bill: Uhh. (pause) I don't remember. I may have not heard you, or I may have looked at you or acknowledged it personally in my own mind, "Well, there's one," or something like that.

Larry: Okay. Maybe it's just my personal baggage about such stuff. It drives me right up the wall. I feel like you are saying to me, "You don't exist. You don't *exist*." And that feels a lot like what I got out of what you were saying earlier, "Hey, you don't exist here, you don't talk, you hide out, you haven't said who you are." Well, I sure the fuck have. (long pause)

You know, I feel incredibly small, being so concerned about such issues. I spend my life swallowing such things. Paying great attention to them, and swallowing them because I know that it's only neurotic turds like me who even pay attention to such events. But the fact of the matter is, I do. The fact of the matter is I feel (pause). I feel like I am the one who isn't heard, isn't listened to, isn't paid attention to, enormously in my life. And that's what I got off of you. It's like, you used me. You used me to get your "let's put the end to politeness" done here. You pressed a button that you knew would pop me. It did. We got something other than politeness happening. But that's your agenda. I haven't been polite here. I'm scared here. I'm not polite. I'm pissed at you for ignoring me, for trivializing that I exist. Fuck you! Son of a bitch! (pause) I'm not your entertainment. (pause) Down at the hamburger stand, after the game, the coach, you, around his whistle says, "Good game, guys. It was a good group we had, huh?" I'm feeling like hammered shit. And I'm so dumb I'm thanking you for it. (long pause) You know, my selfishness is even worse than that. I sit here criticizing you for playing therapist. And the fact of the matter is I'm complaining about you having been a bad therapist once. You've helped pretty well other times. But, uh, I want you to be just one of the bozos on the bus.

Bill: I've done that.

Larry: And I've spoken up, too.

Therapist: Larry, what do you want from Bill?

Larry: You know, what just galled me, Bill, about your saying that I hadn't spoken out, or that you didn't know who I was, was like ignoring me when I was saying I wanted to go to the hamburger stand with you. It's like, I want you to acknowledge that I exist. I want you to stop acting like the relationship that I thought we were starting to have outside is nothing—that I'm not here. (pause) You know, I'm here as best I can. I . . . I can't imagine anybody else who works . . . who . . . who . . . who cares more about . . . who . . . thinks more about, um, trying to be genuine every minute of the day, and walking down the street and every little encounter at the gas station and every damn thing, and you sit here cavalierly in your therapist mode, saying, "man, you know, some day you're going to have to come out and talk." And, you know, I'm not even here disputing the accuracy of it. I'm just saying ouch. I don't like it. And, if this isn't enough, then I don't know what more I can do.

(long pause)

Bill: Do you want me to talk? (pause) I was just noticing how scared I am.

(very long pause)

Bill: I didn't see that as a cheap shot last week. What I imagined was that this group could come to an end soon. And for whatever reason, something that might have moved between us might never happen. Sometimes I'm not really good at caring about other people. And I really don't care about them. Sometimes I'm absolutely indifferent. And so you might want that kind of response from me and never get it. Sometimes I feel absolutely dead cold to my wife, like I could walk out the front door and never see her again, and wouldn't care. That's what it feels like. (pause) And so what I'm dealing with is feeling scared, and also knowing that I run away a lot. I'm not here because I know everything; I'm here because in some parts of my life I know nothing. I didn't mean to hurt you and I didn't think I would hurt you.

Therapist: Do you believe that?

Larry: Yeah, I do.

Bill: I think the other side of it—I think those two things are true, that I neither meant it, nor did I predict it. And when it started rolling, I was thinking that I was glad that I said it. I think we get by too fucking much in this group on brains and style. (long pause) I don't know how to tell myself to be real. And I don't know how to tell other people how to be real. I don't know how to do that.

Therapist: Bill, could you give Larry any of the kind of acknowledgment he's asked for?

Larry: I'm feeling like I'm getting it.

Therapist: Fine.

Larry: I'm sitting here thinking, so what have you gone and done, Larry? Gone and accused Bill of stuff that apparently isn't true, and projected a bunch of stuff from other places on him. I don't know how to tell myself how to be genuine either, and I think the panic over that is a big part of what's driving me.

Bill: The panic that you've done this awful stuff to me?

Larry: No, the panic over I don't know how to tell myself to be genuine. The characterization you made a few minutes ago about me—it's like the truth gets lost between my gut and my mouth. That's so true.

Therapist: There's a filter in there.

Larry: And I'm desperate about it. And part of what I know is that a bunch of the times when I think I'm being authentic, I really feel, it's wrong too.

Therapist: The filter's still operating, you mean.

Larry: I guess.

Bill: Feels crazy, doesn't it?

Larry: Yes. (cries)

Bill: And hopeless.

Larry: Yes.

(long pause)

Bill: What I think is: Sometimes you and I need to get hit very hard. Sometimes we need to jump and scream and hit things, and get confronted like that. And then we start to sound like real human beings because it creates so much emotion and pressure . . .

Larry: Right.

Bill: What's going on, right now, one real thing that's going on for me, is how scared I'm feeling, just talking. It gets me a little dizzy.

Larry: You don't look scared. See, I'm crying. I'm shaking. You don't look scared.

Bill: So what?

Larry: Well, for me—I don't see it.

Bill: For you the play's the thing.

Therapist: Well, I don't know. I think he's saying the same thing to you, Bill, that other people were saying to him last week, that he doesn't see it. That doesn't mean it's not—for both of you—it doesn't mean it's not there, it just means frequently people don't see it. Bill is scared; I believe you, Bill, you're scared. I don't see much fear, I see a little. He doesn't see much, and that doesn't mean that you're doing anything wrong or that he's doing anything wrong, you—you've both got such a built-in filter that a lot of the stuff that's going on, other people do not see, and then they think you're phony. And sometimes you are phony, but often you're not. It's just that there's such a filter there that it doesn't show. You're scared, he doesn't see it. Then, he thinks—then he's not sure he believes you. Because if you're phony, yourself, you know, you get a little suspicious of the other guy. Other people must be phony, too and that's a lot of what's going on with you guys. (pause) And it's why, when you don't see it in the other, it's so upsetting.

Larry: Yes, when you don't *see* it.

Therapist: When you don't see the real feelings in the other one. It's so upsetting because then you begin to project your own phoniness on the other one. And you don't know who's who. And then it gets scary because you, too, don't know whether you are being phony or real.

Like, you know now, Bill, you're being real. You know you're scared. And you know it's just that he's not seeing it. But what happened to you last week, Larry, was people were telling you you weren't real and you got scared that you didn't know whether you were or not. But as you worked through it, and thought about it and felt through it, you decided you were. And they just weren't getting it. And, for both of you, that's a lot of what you have to learn, whether—it is just the filter that's shielding the real or you are making a play of it, which you both do. And it's a real tricky discrimination. But the only way to find out is by looking inside. Like you know you're scared, right?

Bill: Mm-hmm. I am.

Larry: I'm not . . .

Bill: I just was aware of an impulse to jump on you and start beating the shit out of you. (very quiet pause) Did you see that?

Larry: Oh yeah, I got that in spades. I want to do the same.

Therapist: He saw it, I saw it. It's clear in your eyes. It's in your eyes. It's obvious.

Bill: That's good. And I'll tell you what it's about. And I'm just . . . sweating. It's that, you know, we keep working on this, and, closer and closer and closer, and finding me out, being exposed. And, well, I'm just really afraid, you know, that—that somehow you'd get my cover right off, and see what an evil, terrible thing I am.

Larry: Bill, the only thing that I've got, that I haven't said is this: I notice you advertising realness.

Bill: What do you mean?

Larry: Well, about the sweat. It's like, see here, it's real. Dig what I'm saying?

Bill: Mm-hmm.

Therapist: That's like he doth protest too much?

Larry: Yeah.

Bill: All right, well.

Larry: But there isn't any other devastating thing coming to me, it's just, I've got that one perception.

Bill: I really want people to see me. I really want people to see me, I want them to know me, to recognize me, to know all the stuff that's going on with me. Yeah. So I do a lot of advertising. I want you to be sympathetic, I want you to be sympathetic with my fear, and so I'll advertise the realness and the fear, because I don't—I want you to know that that's there, and that might get you to hold back. If I don't tell you I'm afraid, you might not know, and you might just like to say to me, "You fucking scumbag."

Larry: Because I'm not seeing it?

Bill: Yeah.

Therapist: Here, though, Bill, is more feedback. Remember "those drums, those drums, those beating drums." When people hear that, *drama* from you sometimes they label that phony and get turned off. And that doesn't mean it's not real, it is just a style of yours that causes people to attribute unrealness, phoniness, etc., to you, which you may not want to do anything about, or just be aware of, or change, or whatever, but I think that's part of the same thing. It's like his filter; it's a style that has some problems with it, but that doesn't mean that there's anything wrong with you, it just means it's not always effective. (pause) It's why people sometimes will see you phony when you're not.

Larry: I know you're talking about Bill, but it seems right for me too.

Therapist: Or where you're making the most of being real, it's like you're making the most of being real, and it is real, but because you're making the most of it they say, "This isn't real."

Bill: That really works. That really fits. That fits real well. It's like, something happens, and it's real, and I just kind of work it for the next month.

Therapist: Right. Because you're discovering your realness and you're saying, look Mom, I'm real, I'm real, I'm real. And people go, all right, already. You know, it's like, no you're not, you're phony, because if you were real you wouldn't have to make so much fuss about being real, and they don't understand you're discovering your realness and are excited about it.

Bill: It's also like this gatekeeping thing around disclosure. You know, I just imagined that—I sort of don't know when the gates are open. And sometimes I—like I was telling you about this woman at the ski lodge, you know, and I—it was really nice, you know, we were talking for hours in the hot tub and then sitting in the steam sauna and I was singing, you know, I was just really enjoying singing these songs in this little steam sauna up there, and it sounded great, sounded great. She loved it. I mean, I felt like such a hot shit. So I felt like I was a wonderful person. And, uh, like I was being a wonderful person. And the next morning she said, you know, "You want to go on a hike?" and I said, "No, I'm going to go sit in the hot tubs." And she said, "That's all right, I don't have to be entertained," and I just . . . ahhhh. It was really a shot to hear that, because I felt like, you know, your fly's open. That kind of exposure, you know. You're walking along, all of a sudden your pecker flips out. . . . That's real scary for me, and that gatekeeper stuff around disclosing, and it's real scary sometimes, because sometimes I kind of bloop out and I don't know I've done it. And then it's—and then I'm exposed, and it's fucking scary. It's real scary. I was high one time, and a bunch of us sitting around a table, and all of a sudden this woman says to me, are you all right? It felt like, you know, what have I just done, you know? Have I, you know, just done some horrible thing that I wasn't even aware of?

(laughter)

Therapist: And the key to all this, Bill, is that you still think deep down that you are horrible and that somebody's going to find that out. And the truth is that you are magnificent and the only ways that you're—your undesirable qualities are all your attempts to cover up what you think is horrible. And you know that, but I didn't think it would do any harm to tell you. Because people see you, you know, and the more you try to hide something the more they see it.

(very long pause)

Bill: (tears) It's like . . . what I feel like is like I've . . . I'm a jewel that's covered with a ton of shit, and I've forgotten who's home.

Therapist: All right, and what you're doing here so beautifully is you just clear out some of that shit, week to week to week.

Bill: I feel really sad.

Therapist: Breathe and feel it.

Bill: I want to . . . just get away from here, so fast, I imagine just jumping over this railing and just getting out.

Therapist: Just now?

Bill: Just now.

Therapist: Stay here, breathe, feel it. You're among friends.

(long pause, Bill cries)

Bill: I didn't want to say anything because I didn't want to fuck around. I was just thinking how beautiful feelings are, sitting here and just feeling sad and looking at the green leaves outside. There's just something real nice about it.

(long pause)

Therapist: You don't have to say anything.

(very long pause)

Bill: (to Larry) It started out with you and me.

Therapist: Yeah, is this complete?

Larry: Umm. Almost. There's one other thing I wanted to add. When you were talking about, you know, the fly being open, and the unknown—the part of you that flopped out, that you didn't know had been exposed. My version of that has another big baggage hanging onto it, and it's humiliation. I'm wired for humiliation.

Bill: We both are.

Larry: It jumps up so bad it just grabs me right by the throat.

Bill: Otherwise it wouldn't matter if my fly were down.

Larry: Right, it's like, who gives a shit, my fly is down.
Bill: Nice big cock, too.
(pause)
Martin: Or exactly the opposite. (brief but uncontrolled laughter)
(pause)
Therapist: So, are you complete with each other on this? For now?
Bill: See, that's why I was afraid.
Therapist: Why were you afraid?
Bill: I was afraid because you were going to somehow expose me and humiliate me, Larry. And it wouldn't be, "oh, nice big. . . . " It would be like "You call that a penis? You think you're a man? You think you're anything?"
Therapist: Did that happen?
Bill: Did it happen?
Therapist: In this interaction.
Bill: No. No. When I was sitting here, I felt some gratefulness, just for . . . just for, not to anybody in particular, but just to kind of have this experience.
Therapist: Good, Now—but, he did—I want to make a point—he did call you Junior Therapist, you know, and that sort of thing, and that wasn't humiliating. Why not?
Bill: Because I know what I'm doing.
Therapist: Right. There you are. That's the answer. It's like, stay with your own judgment of you. Listen to the feedback, but the final bottom line is what you think and feel. And that's why it wasn't humiliating, because you knew better. You knew you've done good. You knew that you put that out as an act of love. And you knew that when you got Jeff to say that he loved Larry, and that's why he did it, that that too was out of love, and that that was a good move. And that's why you weren't humiliated because you trusted yourself.
Bill: Thank you. That's real true. That part of it—see now, that's real current stuff, and, you know, my fly's down and my cock is out. Yeah, it is. And I know why it is.
Therapist: And you like it.
(laughter)
Therapist: Okay. Are you complete now?
(pause)
Bill: I got a little something I need to do with John. (pause) Actually, I was just thinking about how (pause) I'm just thinking—I'm thinking of tenderness. (pause, sigh, cries)
Therapist: Let it go.
Bill: God. (cries, long pause) Ahh.

Therapist: Breathe in your chest and let yourself feel. (pause)
Bill: Oh. (pause) I don't even know what it was.
Therapist: Doesn't matter. The real feelings are what you guys are trying to reclaim—all you need is that. You don't need analysis or understanding or . . .
Bill: I'm just thinking about women and mother and beauty. Soft. You know, all these pained people I see all the time. And just being held by a loving mother on a beautiful day. You know, just soft. Loved. Ohhh boy. A few minutes ago I finally felt as if I had come home to this—this, where I'm at about the struggle I'm in.
Therapist: Continue. Continue. (pause) Are you done with this part of it?
Bill: Yeah. Thanks, you guys.

INDIVIDUAL THERAPY: PART II

In the next individual session, Larry continued to explore the basis of his falseness and develop the ability to express his real self. In the intervening week, he had several rewarding experiences of assertive self-expression. In this session and in the group session which followed it he continued to be self-assertive and be rewarded in that activity.

Larry: The truth of the matter is, my feelings are dead sometimes. And I have experienced myself a lot in my life as a feeling minefield. That is to say, what was in here was that . . . was a minefield of bad feelings, that they would blow up in my face, that I would see horrible things. In general, I think I've developed strategies for . . . strategies for stepping around bad feelings, just all the time. And it is . . . it is that that I go to . . . my falseness, that the group complains about, I think comes mostly from that. I'm not being scared, being frightened.
Therapist: Of your feelings?
Larry: To a degree no larger than anyone else in the group, my falseness is, more than anything else, fear driven . . .
Therapist: Sure.
Larry: Bill's crack, last Wednesday after I said "Gee Bill, you don't need to advertise your realness quite so much," he said, "You know, for you, the play's everything." Well (pause). No it's not everything. It's something. It's a problem I have. He precision-targeted a real soft spot in me for the purpose of defending himself . . . an observation that only he needed. I know it already. He needs to have it.
Therapist: Ummm-hmmm.

Larry: But, the process of therapy is one in which I somehow am trying to find who I am . . . need to do two sort of contradictory and difficult things at once. One of them is to open up to my feelings, and the other one is to somehow sort of not get trapped by the old ones. You dig?

Therapist: Right.

Larry: And I struggle with the contradiction. Should I just let go with everything? Should I just do my feelings the way they are? Well, sometimes they help me and sometimes they don't. To what extent is the kind of adult balance that that requires similar to the avoidance behavior that I've been doing all my life? To the degree that they're similar, I have a real difficult time separating them out. Bill accurately described the great sensitivity about it. . . . He said, "Larry, when you start talking, it's as if the feeling somehow gets layered over and so by the time it comes out, it's laminated." You know, that's just how I feel, and it's maddening . . . frustrating . . . and basically what I'm doing is protecting myself from not seeing these monsters out of the corner of my eye until I can get them managed and . . . and I lose them in the process. I lose the real in the process.

Therapist: And, so what I think you need to go for is just more feeling, don't worry about getting trapped in it.

Larry: Okay. All right . . . but what has happened in the group is: I feel like at the time when I was opening up the most, I got dumped on for being phony. At the time when I was caring the least about my superficial appearance and my performance, I got dumped on for being concerned about my superficial appearance. I feel like I got tackled after that play was blown dead. And . . .

Therapist: I think you're right.

Larry: Also, so what? I mean, the so what about it is that when I talked to Maria about it, she says, "Do you think these people are saying these things out of hostility?"

Therapist: Well . . . love?

Larry: It doesn't feel like love to me. You keep offering that interpretation. Apparently, I think it's true, but I don't feel it.

Therapist: It's not just love . . . I think it's love and projection. . . . It's love and projection. And . . . accurate perception and other motivations are all mixed in . . . It took a lot of courage for Jeff and Bill to say what they did and, I think, a lot of love. On the other hand, there was some projection there. At the same time, I think there is some justification for the projection. But, when I hear you getting only the attack in it, I think, "Tell me more about how you are putting this together."

(long pause)

Larry: I am, ah. I have been ferociously examining my own internal thinking processes . . . what goes on inside my head, under one form of it or another, is the assumption that there is something wrong with me . . . like I say, since I was a child. When I had my one acid trip and freaked out, that was basically it. It was so . . . it was just an experience of being so strangled by the complexity of . . . of . . . of . . . ah . . . trying to understand my internal mental processes. With that kind of chemical, there's too much going on. . . . But, I'm like that a lot. And I am frustrated and tired and pissed about living that way. I look around, and the average person doesn't beat themselves up and down the block just as an avocation . . . their hobby, their resting state, all the time. I mean . . . it is in that context that the kind of feedback that I'm getting from the group is such a problem for me. I mean . . . I am 30 years or so, at least, into living this way. And, I'm starting to get real angry with it.

Therapist: Mm-hmm.

Larry: Just angry. And, and . . . part of . . . and that's what that remark about not being a friend to myself comes from. I . . . (pause, sharp short exhale) somehow, I feel . . . about coming out of my hole. . . . I don't know how to come out of it smiling very much, but I do know how to come out of it angry.

Therapist: Good. Take that.

Larry: I will. I need it.

Therapist: You have enough ego strength, you're not gonna do anything dangerous. . . . You might embarrass yourself . . .

Larry: (laughter) I might well lose my friends.

Therapist: No, you won't. You might piss them off. But you won't lose them. You may not believe that, but that's my reassurance to you. . . . And they may be just absolutely delighted and relieved to see you where they can really see you. That's what they're asking for most. I'm asking for that too. See if you can find this anger now and tell me about it.

(long pause)

Larry: I feel a bunch of the energy and feeling I had about this recently. I shot out a bunch of suspicions about all of this. The part that I get now . . . has to do with the interactions here. You and I . . . the group meetings. I was feeling pretty miserable. Ahhhh. I was thinking last night. So, now where am I, at three years' worth of therapy here? . . . I'm . . . I'm feeling stuck in a same old way . . . I didn't stay in that condition very long, but that's what I felt for a while. Ahhmmmm. So, this therapeutic process hasn't really gotten to what I needed to get to. It really hasn't gotten me out of this. This group isn't going after reality. They have learned a set of behaviors. A religion. So that's where the suspiciousness goes. I come here to you, I get reassured about it, okay. But, then that somehow mutes me. (pause) I imagined last night you saying, "Larry . . . okay, you think the group doesn't like you. Let's have the group sit and all tell you what they like about you." To which I go, "Stuff it up your nose, Stephen." I'm . . . ah . . . I wouldn't believe them anyhow . . . and, ummmm, and, and . . . HEAR me (struggles for words) that this is what I've got . . . if you want the real me. I don't think you fuckers want the real me. You keep pulling for the real me, but what you really want is this behavior where I'm either broken down and crying or I'm somehow very mellow. But not that I'm venal, suspicious, uhh, I don't know what . . . short-sighted, not able to get the love that they're really feeling. . . . You're right. I don't get it. (pause) But the real me is my feelings. And my feelings are what I don't get . . . that's what Bill, in particular, is telling me . . . for my benefit. I know intellectually that much of what he said is correct. That characterization about how my feelings get overlaid, laminated . . .

Therapist: Whatever his motives are, he's on.

Larry: Yeah.

(long pause)

Larry: Somehow, this business of . . . of getting real and finding out who I am cannot be a lifetime of (pause, sigh) negative, critical self-evaluation and commitments to start something tomorrow and never forget it. You know, it's like . . . it's like . . . Bill's prescriptions about my behavior are not something that I'm going to succeed at just incorporating. . . . I mean, I have got to somehow be allowed to run on automatic. I've got to somehow. . . . It has got to be okay that I am how I am.

Therapist: Especially with the child in you. . . . How do you see the group around that issue?

Larry: I haven't . . . I don't enjoy the group much.

Therapist: I don't know what you mean. Overall or lately?

Larry: No . . . just lately. From feeling real enthused about it. I enjoyed it at other times when I was under attack because I felt that rush of growing. But lately . . . I've thought seriously about just leaving it as an open question whether or not I would go from here to there this evening. Not deciding no, but it gets to be my choice.

Therapist: Right. You're mad.

Larry: Damn right.

Therapist: But not accepted. You feel real nonaccepted.

Larry: That's right. I don't trust . . . I don't believe what they're saying about "we want the real you." The real me is not very pleasant.

Therapist: You don't believe what they're saying.

Larry: That's right. (pause)
Therapist: Do you feel that anyone in there means it when they say they will support you.
Larry: I sure do. I think Martin does it. I think John does it. George does it. I think you do it. So that leaves Bill and Jeff, right?
Therapist: Okay, (laughter) so you're real mad at Bill and Jeff for not accepting you as you are. And for their misperceiving, and for working their own shit out on you?
Larry: And, I'm real mad at me for all the times I don't say my piece. I mean . . . it is there, of course. I agree with their criticism of me. I just—this guy that offended me on the road today, was very useful in that I said my piece.
Therapist: And you feel you haven't done that in the group?
Larry: Right, even last Tuesday, with Bill. I only got half of it. I was still pulling punches like crazy.

The remainder of the session was spent encouraging Larry to give Bill and the group the other 50 percent just as he'd given it to me earlier in this individual session. This week, Larry went directly from his individual session to the group meeting and assertively confronted Bill with his accusation from the prior week, "For you, the play's the thing." Jeff was also present this week and Larry was able to confront him with the lack of acceptance he had felt two weeks before when Jeff had accused him of being patronizing. For months, Jeff had been working on his very negative feelings concerning his own very patronizing father and Jeff was able to acknowledge the possible transference in his statement two weeks earlier. Larry let out a good deal of his anger and resentment during this session and confessed to his distrust of the constancy of the group. He received rather massive positive feedback after doing this and was both surprised and relieved by it. At this point, he remarked, "Now I feel the love. Now I feel it."

Good boys and girls who have inhibited their aggression for fear of humiliation and rejection need the experience of its expression and acceptance again and again to reclaim themselves. For a while, they often do not feel completely seen and accepted unless this "venal, angry, suspicious, hurt" side of them can be expressed, seen, and accepted by others. Some variation on this theme is probably true for all narcissistic characters. Often in this and other groups, I use the group members to provide regular reassurance after an individual member has revealed a part of him- or herself about which he or she is particularly insecure. Either the client or I will ask members of the group to provide that reassurance after the expression of self with which the client is usually so insecure. Almost without exception, the feedback is of an extraordinarily positive nature because we really do want to see each other as we are. We are willing to take the bad with the good. What makes us all most uncomfortable is what is hidden, what we suspect, and what serves as an ambiguous target for our own projections of insecurity.

Clients like Larry also typically need repeated experiences of standing their ground and reclaiming their rights. This Larry was doing intensively, both in and out of therapy, during this period and it was both cute and inspiring. Toward the end of this period, Larry began to be dissatisfied with the "project" nature of this work. He wanted a breakthrough, a flash of insight, a transformation, and was discouraged with these step-by-step gains. He was getting high levels of encouragement and praise from both myself and the members of the group concerning his self-expression, assertiveness, realness, etc., but it wasn't enough.

I made two responses to Larry's dissatisfaction with his work. First, I observed that he was very easy to offend but very hard to praise. He had a hair trigger for humiliation but it was difficult for him to take in and feel good about support or encouragement. This, of course, is characteristic of the narcissistic pathology and, in words less pejorative and diagnostic, I said this to Larry. Second, I observed that Larry was continually grading himself, and the grades were always less than A-plus. His assertions weren't good enough because he was anxious while making them. His new initiations to women were not good enough because the women weren't so outstandingly attractive to him that they constituted the ultimate challenge. His progress, such as it was, was not good enough because it did not represent a leap or breakthrough as he had seen in Martin's case.

But, as I pointed out to Larry in a rare discussion of comparison, Martin's "breakthrough" had occurred after five years of very hard therapeutic work and was a dramatic breakthrough because it involved recovery of an extraordinarily traumatic and repressed series of childhood events. Larry's "child abuse" was, like that of most of us with a narcissistic style, much more subtle. Its healing lent itself to peak experiences, which Larry had had, but not to the kind of dramatic breakthrough that he had witnessed with Martin and to some extent with John. Our American, fast-everything culture leads to an expectation of breakthrough, transformation, and miracles. My experience with everyone who has promised this to me has been a disappointment—and there have been plenty of them. This love affair we have with miracles is consistent with the grandiosity of narcissism and the inherent narcissism of our culture.

I shared all of this with Larry by way of communicating that I thought he was doing as well as he could. Indeed, I thought he was moving fast and I was very gratified by his work. Finally, I characterized his continual grading of himself as a kind of obsessive activity which he had needed up to now to structure his time and bolster his sense of self. Formerly, he had been a workaholic with many episodes of exhaustion and physical illness. He had been socially isolated, without any avocations or pleasure in his life. During the period of recording documented here, all of this had been substantially reversed. Therefore, I suggested to him that this obsessive behavior might, at this point, be habitual but in a very real sense no longer necessary. I suggested to Larry that he was no longer really very disabled psychologically or behaviorally and that his obsessiveness about grading himself might simply represent *unnecessary* psychological pain at this point.

I further suggested that he would probably not stop grading himself very quickly but that he could begin to simply observe himself grading and, if he disapproved of the grading, observe the disapproval. In short, I began to suggest the same kind of intervention used in Phil's case, documented in Chapter IV. I suggested further that the loss of this obsessive crutch might, on occasion, lead to some anxiety, but that ultimately it would lead to a greater sense of his real experience of living. This led to a period of cognitive treatment of this unnecessary emotional pain and very quickly began to result in an enhanced level of self-acceptance for Larry and an enhanced ability to take in the acknowledgment and love for which, by now, he was a very worthy target.

By this time in the work, Larry was personally involved with four women, not all lovers, but all in a companionable male-female relationship. This gave Larry abundant opportunities to acknowledge himself for being an attractive, interesting, and lovable man. He also, of course, had plenty of opportunity to engage in his habit of holding back his own acknowledgment and affirmation of these women for fear of the obligations to which such self-expression could lead. This gave him the opportunity to repeatedly challenge the early training concerning the implicit obligations of others, particularly women, and to live and even love without being restrained by anticipated obligations. Repeatedly, he could engage in the discovery that not all women in the world were like his mother. Most of them, indeed, could accept him as he was, take what he had to give, let him go, and take care of themselves. They particularly could do this if he would allow them to see him for who he really was with his understandable difficulties around commitment, his inability to totally take care of another person, and his continuing need to find and support himself before becoming fully involved in a committed relationship. For Larry, as for all other people introduced in this book, the work goes on.

COMPLEMENTARITY OF INDIVIDUAL AND GROUP TREATMENT

Theoretical considerations and direct experience both confirm the utility of group therapy for individuals with narcissistic issues. It is also clear that group and individual treatment can make unique and complementary contributions to these patients' growth. Finally, my most recent experiment in serving as both group and individual therapist for the same clients suggests that the integration made possible by this dual role can be most beneficial.

More than many patients, narcissistic individuals need group therapy because, in one way or another, they are very isolated. The inferiority and specialness which they feel isolate them from the "ship of humans." There is, in narcissistic individuals, that nagging sense that there is something bad, inadequate, or innately unacceptable about them. It is their continuous attempt to hide this unacceptability that keeps them separate, together with their continuous need to prove specialness, uniqueness, and perfection. I believe that most narcissistic individuals need a special environment which is at once safe and inescapably real. This special environment must pull for and then accept the realness of each member, including his or her vulnerabilities and special gifts.

In the group just presented, Bill often used the group as a place to confess those things about himself of which he was incredibly ashamed, and for which he expected profound disgust and rejection from others. For him, each confessional brought him in touch with incredibly deep emotional pain. Yet, each experience brought him in contact with a reality of self which he did not ordinarily experience and the acceptance he received on each occasion allowed him to internalize an ever-greater degree of self-forgiveness, self-acceptance, and self-love. He, like all other members of the group, provided powerful learning for the others simply by example. The other group members saw their own incredible self-denigration and self-hatred in Bill, and as he forgave and accepted himself, I could see them doing the same. These men recognized their twinship with one another and as they saw the others' beauty in vulnerability and realness, they began to recognize their own. Obviously, these kinds of effects are not nearly so possible in individual work.

The group also provides the narcissistic individual with a social context where he may not otherwise have one. This creates the opportunity for all sorts of therapeutic material which might not otherwise be available. In this group, for example, the men, most of whom were single, often used one another to work through personal issues as they might otherwise have done in the context of a family. These projections, interpersonal patterns, or conflicts could then be dealt with in the group with the therapist's supervision. As illustrated in these transcripts, the group process could then be supplemented by more intensive individual work when appropriate. In general, the group therapy provides an opportunity for guided practice in communication and intimacy very much needed by the typical narcissistic client. In this group, as in others I have led, there was meaningful extratherapy contact, which supplemented and helped create the real social support system these clients needed. As the group contact "networks" out into other meaningful relationships, the effects can be especially profound.

In all of these ways, then, the group provides a testing ground and jumping off place for the individual client's social support system in which the ever-maturing versions of the narcissistic transferences may be realized for the purpose of self-sustenance. These self-other transferential relationships anchor and sustain the self in context. To review, these *"selfobject"* transferences are merger, mirroring, twinship, and idealization (Kohut, 1971). In the mature version of the merger transference, we are simply anchored and sustained by those individuals with whom we can join or meld such that our security in living is enhanced. We are less alone as we fuse in our identification with a few significant others. Second, we need others to mirror us—to really see, understand, prize, acknowledge, value, and treasure us. When this mirroring is for our *real*, as opposed to false, self, we are encouraged to be our *real* selves, to relax, to breathe, to express, and to simply be the one we are. Similarly, we discover, value, and enhance ourselves as we can relate to others who are, in some significant ways, like us. In this group, for example, the realities of twinship for the entire group, and particularly for certain pairs (i.e., John and Martin, Bill and Larry) provided a good deal of the emotional heat, accurate empathy, and self-other acceptance. The recognition of twinship in a real and more mature sense significantly erodes the isolation of the narcissistic person and confirms that he is indeed a member of the human community—that his feelings, vulnerabilities, advantages, and problems are all part of the human experience.

Once idealization is tamed, one can appreciate real attachments to others who are worthy of respect and who embody qualities to which one aspires. These people are not seen as infallible or universally good and wise. Rather, they are legitimately admired for qualities which are valued and they are used as models and mentors in the process of building an ethical life that works. Similarly, ideals, in the more abstract sense, also provide anchors to the self by offering an ideal to be pulled by rather than a perfectionistic standard always to be met. In other words, there is nothing wrong with perfection, just perfectionism. In a group that works, you can often witness the initially more primitive idealization evolve through frustration to its more mature expression. The realness demanded in the group context makes it impossible for any group member to unquestioningly idealize another for very long. And the accommodation required in this process affects the maturation of the idealization transference. This same effect occurs, of course, with the therapist in both the individual and group contexts, though he or she is typically in more control of the timing of this disillusionment-accommodation process in individual therapy.

The group, then, provides the hub of and testing ground for these kinds of human relationships which are self-building and self-sustaining. The group models and demands the reliance on others beyond the potentially regressive dyadic relationship of individual psychotherapy. This spread of reliance directly encourages the discovery and development of self in a social context. It makes real the limitations of what others can do for one, as well as the remarkable possibilities of what can be accomplished in community. It strengthens the self while simultaneously demonstrating the incredible power of interrelationship.

All of these effects can be greatly enhanced by complementary individual psychotherapy. In this setting, there can typically be more focus on an individual's history, working-through of archaic injuries, exploration of transferential aspects of current relationships, and the working-through of a truly dyadic relations. In spite of some risks inherent in the combination or the integration of these two approaches, I have been very impressed by the results of this initial experiment in which I was or had been the individual therapist for each member of the group. While I certainly would refrain from saying "This is the way to do it" on the basis of this one successful experiment, I am certainly encouraged to do it again and to recommend others consider this possibility.

To put it succinctly, the group, over time, began to serve a sort of family function for each member. Each person related to the group as they might to the family and provided many samples of the relating style they employed outside this protected setting. For me to be able to see that provided information which I could not have obtained in any other way. In a sense, it was like doing family therapy and individual therapy simultaneously—seeing the individuals' interpersonal behavior and then being able to deal with it one-to-one shortly thereafter. The group experiences provided invaluable material for the individual sessions, and my participation in both seemed to speed up and smooth out the integration of the two approaches. I could, for example, see more readily where an individual was projecting or setting up an interpersonal game of engaging in idealization, splitting, or some other maneuver which reflected the developmental arrest or pertinent conflict.

It certainly assists in one's reality testing function to have been there for the reality. And, just as the group experience serves to concretely *inform* one's individual therapeutic activities, the individual therapy content serves to *inform* your intervention in the group context. The greater knowledge that the individual treatment gives around genetic history, conflict, and developmental arrest can be most profitably used to gauge the level and type of intervention which might be most effective in the more public group context. In short, the major advantage of this type of integration is that the material in each form of psychotherapy informs the interventions in the other and helps assure that the two forms of therapy will be used in a complementary fashion.

There are, of course, risks in doing it this way. In discussing this with colleagues, I have learned that some groups have had difficulties when some individuals were in individual therapy with the group leader while others were not. This kind of arrangement can, of course, lead to a sort of in-group/out-group division, counterproductive for all concerned. Particularly where the therapist is narcissistic and interested in building a following, this kind of arrangement could be lethal. Also, the group experience does, to some extent, blemish the special dyadic experience that some clients desperately need. When such dyadic needs are great, group involvement may need to be delayed until the dyadic issues have been adequately worked through or separated from the individual work. Character disorders involving schizoid, oral, and symbiotic pathologies might be particularly prone to this kind of risk.

The primary disadvantage I experienced in this particular experiment was the impossible task of modulating my therapeutic interventions so that they optimally met everyone's needs simultaneously. With some clients, for example, I know I can be relatively self-disclosing, whereas with others I know it is best to be more the contentless, blank screen which stimulates projection. In the group context, however, it is impossible to do both simultaneously. Once I disclose something for the benefit of one patient, it has been disclosed to the others, perhaps to their detriment. Similarly, some clients need us to be very safe, accepting, and nonconfrontational for quite a while, while other clients require us to be confrontive. While this kind of differential response to clients can certainly be practiced in the group context, the client who needs safety will obviously observe the confrontation of another, and this may disrupt the transference in the individual sessions. In addition, group members will model the therapeutic responses of the therapist but may not have the same level of theoretical or individual historical knowledge to similarly moderate their response. While the therapist can certainly have some influence on this, it does present another potential problem. Relative to these kinds of differential therapeutic responses, clients may also begin to develop rivalries with one another around the comparative aspects of their dyadic relationship with the therapist. Though a useful area of exploration for many clients, these rivalry issues are often difficult for the therapist to handle.

The foregoing is just a brief list of the potential risks of this kind of combined therapeutic approach. I'm sure there are others. But each risk is also an opportunity. Often these kinds of issues lead to productive uncovering of conflict, arrested development, transference reactions, etc. Like everything else in psychotherapy, we need in this circumstance to make the best informed choices we can and proceed according to our judgments. Some clients will need to be screened from this dual therapeutic involvement, at least for a time, and our group therapy behavior under these special circumstances must be informed by our theory and experiences.

All things considered, I have been tremendously encouraged and enriched by this particular kind of group involvement. Because of the prior individual involvement with me, I believe the group took off much more quickly than would otherwise have been the case. These men got down to the business of constructive intimacy and therapeutic work with minimal resistance and delay. There were also untold and unanticipated benefits for me as a therapist and teacher as a function of working in this dual and integrative role. In short, the advantages far outweighed the disadvantages. I plan to repeat this experiment, being careful in the selection of group members and vigilant regarding the potential risks, but committed to exploring the limits of this combined approach.

The healing of any narcissistic character disorder or narcissistic style involves a transformation around the issue of self-regard on the one hand and enhancement of social concern on the other. Well orchestrated group work serves both of these interrelated objectives beautifully. Through all the processes outlined, it encourages greater self-acceptance and demands greater awareness of and involvement with others. Sooner or later, group therapy is probably indicated for most individuals who exhibit any significant degree of narcissistic pathology, for the discovery, development, and healing of the true self requires a social context. When such a context is optimally functional, the self cannot fail to grow and to nurture what nurtures it.

CHAPTER VIII

TRANSFORMATION: *POSSIBILITY OR FALSE PROMISE?*

> The tragic hero who is the protagonist of the great tragedies, which must be counted as among the most precious cultural possessions of mankind, is a man, who, despite the breakdown of his physical and mental powers (e.g., Oedipus) and even despite his biological death (e.g., Hamlet), is triumphant because his nuclear self achieved an ascendancy which never will, indeed which never can, be undone.
>
> — Heinz Kohut, 1984, p. 37

WHAT IS TRANSFORMATION? It means, first, a *shift* from compensation for a lack of self to an expression of that self. Even when the self so expressed is fragile, immature and frightened, the transformation involves a commitment, more or less conscious, to find, express and develop it. Such a commitment takes courage and the courage required begins itself to serve as a bulwark of the self. As outlined earlier, one profound sign of this shift occurs when a person begins to use others to discover and support who he or she really is, rather than continuing to use others to aggrandize the false compensation.

The shift in orientation is usually, if not always, gradual and uneven. The habits of a lifetime, which typically ward off overwhelming emotion and profound disorganization, cannot yield immediately even to the most courageous and conscious commitment. Like the shifts in consciousness which occur in early childhood, some time is needed for accommodation to a radically new way of experiencing the self, others, and life itself.

Still, it is during this initial *shift in orientation* to life that the marker events of a transformation will often be most profound. The peak experiences of such a transition will look most like the lightning bolt changes associated with the contemporary use of the word "transformation." I have, in fact, used this word reluctantly for this reason: It often implies sudden, complete and lasting metamorphosis. In the area of characterological change, this is a comforting but deceptive illusion which leads either to the pain of disillusionment or, worse yet, to the brittlely maintained lie of having been transformed. Such a lie is used in the service of the false self and furthers a real transformation only insofar as it hastens the eventual fall from false grace which will motivate the true shift.

Many in the transformational movement have been irresponsible by encouraging, either explicitly or implicitly, this illusion. They have fostered change by wholesale identification—a classic form of transference cure—thereby retarding the acceptance of the real contribution that their philosophies and technologies could make to a true evolution of consciousness.

Transformation as just described is a false promise. Transformation which begins with a *shift* and is followed by continuing, if uneven, *evolution* is a very real possibility. This continuing evolution involves the building of structure, the uncovering and resolution of conflict, and the evolution of a truly mature wisdom which continues to develop throughout life.

If we grant the proposition that characterological change inherently requires time, the question still remains whether such change can be accelerated or made less painful. Furthermore, we need to continue to explore whether such change can be accomplished with less *professional* time, even though the absolute time for change may remain relatively long. I believe the answer to the latter question is an unqualified yes, and that an eclectic psychotherapy solidly grounded in a *comprehensive* theory can accomplish that goal. The addition of active strategies for building structure and resolving conflict in the psychotherapeutic process can reduce the frequency of required therapeutic sessions and therefore reduce the investment of professional time. If, for example, we can accomplish the same therapeutic change with one session a week rather than four, we have reduced the cost in professional time by 75 percent, even if there is no change in the absolute length of time required for the change. My experience suggests that such an accomplishment is a contemporary reality.

There is also good reason to believe that enhancement of the therapeutic process and reduction in professional time can be effected by the implementation of various therapeutic modalities. Some of the possibilities for the integration of group and individual therapy have been illustrated in the last two chapters. Among other things, a group experience broadens the base of social support, provides the opportunity for increased generalization, and dramatically increases the possible therapeutic interventions while at the same time reducing the personal cost and professional time required. Marathon group experiences, so popular in the transformational movement, share or amplify all of these advantages, while contributing additional ones. Among other things, marathon experiences wear down defenses through the pressure of the continuous time involvement. In addition, they usually result in at least some peak experiences of breakthrough for some participants, which serve a positive modeling effect. When such breakthroughs occur, they provide at least a glimpse of how life could be without the constraints of one's scripts and defenses. I believe that in most, if not all, cases such breakthroughs require continuing group or individual work which self-consciously aims at consolidating and integrating the changes experienced during the peak time. Thus, an integration of all three therapeutic modalities—individual, group, and marathon—might very well accelerate the process, mitigate the necessary pain involved and save professional time, thereby making such characterological transformation available to more people.

Whatever the ultimate solutions, I believe we are obliged to stay empirical in our quest for better treatment. It is such empiricism which leads me to the conclusion that real characterological change takes a significant amount of time and involves the experience of necessary emotional pain. It's important that we not lie about that and artificially give people what they've always wanted: quick, painless solutions to life's most basic problems. By the same token, it is our obligation to remain open to the possibilities of such change with less absolute or professional time involvement and to pursue the exploration of strategies with potential for realizing that end. We have already made progress in these ways and further progress is possible. But real progress will be made by hard work on the problem, not by the nurturance of magical illusions.

Characterological change, while rewarding, is stressful. It requires the stretching of our current repertoire throughout the years of evolution. Any bulwarks to the self which enhance the experience of self as secure and supported will help. Anything that provides an anchor to the self will increase the capacity to endure the stress which can transmute to greater structure. In organizing our thoughts about such self-sustenance, we may think of such bulwarks of the self at three levels: (1) individual-systemic, (2) social-cultural, and (3) conceptual-spiritual.

At the individual-systemic level, the currently known strategies are commonly found in stress management programs. These include programs of relaxation, meditation, exercise and diet. These extraordinarily valuable tools, so often ignored by psychotherapists, aim for a normally functioning physical self which can then support the complexities of human living. Therapists will vary in the degree to which they feel it appropriate to play a central role in this. At minimum, however, it could be part of a therapist's supportive and ego-enhancing function to support work at this level. Too much "noise" in the physical-mental system will render characterological change impossible. To assist and support the reduction of such noise by the methodologies mentioned, and perhaps by others still to be discovered, will lay the ground work for the evolutionary process of change.

At the social-cultural level, the bulwarks of the self include the self-sustaining aspects of the family and community. A deep understanding of the continuing need for sustaining *selfobjects* on the part of both therapist and client will lead to an increasingly self-conscious attempt to construct and sustain a socially supportive environment in which true characterological evolution can occur. An appreciation of the continuing need for ever maturing relationships, which contain the sustenance of merger, twinship, mirroring, and idealization, can lead one to self-consciously build such socially supportive relationships, as well as to provide them for others and take genuine pleasure in the humanity possible in them. Indeed, a good deal of the "humanizing" of the narcissistic style is in accepting and embracing one's *human* nature, which includes the hunger for and satisfaction in these relationships. Central to the therapist's contribution, of course, is his or her own genuine humanity in the therapeutic relationship itself. It is often the case that the therapist is the chairperson of the welcoming committee back to the essential human condition. A therapist lost in technique of whatever kind can never truly serve that function.

Finally, any reading of history cannot fail to reveal the overwhelming power of values and ideals in sustaining a person or a people through stress and adversity. Values give shape and purpose to life and have repeatedly sustained individuals through situations of stress that otherwise would be totally overwhelming.

Anatoly Shcharansky is a contemporary example of one so sustained by his moral convictions and ideals. Shcharansky was imprisoned for nearly ten years, often under the most torturous conditions, and subjected to many overwhelming tests, including long periods of isolation. In *Shcharansky: Hero of Our Time* Gilbert tells his long, courageous story and sheds a good deal of light on how a man such as this could sustain himself under such conditions. Following his arrest in 1977, Shcharansky was imprisoned, tortured, threatened with execution, and otherwise abused for 16 months before being brought to trial. In this trial, where he was unrepresented by counsel and not allowed defense witnesses, Shcharansky behaved calmly, pleading not guilty and rebutting his accusers with dignity. In his final speech he said:

> Five years ago I submitted my application to leave for Israel. Now I am further than ever from my dream. It would seem to be cause for regret. But that is not the case—I am happy. I am happy that I have lived honestly, in peace with my conscience, and never compromised, even when threatened with death.
>
> I am happy that I helped people. I am happy that I knew and worked with such honest and courageous people as Sakharov, Orlov, and Ginzburg, who are carrying on the traditions of the Russian intelligentsia. I am happy to have been a witness to the renaissance of the Jews in the U.S.S.R. I hope that the absurd charges against me and the whole Jewish immigration movement will not hinder the liberation of my people. . . . To the members of the court, who have merely to confirm a predetermined sentence, I have nothing to say. (Reddaway, 1986)

This and other extreme examples of courage and self-constancy under the most disorienting and threatening conditions dramatically illustrate the self-sustaining role of ideals and moral values. As psychotherapists, it is usually not our role to suggest such particular values, but we can acknowledge and support them, thereby enhancing their self-sustaining function. An appreciation of the important role of values, ideals, and spirituality in life is a very important prerequisite for a therapist involved in the evolution of character change. "Heroes" like Shcharansky also serve a selfobject role for the rest of us in our relatively minor struggles for cohesion under stress. And their successful strategies in such extreme circumstances provide useful information about how the stress of characterological change can be managed. Shcharansky, for example, has shared how he kept his sanity in these torturous circumstances. He repeatedly kept himself "fixed in that same constellation of relationships of which I've been part in previous years." He reports to repeatedly summoning up:

> pictures from my past, thoughts about history and tradition, the Hebrew language and books I've read, all that stayed in my memory from my study of mathematics and chess, even visits to the theater, and of course the ability to laugh—not at jokes or clever plays on words, but as if I was a spectator viewing the world from the sidelines, without undue melodramatics, discovering many interesting things, both comic and absurd at the same time. All these devices were employed . . . in a struggle that I had to conduct within myself, or, more correctly, with my fear.

Shcharansky exibits here the kind of humor and acceptance of transience that Kohut lists as characteristic of a transformed narcissism. There is sufficient cohesion of self that one can loosen one's attachment to self and even transcend the self. In spite of man's continuing dependence on external social factors, he retains, sometimes to an unbelievable degree, the internal ability to construct or reconstruct what is sustaining. There is no question but that this ability can be employed and strengthened in the heroic struggle of maintaining the self through characterological change. It is, of course, true that such cognitive mediation can be used in the service of defense, particularly denial. The lie of transformation presented at the beginning of this chapter is an example of this defensive, non-evolving stance. But because of our classic training, we therapists often are too attuned to the defensive role of ideals and values and too skeptical of their essential role in the maintenance of a secure sense of self within which the stress of change can be endured. The work of Kohut (1984) and Frankl (1962, 1969), among others, can serve as profound antidotes to this scientific conservatism.

The promise of characterological transformation can be fulfilled best in the context of the security provided by all of the bulwarks to the self thus far reviewed. Over the last 20 years, I have had the experience of being guide to others and being guided by others in a very different context. I have led and been led in challenging recreational activities such as mountain climbing and skiing, which pull for growth while stimulating fear. In these contexts, I have also learned that the most growth and pleasure come when two basic conditions are satisfied by the guide: (1) He promotes security by competence in the activity and in understanding the student and his needs; he inspires trust through the integrity and generativity of his intention. (2) He is able to appropriately "dose" or sequence those activities which push the student's limits or provoke his fear. These same factors operate in guiding characterological transformation. In the context of safety, the character structure must be challenged. The challenge provokes discomfort, but it is in working through the discomfort that change is realized.

So the transformation will be furthered by whatever will optimally challenge the client's structure. We have many strategies for doing this, from conventional confrontation and interpretation to the more unconventional procedures of Gestalt and bioenergetic therapy. We can keep discovering new techniques which accomplish this purpose. But, whatever the techniques, what will remain critical is the context of safety and support and the "dosing" of the challenges so that they can be optimally used to achieve change. On some occasions, particularly with narcissistic individuals, it may be necessary for the individual to suffer a series of devastating failures—"to bottom out"—before being willing to even consider giving up the compensation. This should be avoided wherever possible, of course, and a therapist, called in soon enough, can certainly have a role in preventing this outcome. The holding environment created by individual or group therapy, as well as that enhanced by a therapeutically supported environment of family and community, can serve to prevent a crisis which produces severe dysfunction or results in downward mobility. With the possible exception of Larry's case, this "bottom out" was avoided in all the cases reviewed in this book, even though the affective consequences of the confrontation with self were extremely disruptive for several individuals (e.g., Martin and John). But we therapists can do only so much. Sometimes the false compensation must break rather than melt and we must deal with that reality.

For an impaired character structure to truly evolve, there must be a confrontation of the real self which inevitably contains powerful archaic affects, unrealizable demands, and a frightening void where there should be structure. A confrontation of all that is necessarily difficult, and it serves our clients when we tell the truth about this. Existence, much less change, is not pain free. However, to the extent that the pain can be appropriately "dosed" and therapeutically used, it needn't be repeated.

Any psychotherapy which deserves that label is a process which initiates characterological change. When best accomplished, the change process will outlive the course of therapy and continue throughout life. Psychotherapy which initiates such change can be short-term or long-term, but the change process itself is long-term. This certainly was the case in Chuck's short-term therapy (see Chapter V), as it often is in cases where the initial structural resources are strong and a short-term course of psychotherapy is initiated by a life crisis such as divorce or the death of a spouse. Horowitz (1986) reports this same effect—initiating a long-term change through short-term bereavement therapy—when the person is initially rich in ego structure. But even long-term therapy is not over when the therapeutic contact ends. Rather, at the end of successful long-term treatment, an individual possesses the structure and resources to arrange for his milieu of support, both internal and external, and to arrange for his own "dosing" of life's challenges.

So, therapy, like life, is a process—a journey. To be guided on that journey is part of our legacy as humans. And so, of course, is to be a guide. To be led means to allow oneself not to know. To lead flexibly means to know with the openness, at any time, not to know and thus to learn.

APPENDIX

THE FOLLOWING ARE processes referred to in the text which were outlined in the first volume of this series: *Characterological Transformation*. They are reproduced here with minor editing for the reader's reference. This is in no way an exhaustive outline of processes but only an explication of those mentioned in this volume.

INTERNAL PROCESSES

Focusing

The process of focusing (Gendlin, 1978) is an example of a relatively less intrusive body-oriented approach which does not require movement on the part of therapist or client. It is useful for a wide range of therapeutic applications.

The following is a brief description of Gendlin's focusing process in six steps.

Step 1: Clearing a space

As with many other processes involving attention to internal processes, this one begins with a procedure aimed at facilitating uninterrupted internal attention. Gendlin prescribes an initial clearing process in which you list all of the things which are troubling you at the moment. Don't get hung up or stuck on any particular problem but simply allow the list to emerge, temporarily putting each item on the shelf. This meditative attitude of letting things come up and go by is represented in many such techniques. When you seem to have the list completed, Gendlin suggests that you use the sentence, "Except for all of this, I am fine." Often, this sentence will lead to other items for the list until it seems completed. At this point, you may experience a settling down or settling in such that you can say with some confidence, "Except for all of this, I am fine."

As is true of the listing of reluctances or resentments outlined earlier, a common result is a kind of detachment from the list itself. While it is all so, there is a release in the listing and a disengagement which can come from separating the list from yourself. As with other Gestalt processes, this one demands awareness which goes beyond what is already consciously realized. In this, there is both clearing for the process of focusing and the beginning of the process itself.

Step 2: Feeling for the problem

In this step, you begin the process of *feeling for* the essence, heart, or core of the trouble. Essentially, you ask your body to send you the message in a kinesthetic, sensory way. You avoid labeling, understanding or analyzing, but give yourself time to feel the message in the language of the body rather than in the language of the mind. All of us, will almost automatically tend to analyze and jabber during this second step. What is required is patience and time for the feelings to present themselves. The body generally speaks more slowly and, particularly where unpleasant emotions are concerned, there are often well-established habits of mental exercise which close off feelings.

Gendlin suggests that in this second phase, you ignore the details of any concern and just feel for the totality of the problem. He suggests such questions as, "What does this whole problem feel like?" "What whole problem feels worst on this particular day?" "What does this whole thing feel like?" In this second step, you are trying to arrive at the single whole *feeling* that includes all that is central in the sadness. Just as it is important not to intellectualize or analyze the feeling, it is also important not to try to change it—simply hold and deepen it. It is like calling up the central feeling you have when thinking of a certain other person. The details, the visual experience, the understanding of that person may be there, but they are not essential to the feelings called forth as you think of that person.

This part of the process is in some ways the most difficult, especially for a schizoid client, because it is teaching him a new language—a sensorily based form of communication with himself which will be relatively foreign. There will be some real difficulty in describing in words the language and messages of sensation.

Step 3: Finding the crux

The process of focusing is essentially a training for communicating with the feelings, the body, or the unconscious. The secret of this kind of work involves asking open-ended questions and waiting for answers, avoiding any rational, conscious mind responses arrived at rationally. This third step may be the most difficult to explain and differentiate from the ones preceding and following it. It, too, involves the asking of verbal questions and remaining open to answers which are often nonverbal, kinesthetic or visual. The key questions in this third step are, "What is the crux of this problem? What is the worst of it? What is the main thing in it that makes me feel bad?" You then wait for the answer to come.

Gendlin indicates that in this phase of the process you may find the problem changing. That change will be at a feeling level, so that you know that you are making progress in this third step if there is a definite shift in bodily feeling. You know that you are on the right track in answering the crucial question of the third step when the bodily shift suggests, "This is right, this is it." The shift resembles that feeling you have had when you suddenly remembered something you knew you had forgotten but couldn't place what it was, or when you have recalled where you left something you had lost.

In this third step you may begin to come up with a verbal label or discover an image which gives some understanding of the crux of the problem. While this is all right, it is not necessary and it is more important to slow this process down than to rush to complete it. We learn to use a new language correctly much more slowly than we can use the old one and it is always a temptation to return to the ease of the old language. If you slow down the process of focusing, you are more likely to be learning the new language of feelings. The secret of focusing is to ask open-ended questions and then wait for the body, "the part," the unconscious, or whatever you want to call it to slowly give you the answer.

Step 4: Labeling

In this step, at last you begin to ask for pictures or words which come from the feeling and, in effect, label it. Once again, however, the process is not from the top down but from the bottom up. The label must flow out of the feeling rather than be imposed upon it. Essentially, you are looking for something you don't know already and the old labeling and understandings will not give you the kind of body shift that is the measure of a successful focusing process. In this fourth step, you may ask of yourself, "What is this feeling?" and then wait for the words or images to emerge or pop up out of the felt sense. Frequently, this labeling may quickly and naturally fall out of the third step and that is fine as long as the label comes from the feeling and there is that concomitant shift in the body which signals a completion, resolution, or change. The bodily shift in this fourth step will often involve an "aha" or a "that's it" which signals that more has been accomplished than the repetition of some old insight or way of looking at things.

Step 5: Checking back with the feeling

In this step, you simply check the image or label received in step 4 with the felt sense of the problem to see that there is a fit. You ask in this step, "Is this right?" Once again, wait for the response to this question to be felt rather than thought. If the sensation which answers the question is a confirming, settling one, you can move on to the next step. If the felt response is less settling, wait and see if a more precisely fitting label or image emerges from the feeling. Whatever the answer is in this step, it is important to hold on to the feeling rather than to stop feeling it once you have a label for it. You must have the feeling and the label together before you can check one against the other. In this step, too, the feelings may change. It is advised that you allow all of this to flow—to let both the words and the feelings shift until there is a match. When that occurs, let yourself feel the feeling and experience the words for a minute or two.

It is important to let the feeling be, and not try to change it. It is during these minutes that there can be a continued changing, releasing, moving, and resolving. Often the tendency is to rush on and escape or change the feeling. It is important to counter this tendency and stay with the feeling and its matching label for a while.

Step 6: Recycling at deeper levels

In succeeding rounds of this exercise you look for successive feeling experiences and their accompanying labels at deeper and deeper levels. You assume, for example, that what you have arrived at so far may be only the first layer of this feeling state. By returning to Step 2 you ask again, "What is the whole felt sense about that problem?" Again the body, the feeling, or the unconscious is allowed to begin to present that answer slowly. In repeating the third step, you again ask for the crux, and in the fourth for the label. In the fifth step you again ask for the match between words or images and the felt sense. This process can seemingly go on indefinitely, as ever deeper experiences of settling and shift occur around the feeling or the derivatives of that feeling which emerge as the process evolves. The stopping point may be dictated by the end of the therapeutic hour or, more fortunately, by coming to a place at which the shifts and settling in the body signal that one has arrived at an appropriate place to stop.

The focusing process involves learning a new language. It takes time and practice and an increasing faith in one's ability to communicate with one's own body and unconscious. This may be very much a *foreign* language and much repetition and patience may be required. Very often, I have found that hypnotic trance induction is particularly useful for the initial stages of the process to encourage the client to suspend his ordinary conscious judgments while he learns this new, often threatening language.

The preceding is only a brief outline of Gendlin's focusing process, and while this description may enable you to understand it, it may not be enough to allow you to practice it effectively. Gendlin's book covers many of the difficulties which people typically have in learning the process and, though repetitive, gives the reader a deeper understanding of the process, so that it becomes possible to guide others through focusing after one has been through it again and again in the process of reading the book. Because this is a new language for most therapists, as well as clients, the repetitive and even drilling nature of Gendlin's book is, I think, often necessary and beneficial.

Reframing

Bandler and Grinder (1979, 1982), in their application of neurolinguistic programming to the clinical situation, have institutionalized some basic insights into general sets for therapeutic work, as in the specific process called *reframing*. The reframing process outlined here can be very useful in helping a client orient to appreciating the function of his resistance or symptoms, as well as in coming up with new ways of accomplishing that function. The reframing process per se is predicated on the useful fiction of separating one's ego states or ways of being into "parts," as has been done in much of Gestalt therapy and transactional analysis. The process itself involves communication with and between these parts, with a focus on understanding the underlying *intention* or purpose of the troublesome "part" and then finding new, less troublesome behaviors or attitudes which accomplish that intention. A brief overview of the reframing process is given below, followed by detailed instruction for its use.

The reframing exercise may be aimed at any problematic behavior, attitude, or feeling. After identifying the target of the process, it is often useful to produce in the client a state anywhere from mild relaxation to deep hypnotic trance before proceeding with the following steps. In this altered state of consciousness, the client is asked to establish communication with the part of him that generates the problematic pattern. Having established communication, he is then asked to discover the positive intentions of that part. Following this, he is asked to contact that part of him which is creative and ingenious. Using all the resources of his creative part, he is asked to generate new ways of accomplishing the intentions just discovered. Next, the part in charge of generating the problematic pattern is asked to examine, correct, or assist the creative part in perfecting those new solutions until they are acceptable all around. When all new solutions are acceptable, the part in charge of generating the former problematic pattern is asked to take responsibility for generating these new solutions in the appropriate contexts. Finally, the client is asked to check and see whether there are any remaining considerations which would prevent him from adopting the new solutions.

The process does not, of course, always go as smoothly as outlined, nor does it always produce immediate or profound change. Yet, I have found the outline of this reframing exercise to be extraordinarily valuable in changing my own and my clients' orientation to the problems brought up in psychotherapy, particularly the problems of resistance. All resistance is essentially self-protective and much can be achieved when this is fully appreciated by both client and therapist. Once this is known, many measures can be taken to accommodate resistance's self-protective intent. Following is an outline and suggested text for Bandler and Grinder's reframing process. The process itself can vary considerably and often certain steps may be deleted or expanded for a given case. The outline is deceptively simple in that the exercise does not always go as smoothly as presented and much additional work will often be needed just to complete one step. Yet, this process, like many coming from Bandler and Grinder, represents a masterful integration of a number of therapeutic principles and offers a useful guideline for an entire course of therapy, particularly around resistance issues.

Reframing outline

1) Identify the pattern or problematic situation to be addressed.
2) Establish an altered state.

   Through relaxation or hypnotic induction, establish an altered state of consciousness in which the person is more inwardly focused and more capable of suspending disbelief than in his usual conscious state.
3) Establish communication with the part that generates the problematic pattern or problematic situation.

   "Now as you are focused deeply inside and aware of yourself, I would like you to remember a time when this problematic pattern occurred. I'd like you to be highly aware of the situation and more and more in contact with that part of you which generated it. As you do this, I want to prepare you for the question that I will soon ask you. When I ask this question, I want you to become exquisitely aware of any changes that occur inside you. It may be a feeling or an image, or you may hear a word or sound. Just be exquisitely aware of the change. The question is, 'Will the part of you that creates this situation communicate with us in consciousness?'" Wait and ask the client to signal nonverbally when some change or changes have occurred. When you see the signal, continue, "Good. If those changes represented a yes, a willingness to communicate, I would like that part to intensify the changes to further signal that yes. If it is a no, I'd like to diminish the intensity of the changes to signal no." Assuming the answer was yes and the signal intensifies, continue, "Good, now diminish the signal so that you know what a 'no' will look and feel and sound like. Now, I have another question for this part of you. It is this: 'Are you aware of your positive, beneficial intention in creating this situation?'" Assuming a yes, move on to the next step.

4) Elicit the intention of the pattern or situation, "Will the part of you that creates this situation be willing to communicate it to us?" Assuming a yes, "Do that now."
5) Generate new solutions to satisfy the intention.

   There is a part of you which is creative and ingenious. It is the part which you have used on other occasions when a problem needed a novel solution. When the old ways did not fit, or when you came up against a new situation which required a different approach, the part emerged. Perhaps in your personal life or your work or in fixing something. Let this part emerge now—allow it to begin to generate new solutions to satisfy the intention we have just uncovered. Allow it to present at least three new alternatives and signal me when this is done. You may not be aware of all the solutions that you create now and those discoveries may continue for some time to come." When the new solutions have been generated and shared, move to the next step.
6) Integrate the new solutions.

   "Now I want to ask that part of you which creates the pattern or situation to pay attention and answer another question. 'Will you accept the new solutions and accept the responsibility for generating them when your intentions need to be fulfilled?'" This step will provide very useful opportunities for editing out and adding new solutions if there are objections to the solutions already generated. There can be a dialogue created here between the part which creates the pattern and the creative part which suggests the solutions. When this is accomplished the client is ready for the final step.
7) Check for ecological balance.

   "Now go deeply inside yourself and see if there is any other part of you which is holding back or concerned about the solutions and agreements that have been made here." This, too, is a very useful step for editing and adding solutions. The basic idea here is that whatever solutions are generated should not violate any other part of the person or any of his other intentions. Once this editing is performed, the process is complete.

An exercise of this kind can take from a half hour to many sessions of intensive work. Indeed, as indicated before, this overall outline can encompass a good deal of the therapeutic process itself. In cases in which the person is unaware of the intention or the part responsible is unwilling to communicate or share that intention, the whole process can be done at a level outside conscious awareness. This is not at all difficult for therapists who are comfortable with hypnotic procedures, though it probably will be uncomfortable for anyone who is not. Those therapists uncomfortable with the useful fiction of parts communicating through internal sensory experience may not wish to use this process at all. But they will be assisted, I think, in acknowledging and following the basic underlying intention of this process—appreciation and respect for the intended function of any persistent pattern and assistance in generating more evolved methods for fulfilling that purpose.

ACTIVE PROCESSES

The following are processes derived from bioenergetic therapy. All but the last one, "The Stool" are used to enhance grounding in the client. Grounding processes are employed to bring the client into greater contact with himself and the environment. They may stand on their own or be used as preparatory for affective release work.

Standing on one leg

A number of variations of simply standing on one leg can be used to bring more energy and charge into the legs. The simplest variation involves a simple alternation such that you stand on one leg attending to the foot's contact with the ground and feeling the charge building in the leg. Then, after a time, shift to the other leg and repeat the process. A second variation brings more charge to the legs. Stand on one leg with the knee bent and extend the other leg behind you for support only, so that all of your weight is resting on one leg. Hold this until vibrations have been established for 15–30 seconds. Repeat this with the other leg.

Putting the foot down

In this exercise, you simply stomp your feet alternatively on the floor. It is often useful to experiment with the way in which this is done, altering the angle of the blow, stomping with the heel only, etc. This action is also, obviously, of metaphoric value and can be used literally when the person needs to "put his foot down." When the exercise is used in this fashion, add appropriate verbalizations, such as "No; I won't; stop it," etc.

Squatting against a wall

Stand against a wall and then go into a squat with your back flat against the wall. Cup your hands behind your head, keeping your breathing full and open. Sustain this posture at least to the point of vibration. This posture is particularly useful for building a good solid energy charge in the legs and for strengthening. It is a useful exercise to recommend for self-administration.

Jumping

Jumping may be used in any number of variations, not only in improving grounding but for other sensory experiences involved in this process. Some of the variations are as follows:

1) Jump up and down, banging the feet on the floor, like a protesting child.
2) Jump for height, but land flat-footed for a solid sense of the ground.
3) Lean back on the heels and try to jump from this position. This illustrates that the heel rest posture, typical of the oral character, is not only a "pushover" position, but also one from which one cannot very well "take a leap."
4) Jump from and return to the ground with the toes, giving the experience of springing up, "taking a leap," and returning lightly to the ground.
5) For a self-administered exercise, regularly use a jumprope or small trampoline for jumping. Concentrate attention on feet and legs.

Forward position

Demonstrating as I give the instructions, I lead the client into one of the most basic bioenergetic positions. "Let your head drop down to your chest and slowly allow the upper part of your body to bend forward until your fingertips touch the floor. Bend your knees and breathe. Now begin to add a little movement. As you breathe in, bend your knees a little more. As you breathe out, straighten them a bit, but not to the point of stiffness. Let yourself have nice and easy breathing and move up and down to the rhythm of your breathing. Shift your weight slightly forward so that you are sure to *push* your body up as you breathe out. Let your feet and legs do the work. Feel your feet and legs and let your upper body just hang. Be sure to leave your fingertips on the floor so that just your lower body is moving while your upper body simply breathes and hangs out." The length of time of this process will vary depending on the tolerance and needs of the client. After it

Figure 1. Forward position

is finished, it is always useful to ask for some feedback or debriefing about it. This process enhances grounding in the literal, physical sense, as will the two that follow.

Footwork with the dowel

For this exercise, a three-fourth to one and one-fourth inch dowel approximately two and one-half feet long is required. I usually place the dowel in front of the client and say, "Begin by rolling your feet over the dowel which I've placed in front of you. First one foot and then the other. Allow the muscles in the bottom of your feet to relax and notice those points which hurt. When both feet seem sufficiently relaxed, walk across the dowel, starting just below the toes and proceeding slowly back to the beginning of the heel. This will probably hurt in places and that's okay as long as you don't force it and bruise a muscle. Adjust your weight as you walk so that you can feel your feet and perhaps feel the pain but don't be too hard on yourself. Breathe. Now repeat this one to four more times. Now come off the dowel, bend your knees, breathe, and feel the increased sensation in your feet."

The stool

The bioenergetic stool is a custom made tool for this work which may be purchased from Realto Furniture, 214 Sullivan Street, New York, NY 10012. It is a stool approximately three feet high and resembles a sawhorse, though it is narrower in width. The stool is padded at the top so that the client may extend himself over it in various applications. The most common application of the stool involves another form of the bowed back stretch. When I first introduce the stool to clients, I typically demonstrate the desired posture. I lie on my back over the stool with the top of the stool just below my shoulder blades. This point is exactly corresponding to a woman's bra line across the back. I extend my arms back and with each exhalation attempt to stretch my back by lowering both my hips and shoulders as much as possible. The same stretch may also be accomplished over the arm of a

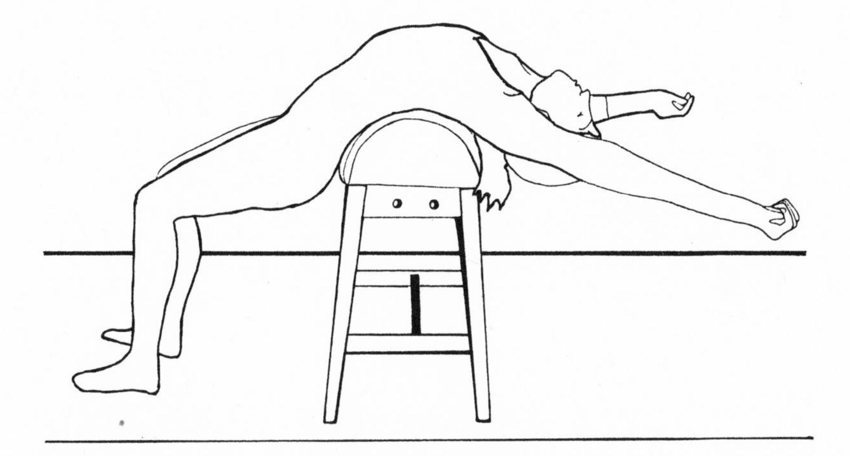

Figure 2. The stool

typical sofa or over a large towel placed on top of an ordinary stool. Though the height of the sofa arm or ordinary stool may be lower than would be optimally desired, these more common structures can be used for any self-help stretches prescribed for the client. This stretch opens the chest, bringing movement to chest breathing and expansion in the abdominal region, lower back, shoulders, etc.

REFERENCES

Abend, S., Porder, M., & Willich, M. (1983). *Borderline patients: Psychoanalytic perspectives*. New York: International Universities Press.

Alder, G. (1985). *Borderline psychopathology and its treatment*. New York: Jason Aronson.

Bandler, R., & Grinder, J. (1982). *Reframing*. Moab, Utah: Real People Press.

Bandler, R., & Grinder, J. (1979). *Frogs into princes*. Moab, Utah: Real People Press.

Beckwith, L. (1979). Predictions of emotional and social behavior. In J. D. Osofsky (Ed.). *Handbook of infant development* (pp. 671–706) New York: Wiley.

Beres, D. (1956). Ego deviation and the concept of schizophrenia. *Psychoanalytic Study of the Child, 11*, 164–235.

Berne, E. (1964). *Games people play*. New York: Grove Press.

Birns, B., Barten, S. & Bridger, W. (1969). Individual differences in temperamental characteristics of infants. *Transactions of the New York Academy of Sciences, 31*, 1071–1082.

Blanck, G., & Blanck, R. (1974). *Ego psychology. Theory and practice*. New York: Columbia University Press.

Blanck, G., & Blanck, R. (1979). *Ego psychology II: Psychoanalytic developmental psychology*. New York: Columbia University Press.

Boadella, D. (1977). *In the wake of Reich*. Ashley Books.

Bowlby, J. (1969). *Attachment and loss. Vol. I: Attachment*. New York: Basic Books.

Bowlby, J. (1973). *Attachment and loss. Vol. II: Separation: Anxiety and anger*. New York: Basic Books.

Bowlby, J. (1960). Grief and the mourning in infancy and early childhood. *Psychoanalytic Study of the Child, 15*, 9–52.

Bronson, W. C. (1966). Central orientations: A study of behavior organization from childhood to adolescence. *Child Development, 37*, 125–155.

Cameron-Bandler, L. (1985) *Solutions: Practical and effective antidotes for sexual and relationship problems*. San Rafael, CA: Future Pace, Inc.

Chessick, R. D. (1985). *Psychology of the self and the treatment of narcissism*. Northvale, NJ: Jason Aronson.

Davanloo, H. (1980). A method of short-term dynamic psychotherapy. In H. Davanloo (Ed.). *Short-term dynamic psychotherapy*. New York: Aronson.

Dilts, R., Grinder, J., Bandler, R., Bandler, L., & DeLozier, J. (1980). *Neurolinguistic programming Vol. I: The study of the structure of subjective experience*. Cupertino, CA: Meta.

Emde, R. N., Gaensbauer, T. & Harmon, R. (1976). Emotional expression in infancy. *Psychological Issues, Monograph 37*.

Emde, R. N., & Robinson, J. (1978). The first two months: Recent research in developmental psychobiology and the changing view of the newborn. In J. Noshpitz, & J. Call (Eds.). *American handbook of child psychiatry*. New York: Basic Books.

Fraiberg, S. (1969). Libidinal object constancy and mental representation. *Psychoanalytic Study of the Child, 24*, 9–47.

Frankl, V. (1962) *Man's search for meaning: An Introduction to Logotherapy* Boston: Beacon Press.

Frankl, V. (1969) *The will to meaning: Foundations and Applications of Logotherapy*. Cleveland: World.

Freud, A. (1936). *The ego and the mechanisms of defense*. New York: International Universities Press, 1967.

Gendlin, E. T. (1978). *Focusing*. New York: Everest House.

Gilbert, M. (1986). *Shcharansky: Hero of our time*. New York: Viking/Elizabeth Sifton Books.

Giovacchini, P. (1975). *Psychoanalysis of character disorders*. New York: Jason Aronson.

Goldberg, A. (1985) (Ed.). *Progress in self psychology*. New York: Guilford Press.

Greenacre, P. (1959). Certain technical problems in the transference relationship. *Journal of the American Psychoanalytic Association, 7*, 484–502.

Grinker, R., & Werbel, B. (1975). *The borderline patient*. New York: Jason Aronson.

Harlow, H. K., & Harlow, M. H. (1966). Learning to love. *American Scientist*, 54, pp. 244–272.

Hartmann, H. (1964). *Essays on ego psychology*. New York: International Universities Press.

Hartmann, H. (1958). *Ego psychology and the problem of adaptation*. New York: International Universities Press.

Hilton, R. (1980). General dynamics of character structure development and the therapeutic process. In Cassius, J. (Ed.). *Horizons in bioenergetics: New dimensions in mind-body psychotherapy* (pp. 178–197). Memphis, TN: Promethean Publications.

Horner, A. S. (1979). *Object relations and the developing ego in therapy*. New York: Jason Aronson.

Horowitz, M. (1986). Personal communication.

Jacobson, E. (1964). *The self and the object world*. New York: International Universities Press.

Johnson, S. M. (1985). *Characterological transformation: The hard work miracle*. New York: W. W. Norton.

Keleman, S. (1981). *Your body speaks its mind*. New York: Simon & Schuster.

Kernberg, O. (1975). *Borderline conditions and pathological narcissism*. New York: Jason Aronson.

Kernberg, O. (1976). *Object relations theory and clinical psychoanalysis*. New York: Jason Aronson.

Kohut, H. (1966). Forms and transformations of narcissism. *Journal of American Psychoanalytic Association, 14*, 243–272.

Kohut, H. (1971). *The analysis of the self*. New York: International University Press.

Kohut, H. (1977). *The restoration of the self*. New York: International University Press.

Kohut, H. (1978). *The search for the self*. Ornstein, P. (Ed.). New York: International Universities Press.

Kohut, H. (1984). *How does analysis cure?* Chicago, IL: University of Chicago Press.
Kohut, H. (1985). *Self psychology and the humanities: Reflections on a new psychoanalytic approach*. Strozier, C. (Ed.). New York: W. W. Norton.
Lowen, A. (1958). *The language of the body*. New York: Collier.
Lowen, A. (1967). *The betrayal of the body*. New York: Collier.
Lowen, A. (1983). *Narcissism: Denial of the true self*. New York: Macmillan.
Lowen, A., & Lowen, L. (1977). *The way to vibrant health*. New York: Harper & Row.
Mahler, M. S. (1969). *On human symbiosis and the vicissitudes of individuation*. New York: International Universities Press.
Mahler, M. S. (1972). Rapprochement subphase of the separation individuation process. *Psychoanalytic Quarterly, 41*, 487–506.
Mahler, M. S., Pine, R. & Bergman, A. (1975). *The psychological birth of the human infant*. New York: Basic Books.
Malan, D. H. (1979). *Individual psychotherapy and the science of psychodynamics*. London: Butterworths.
Masterson, J. (1976). *Psychotherapy of the borderline adult*. New York: Brunner/Mazel.
Masterson, J. (1981). *The narcissistic and borderline disorders*. New York: Brunner/Mazel.
Masterson, J. (1985). *The real self: A developmental, self, and object relations approach*. New York: Brunner/Mazel.
Matheny, A. P., Riese, M. L., & Wilson, R. S. (1985). Rudiments of infant temperament: New born to nine months. *Developmental Psychology, 21*, 486–494.
Miller, A. (1981). *The drama of the gifted child*. New York: Basic Books.
Miller, A. (1984). *Thou shalt not be aware: Society's betrayal of the child*. New York: Farrar, Straus, & Giroux.
Muller, E. (1982). L'Analyse du caracter a la Rumere de la psychologie de l'ego. *Analyse du corps*, Vol. I, p. 1.
Norwood, R. (1985). *Women who love too much: When you keep wishing and hoping he'll change*. New York: Pocket Books.
Orme-Johnson, D. W., & Farrow, J. T. (1977). Scientific research on the transcendental meditation program. *Collected Papers, Vol. I*. New York: Mahraishi European Research University Press.
Prather, H. (1980). *There is a place where you are not alone*. Garden City, NY: Doubleday.
Reddaway, P. (1986) Mensche, A Review of *Shcharansky: Hero of our time*. In *New York Review of Books*. XXXIII, 14, pp. 13–18.
Reich, W. (1942). *The discovery of the orgone, V.I.: The function of the orgasm*. New York: Orgone Institute Press, Inc.
Reich, W. (1949). *Character analysis, 3rd. ed*. New York: Orgone Institute Press, Inc.
Settlage, C. F. (1977). The psychoanalytic understanding of narcissistic and borderline personality disorders: Advances in developmental theory. *Journal of the American Psychoanalytic Association*, 25, pp.805–833. Reprinted in *Rapprochement: The critical subphase of separation-individuation*, Lax, R. F., Bach, S., & Burland, J. A. (Eds.) (pp. 77–100). New York: Jason Aronson.
Silverman, L. H., & Weinberger, J. (1985). Mommy and I are one: Implications for psychotherapy. *American Psychologist, 40*, 1296–1308.

Spitz, R. (1965). *The first year of life*. New York: International Universities Press.
Thomas, A., & Chess, S. (1977). *Temperament and development*. New York: Brunner/Mazel.
Thomas A., & Chess, S. (1980). *The dynamics of psychological development*. New York: Brunner/Mazel.
Tolpin, P. (1983). A change in the self: The development and transformation of an idealizing transference. *International Journal of Psychoanalysis, 64*, 461–483.
White, E. (1983). *States of desire*. New York: E.P. Dutton.
Winnicott, D. W. (1953). Transitional objects and transitional phenomena. *The International Journal of Psychoanalysis, 34*, 89–97.
Winnicott, D. W. (1965). *Maturational processes and the facilitating environment*. New York: International Universities Press.
Wolf, E., Gedo, J., & Terman, D. (1972). On the adolescent process as a transformation of self. *Journal of Youth and Adolescence, 1* 257–272.
Wolf, E. (1979) Transference and countertransference in analysis of disorders of the self. *Contemporary Psychoanalysis, 15*, 577–594.

INDEX

abandonment depression, 44, 45, 59
  see also annihilation-abandonment crisis
Abend, S., 28
Adler, G., 12, 28, 29, 40, 59
adolescence, 30, 119
affect, real self and, 156–59
affective objectives, 71–74
affective therapies, 5, 6–7
  see also bioenergetics; Gestalt therapy
affirmation, 172, 173
"All That Jazz" (film), 114
analytic psychotherapy:
  regressive states in, 89
  working-through in, 136
annihilation-abandonment crisis, 59–60, 62, 103–8, 138–39
  psychological defense building and, 112
  real self and, 147, 153–56
  therapeutic errors and, 153–54
anxiety, 33, 170
  masochism and, 33–34
  self-expression and, 160
  separation, 21, 23–25
autism (primary narcissism), psychopathy and, 15–17
autonomy, guardianship of, 106, 128, 143, 168
awareness-relaxation exercises, 94–95

"Back to the Future" (film), 118–19
Bandler, R., 108, 167, 265–68
Barten, S., 37
Beckwith, L., 37
behavioral-social objectives in treatment, 74–76
Beres, D., 13
Bergman, A., 12, 17
Berne, E., 134
bioenergetics, 5, 6–7, 9, 32
  borderline narcissist and, 88–90
  contractions and, 125
  depression treatment and, 94–96
  exercises for, 94–95, 121–24, 126–27, 268–71
  five-step reconnection with biological reality in, 121–24
  masochism and, 34
  narcissistic style and, 91
  outside of therapy, 127, 148–49
  psychopathic character as viewed by, 65–67
  somatic awareness and, 86
  treatment of false self and, 120–28
bioenergetic stool, 94, 122, 271
Birns, B., 37
Blanck, G., 13, 33, 40, 170
Blanck, R., 13, 33, 40, 170
Boadella, D., 14
borderline individual, 28–29
  see also symbiotic character
borderline narcissism, 59, 88–92, 101–2, 112–13
  countertransference and, 82–83
  defenses of, 88–90, 112
  empathy and, 138, 140
  evocative techniques and, 88–90, 121
  mobilization in, 138–41

borderline narcissism (*continued*)
narcissistic style compared with, 150, 151
reparenting processes and, 108
borderline triad, 147
Bowlby, J., 23
"Breakfast Club, The" (film), 156
Bridger, W., 37
Bronson, W. C., 37

Cameron-Bandler, L., 165
chameleon psychopath, 65–67
change history procedure, 119
character analysis, 4–6, 10, 14
temperament and, 37
see also specific character types
character disorder, 87–92
depression and, 96–113
see also narcissistic character disorder
Characterological Transformation (Johnson), 4, 6, 9, 10, 14–15, 94, 108, 123, 170
character style, 87–96
depression and, 92–96
see also narcissistic style
Chess, S., 37
Chessick, R. D., 28
chest, bioenergetics and, 121–22
child abuse, undoing pattern and, 117–18
choking, 122
client-therapist relationship:
empathy in, 123–24
intimacy in, 124, 155–56
manipulation in, 81–82
trust in, 72, 80–81
cognitive objectives in therapy, 67–71
cognitive therapy, 32
conceptual-spiritual therapy, 256–58
conflict model, 9, 37–38, 136
consciousness, evolution of, 12; *see also* developmental psychoanalytic theory
countertransference, 77–84
real self and, 82–84
therapeutic errors and, 153–54
therapeutic set and, 77–82

Davanloo, H., 173
defenses, 5, 14, 40, 45, 62–64
of borderline narcissist, 88–90, 112
narcissistic style and, 90–91, 122
of pure narcissist, 57, 62
undoing pattern and, 116–20
deficit model, 9, 37–38, 136
denial, 116
undoing pattern and, 117–18
depression, 48, 63–64
abandonment, 44, 45, 59; *see also* annihilation-abandonment crisis
character disorder and, 96–113
character style and, 92–96
treatment of, 92–113
developmental psychoanalytic theory, 4–10, 167
integration in models of, 5–9
model of, 9–10, 12–38
see also ego psychology; object relations; self, self development
differentiation, 22–25, 34
Dilts, R., 167
disability, in body vs. life, 87
disavowal, 55

ego psychology, 4–6, 8–9, 10, 13, 14
arrested development and, 4–5, 14, 15, 18–20
optimal frustration and, 20–22
Emde, R. N., 13, 16, 23
empathy:
borderline narcissist and, 138, 140
client-therapist, 122–24
need for, 125
therapist, 84
energetic expression, 10, 64–67
see also bioenergetics
Erhard, Werner, 62, 219
est training, 62
exercises:
in bioenergetics, 94–95, 121–24, 126–27, 268–71
focusing, 261–65
real self-upside and, 159, 168–69
reframing, 265–68
"What Are You Experiencing?," 168–69
existential shift, 142–44

extratherapy behavior, structuring of, 127–28, 148–49
eyes, bioenergetics and, 123

false self, 11, 40, 41–42, 44–48
  client manipulation and, 81–82
  defensive functioning of, 62–63
  identity formation and, 53–60
  narcissistic compensation and, 45–46
  of oral character, 58
  -real self dialogue, 128–34
  schizoid, 58
  of symbiotic character, 58
  threats to, 29
false self, treatment of, 114–44
  energetic interventions and, 120–28
  existential shift and, 142–44
  mobilization in borderline narcissist and, 138–41
  necessary vs. unnecessary pain and, 134–35
  undoing and, 116–20
  working-through and, 118, 119–20, 135–38
Farrow, J. T., 173
feeling:
  in treatment of symptomatic self, 84–85, 100–101
focusing, 261–62
footwork with the dowel, 270
forward position, 269–70
Fraiberg, S., 21
Frankl, V., 258
free association, 126–27, 174–75
Freud, Anna, 13
Freud, Sigmund, 34, 35, 127
frustration, optimal, *see* optimal frustration

Gaensbauer, T., 13, 16, 23
Gedo, J., 12
Gendlin, E. T., 108, 261–65
Gestalt therapy, 5, 6, 9, 32, 168
  borderline narcissist and, 88–90
  false self-real self dialogue and, 128–34
  frustration principle and, 155
  narcissistic style and, 91, 151
  outside of therapy, 148–49
  role-playing process in, 127, 151
  "two-chair" procedure in, 129
Gilbert, M., 257
Giovacchini, P., 28, 29
Goldberg, A., 12
grandiosity, 25–31, 33, 42
  bioenergetics exercise on, 126
  narcissistic compensation and, 45–46
  in practicing phase, 25–27
  rapprochement and, 27–31, 41
  real self formation and, 61
  treatment of false self and, 125–26
  treatment of symptomatic self and, 84–85
Greenacre, P., 25, 106, 143
Grinder, J., 108, 167, 265–68
Grinker, R., 28
grounding, 121, 126
group therapy, 11, 101, 116, 168
  advantages of, 254–55
  complementarity of individual therapy and, 247–52
  family function of, 250
  narcissistic character disorder and, 191–204, 208–13
  narcissistic style and, 116, 228–40, 247–52
  risks of, 251–52
growing up, therapeutic objectives and, 68, 74
guardianship of autonomy, 106, 128, 143, 168

Harlow, H. K., 17
Harlow, M. H., 17
Harmon, R., 13, 16, 23
Hartmann, H., 13
Hilton, R., 14, 35
hips, bioenergetics and, 122
Horner, A. S., 12, 28, 29
hypnotic therapy, 32, 113, 165, 170–71
  borderline narcissist and, 88–90
  narcissistic style and, 91
hypochondriacal preoccupation, 63, 85–87

"I am" meditation, 121
idealization, 33, 45–48, 50, 52–53, 64
  of children, 29, 45
  of parent, 27, 46

idealization (*continued*)
rapprochement phase and, 27–28, 29, 46
of therapist, 80, 106–7, 164
transference, 20, 164, 172, 248, 249
ideals and values, stress management and, 256–58
identity formation, 53–60
"no" and, 32–34
illness, psychosomatic, 63, 85–87
individual differences, character formation and, 37
individual-systemic level, stress management at, 256
individual therapy, 11
complementarity of group therapy and, 247–52
narcissistic character disorder and, 204–8, 213–17
narcissistic style and, 221–28, 240–52
individuation, *see* separation-individuation
internalization:
promoting transformative, 170–73
transmuting, 21–24
intimacy, client-therapist, 124, 155–56
isolation, narcissism and, 64, 74

Jacobson, E., 12
jumping, 269

Keleman, S., 14
Kernberg, O., 12, 32
Kohut, Heinz, 10, 12, 28, 31, 32, 35, 63, 102, 103, 105, 110
analytic therapy compared with theater by, 89
"experience near" description of self and, 15
optimal frustration concept of, 20–22, 170
on quiet competence, 79, 143
real self formation and, 61–62
"tragic man" of, 62, 253
on transference, 50–52, 248
on transformation, 68, 258
vertical and horizontal split concept of, 54–57
working-through and, 136–37

limitations, 41, 43, 250
of therapist, 83
treatment of false self and, 115–16
Lowen, A., 14, 33, 35, 40, 94, 177
Lowen, L., 94

Mahler, M. S., 8, 12, 15, 17, 22–23, 106
separation-individuation model of, 22–34, 42
Malan, D. H., 173
manipulation, in client-therapist relationship, 81–82
masochism, 33–34
Masterson, J., 12–13, 28, 32, 44, 59, 147, 161
mate selection, undoing pattern and, 117
Matheny, A. P., 37
meditation, 172–73
"I am," 121
memory, recognition, 21
merging transference, 50–51, 52, 172, 248–49
Miller, Alice, 35, 36, 40, 43–44, 49
mirror transference, 51–52, 172, 248, 249
mobilization, 127
in borderline narcissist, 138–41
mothers, 45
"good enough," 43
stage, 44
mother-child symbiosis, 17–20
Muller, E., 14

narcissistic cathexis, 43, 45, 48, 78
narcissistic character disorder, 4, 11, 53
identity formation and, 56
integration of group and individual therapy and, 190–218
narcissistic character structure, 10, 39–76
behavior, attitude, feeling and, 46–67
borderline, *see* borderline narcissism
collapse of false self and, 57–59
energetic expression and, 10, 64–67
etiology of, 39–46, 65
identity formation and, 53–60
normal, 4
object relations and, 40, 41, 48–53

other-directed individual and, 52
primary, *see* autism
pure (narrow), 9, 40–41, 57, 59, 62, 65, 72, 157
symbiotic character compared with, 50
therapeutic objectives and, 31, 67–76
three expressions of, 55
treatment and, *see* false self, treatment of; real self; symptomatic self, treatment of
see also narcissistic character disorder; narcissistic style
narcissistic compensation, 45–46, 55, 70
narcissistic injury, 39–41, 44, 57, 78, 124
compensation and, 45–46
rage and, 157–58
treatment of symptomatic self and, 84–85
narcissistic rage, 57, 73, 101, 154–55, 157–58
narcissistic style, 3–4, 11, 78, 88
borderline narcissism compared with, 150, 151
collapse of false self and, 57–58
defenses and, 90–91, 122
evocative techniques and, 91, 122, 151
group therapy and, 116, 228–40, 247–52
identity formation and, 56
integration of group and individual therapy and, 219–52
intrapsychic struggle of selves in, 149–53
pain and, 115
real self and, 154–55
see also narcissistic character structure
narrow (pure) narcissism, 9, 40–41, 57, 59, 62, 65, 72, 157
necessary pain:
aiming of, 136–37
claiming of, 135–36
naming of, 136
taming of, 137–38
unnecessary pain vs., 134–35, 137–38
neck, bioenergetics and, 122
neurolinguistic programming, 113, 119
reframing and, 265–68
resource accessing in, 165
neurotic character, 92
"no," identity formation and, 32–34
Norwood, Robin, 117
nuclear self, 61; *see also* real self

object constancy, child on the way to, 32–34
object relations, 5–6, 8–9, 10, 40, 41, 42
developmental psychoanalytic theory and, 12–38
merging transference and, 50–51, 52
mirror transference and, 51–52
narcissism and, 40, 41, 48–53
twinship transference and, 51
Oedipus complex, 34–36
optimal frustration, 20–23, 25, 30–32, 63
in therapy, 31–32, 38, 108
oral character, 32, 40, 58, 91
collapse of false self in, 47, 58
narcissist compared with, 47
practicing and, 26
separation anxiety and, 24–25
symbiosis and, 18–20
transference and, 20
"Ordinary People" (film), 156
Orme-Johnson, D. W., 173
other-directed individual, narcissist as, 52

pain:
narcissistic style and, 115
necessary vs. unnecessary, 134–35, 137–38
physical vs. psychic, 68
as signal, 68–69
see also necessary pain
parents:
"good enough," 43
idealization of, 27, 46
narcissism and, 40, 43–45, 53
real self development and, 43
real self rejected by, 43–44
see also mothers
parent transplant, 109

pelvis, bioenergetics and, 121
phallic character, 92
phenomenology:
  of client reality, 78
  of self, 4, 9, 10, 12
Pine, R., 12, 17
Porder, M., 28
practicing, 8, 25–27
Prather, Hugh, 145, 190
psychoanalysis, 7, 9, 31–32, 38
  "new," 36, 167
  Oedipus complex in, 34–35, 36
psychopathic character, 65–67
psychopathy, autism and, 15–17
psychosomatic illness, 63, 85–87
psychotherapy:
  empathy in, 84
  trends and, 7
  see also specific therapies
pure (narrow) narcissism, 9, 40–41, 57, 59, 62, 65, 72, 157
putting the foot down, 268–69

quiet competence, 79, 143

rage, narcissistic, 57, 73, 101, 154–55, 157–58
rapprochement, 8–9, 26–33, 46, 147
  developmental tasks of, 31
  grandiosity and, 27–31, 41
  narcissism and, 26, 28, 29, 39–44, 47, 49
  vulnerability in, 42–43
reaching squat, 95
reality:
  biological, bioenergetics and, 121–24
  rapprochement with, 8–9, 26–32
reality relatedness, 40
real object, 43
real self, 11, 46, 145–89
  affect and, 156–59
  annihilation-abandonment crisis and, 147, 153–56
  bioenergetics and reconnection with, 121–24
  case examples and, 149–53, 173–89
  countertransference and, 82–84
  -false self dialogue, 128–34
  formation of, 60–62
  internal crises in emergence of, 147
  parental assistance in development of, 43
  parental rejection of, 43–44
  promoting transformative internalizations and, 170–73
  reframing and, 148
  self-image or self-concept vs., 53–54
  therapeutic tasks in relation to, 147–48
  upside of, 159–70
  upside vs. downside of, 145–46, 152
recognition memory, 21
recognition smile, 16–17, 23
Reddaway, P., 257
reframing, 148, 265–68
Reich, Wilhelm, 14, 134
Reichian therapy, 6–7
reparenting processes, 108, 142
resistance, bioenergetic work and, 124–27
resource accessing, 165
Riese, M. L., 37
Robinson, J., 16, 23
Rogers, Carl, 43
role-playing, in Gestalt therapy, 127, 151

schizoid character, 32, 40, 91
  bioenergetic eye work and, 123
  collapse of false self in, 58
  narcissistic character compared with, 53, 66
  stranger anxiety and, 24–25
  symbiosis and, 18–20
  transference and, 20
secondary gain, 119
self, self development, 4–6, 8–9, 10, 12–38
  abstractions of, 167
  arrest in development of, 4–5
  experience of, 61
  false, *see* false self; false self, treatment of
  masochism and, 34
  optimal frustration and, 20–22
  real, *see* real self
  relaxed boundaries and, 90
  symptomatic, *see* symptomatic self; symptomatic self, treatment of
  see also separation-individuation

self-acceptance, 160
self-care, 160
self-concept, 53–54, 62
self-image, 53–54, 62
self-mobilizing functions, 107
selfobjects, 43, 171–72, 248–49, 256
self-parenting, 127–28
self-preserving strategies, 5
self-representation:
  failures in, 40, 41, 49
  identity formation and, 53–60
senses, renewal of, 159
separateness, 41
separation anxiety, 21, 23–25
separation-individuation, 7–9, 21–34
  child on the way to object-constancy in, 32–34
  differentiation in, 22–25
  optimal frustration and, 21–22
  practicing phase of, 8, 25–27
  rapprochement phase of, *see* rapprochement
Settlage, C. F., 31
sex, character disorders and, 29–30
sexual abuse, undoing pattern and, 117–18
sexual experiences, relaxed boundaries in, 89, 90
sexuality:
  energetic expression and, 66
  Oedipus complex and, 34–36
Shcharansky (Gilbert), 257
Shcharansky, Anatoly, 256–58
Silverman, L. H., 13, 19
smile, recognition, 16–17, 23
social-cultural level, stress management at, 256
social support systems, 109–10
soothing, 107–9, 127, 170–71
Spitz, R., 16–17
splitting, 27–28, 33, 45, 99
  group therapy and, 101
squatting against a wall, 269
stage mother, 44
standing on one leg, 268
Sting, 114
stool, bioenergetic, 94, 122, 271
stranger anxiety, 23–25
stress:
  of characterological change, 255
  management of, 256–58
superego, 35
"Superman II" (film), 118–19
symbiosis, 22, 23, 41
  mother-child, 17–20
symbiotic character, 28–30, 33, 42, 91
  collapse of false self in, 58
  narcissist compared with, 50
  treatment objectives for, 31
symptomatic self, 11, 63
  cognitive objectives and, 68
symptomatic self, treatment of, 77–113
  character disorder and, 87–92, 96–113
  character style and, 87–96
  countertransference and, 77–84
  depression and, 92–113
  psychosomatic illness and hypochondriasis and, 85–87
  therapeutic set and, 77–82
  worthlessness, grandiosity, and the narcissistic injury in, 84–85

temperament, character and, 37
Terman, D., 12
theater, analytic therapy compared with, 89
therapeutic objectives, 67–76
  affective, 71–74
  behavioral-social, 74–76
  cognitive, 67–71
therapeutic set, countertransference and, 77–82
therapists:
  breach of trust by, 80–81
  client attacks on, 57, 153, 154–55, 158
  empathy of, 84
  errors of, 153–54
  "good enough," 158
  idealization of, 80, 106–7, 164
  limitations of, 83
  narcissism of, 78–79
  quiet competence of, 79, 143
  see also client-therapist relationship
therapy:
  issue of continuance of, 110–12
  optimal frustration in, 31–32, 38, 108
  see also specific kinds of therapy

Thomas, A., 37
toilet training, 18
Tolpin, P., 12
"tragic man," 62
trance work, 165
transference, 7, 20, 31–32, 89
  idealization, 20, 164, 172, 248, 249
  merging, 50–51, 52, 172, 248–49
  mirror, 51–52, 172, 248, 249
  negative, 97, 99–101
  twinship, 51, 172, 248, 249
  see also countertransference
transformation, 11, 49, 68, 253–60
  defined, 253
  evolution in, 254
  shift in orientation in, 253–54
transformational psychology movements, 79
transmuting internalization, 21–24
trust, in therapeutic relationship, 72, 80–81
twinship transference, 51, 172, 248, 249
"two-chair" procedure, 129

understanding of the narcissist, 103–4
undoing, 116–20
  timing of interpretation of, 119–20
unity-individuation, 42
unnecessary pain, necessary pain vs., 134–35, 137–38
"upward displaced psychopath," 65–66
used child, 39–76
  girls vs. boys as, 29–30
  see also narcissistic character structure

values and ideals, stress management and, 256–58
vocalization, bioenergetics and, 122
vulnerability, 42–43

Weinberger, J., 13, 19
Werbel, B., 28
"What Are You Experiencing?" exercise, 168–69
White, Edmund, 141
Willich, M., 28
willingness to change, 143
Wilson, R. S., 37
Winnicott, D. W., 13
wisdom, 68
Wolf, E., 12
Women Who Love Too Much (Norwood), 117
work, undoing pattern and, 117–18
working-through, 118, 119–20, 135–38
worthlessness, 45–46, 78, 84–85